The Complete Guide to North American Trees

The Complete Guide

to

North American Trees

CARLTON C. CURTIS

and

S. C. BAUSOR

COLLIER BOOKS, NEW YORK, NEW YORK

COLLIER-MACMILLAN LTD., LONDON

FIRST COLLIER BOOKS EDITION 1963

This Collier Books edition is published by arrangement with Chilton Company—Book Division

Third Printing 1971

Parts of The Complete Guide to North American Trees were formerly published as A Guide to the Trees

The Macmillan Company
866 Third Avenue, New York, N.Y. 10022
Collier-Macmillan Canada Ltd., Toronto, Ontario

Printed in the United States of America

*To JACK and MARY,
and Their Companions in the Out-of-doors,
Wherever They May Be*

Contents

Contents

The Complete Guide to North American Trees

The Complete Guide to _____

Introduction

EVERYONE SHOULD KNOW the trees of his neighborhood. Nothing adds more attractiveness to the country or gives more benefit and enjoyment to the people. If one could see lands that have been stripped of their forests the truth of this statement would be apparent. Many places in the old countries of the East, and indeed some sections of our own country, have been transformed from beautiful and fertile fields into barren and repulsive regions by the removal of the forests.

Not only are the trees themselves a great loss, but the fertility of the soil goes with them. The trees are the great conservers of water. The soft earth with its carpet of leaves permits the rains to settle down slowly into the ground, and this water supplies the brooks and rivers. With the removal of the trees the ground becomes hard; the rains do not penetrate the soil, but run off quickly over the surface of adjacent fields. This results in carrying away the topsoil of these fields and making them unfertile; it also causes the springs and brooks gradually to dry up, which means a loss to all the surrounding country.

It is only within the past few years that we have begun to realize what the forests mean to our country. With the rapid increase of the population it is necessary that something be done to prevent the wasting of land; and to preserve and enlarge our forests, if we are to have places where the out-of-doors can really be enjoyed.

Our North American forests were once the finest to be found in any temperate country. No other region had such a variety of valuable and beautiful trees; no other land is so favorable to their growth. Originally the United States alone had over eight hundred million acres of forest. Today less than one hundred and thirty million acres remain untouched, and half of this is on the Pacific coast. This remnant is being consumed so fast that the end is in sight.

It is reported that a single issue of a Sunday paper requires the destruction of fifty-four acres of timber. One might well ask, which is mightier, the pen or the ax? Our forests have been in continuous possession of the country from a time long antedating the appearance of man upon the earth; and we are destroying this inheritance four times faster than it is being produced. A large forest tree that is cut down and converted into paper in a few days' time may take one hundred years to grow.

But the fact that trees cannot be grown quickly should not prevent our going forward with the work of reforesting. The Forestry Service estimates that we have in the United States over four hundred million acres of land suitable only for forests, eighty-one million acres of which is east of the Mississippi River. Every state has thousands of acres of such land, which if properly managed would meet our needs for all time. Some towns of Europe own and utilize such tracts for forestry purposes and derive a revenue from them that meets all expenses, so that the people are free from taxation.

In every section there are attractive and useful plants now threatened with extinction. This is due to the ignorance of people and their consequent thoughtlessness. If one really comes to know a tree he will have a respect for it. It has a personality as striking as his own and is in many ways more sensitive to the treatment it receives. It is less brutal and harmful to tear out a handful of hair from a person's head than to tear off the branches from a tree; such treatment endangers the life of the tree or prevents it from reaching its full growth. If one must remove any part of a plant it should be done with a sharp knife. Also remember that one or two sprays reflect more beauty than an armful or a carful; furthermore you escape the disgrace of being seen with the slaughter.

Those who really love the out-of-doors prefer to leave growing things where they can flourish and where other people can enjoy them. Every one can be of service in helping to remedy this unfortunate situation; and it is encouraging to note that the spirit of fairness and appreciation is decidedly growing.

The influence of the Scout movement among the boys and girls of our country cannot be overestimated in promoting a spirit of good citizenship and good sport in the use and enjoyment of the woods and fields. This outline will acquaint them with our inheritance and put them in sympathy with maintaining it; and also will enable them to use the numerous and more extensive books dealing with this subject.

No work can be undertaken that will be of greater benefit to you than this work of identifying your trees. It develops a keenness of observation and a power of judgment as no other subject does. John Stuart Mill took up work of this nature as part of his training for his work in economics.

You will at first be amazed at your inability to see and to form a correct judgment. You are dealing with living things that show almost endless variations. Acquiring the power to see clearly and accurately these features and to give them due weight is training that will be of the greatest assistance to you in any work that you undertake.

A general idea of the unseen activities within a tree, beyond giving an understanding of tree structure, cannot help but add to an appreciation of all trees, as well as prove an incentive for furthering an acquaintance with them.

A living tree rivals the activity of a busy factory. As a manufacturing plant, a tree may be considered, for simplicity's sake, to have three main parts—the roots, the leaves, and the woody structure between them.

The roots, besides anchoring the tree, act as agents for selecting the raw materials of manufacture from the soil and bringing them to the tree factory. These materials are water and mineral salts dissolved in water.

The leaves are the food-manufacturing laboratories of the factory. They "breathe in" carbon dioxide from the air and utilize the sun's light energy to combine this gas with the moisture from the roots, thus producing the simple sugars which are the basic food of the tree.

The woody structure—trunk, limbs, branches, twigs—in addition to holding the leaves up where sunlight and air will be available to them, act as the "intramural" transportation system of the factory, conducting raw materials and foods between roots and leaves.

The water and dissolved mineral salts absorbed by the roots are "pulled up" in columns through the outer, newer layer of wood by capillary attraction and the osmotic action induced by the evaporation of water from the leaves. This loss of water through the leaves is called transpiration. A single Birch tree may transpire 700 to 900 gallons of water during a single summer day. An Oak tree has been estimated to lose a daily average of 250 gallons throughout the growing season. This enormous transpiration, plus chemical use of water in food-building, causes a continuous flow of sap from the roots to the topmost twigs.

The mineral salts absorbed in solution by the roots are not in themselves, strictly speaking, foods; they are "nutrients"—raw materials. The tree manufactures its own essential food in the leaves. The process by which it does this is called *photosynthesis*—literally, a putting together by means of light. The *chlorophyll*, or green coloring matter in the leaves, is the chemical agent which utilizes the energy of the sunlight to transform the carbon dioxide from the air and the moisture from the roots into the simple sugars which are the building blocks of all the organic substances composing the dry matter of the tree —carbohydrates, fats, proteins, cellulose, organic acids. From 40 to 50 per cent of the dry weight of the tree is the simple element carbon. All of this carbon is obtained from the carbon dioxide "breathed in" by the leaves. Since only .03 per cent of the atmosphere is carbon dioxide, trees require a vast amount of air to meet their need for carbon. In the process of photosynthesis, as much oxygen is liberated as carbon dioxide is consumed. The respiration of leaves, therefore, reverses the process of animal respiration, restoring to the air the oxygen consumed in human lungs.

The foods produced in the leaves and not used there flow back again through the woody structures to all parts of the tree, even to the roots. Some of this food is converted into plant tissues as the tree grows. Some of it is stored for future use—as in seeds or fruit. The rest of it is converted into the energy by which the tree performs its work. For trees, like animals, do work—an amazing amount of work! Think of the energy required to thrust thousands of rootlets through the soil, to split open obstructive rocks, to lift the tremendous weight of leaves and branches sometimes hundreds of feet into the air, to push out and build the rapidly growing tissues of root-tips, buds, flowers, leaves, and stems! Every living cell of the tree is a food-consuming furnace.

The chemical laboratories in the leaves, therefore, cannot afford to be idle. For that reason the branching of a tree is so designed as to place the leaves in the most favorable position for intercepting the sunlight with which they do their work. True, the characteristic branching of a particular species may sometimes be modified by wind and storm or other external forces, such as physically contending neighbor trees, but the distortion of tree shapes observable in crowded grove or forest is usually due to the trees' own attempts to outstrip one another in the competition for sunlight. In your field excursions you can observe how well most trees have achieved a leaf-placement of maximum exposure to the sun. A glance upward from near the trunk of a field-grown tree will show how beautifully the leaves are spaced so that little of the open sky is visible. In a dense wood it will be obvious how each tree strives with its neighbor for a place in the sun, and how the less successful, overtopped, are forced out of the race by light starvation.

Two types of trees may be recognized by their habit of losing or retaining their foliage after a season's growth.

Following a garish display of reds, yellows, orange, and brown, the deciduous trees drop their leaves in the autumn, and their branches remain barren until the coming of spring.

In the evergreen trees the leaves of one season overlap those of the following, so that the fall of leaves may escape notice. Some species lose their older leaves soon after the appearance of the new ones, while others may retain their leaves for two, three, or more years.

In the forest the dead leaves continue to exert their influence on the living vegetation, for in decay they return to the topsoil the minerals which were absorbed from greater depths by the roots. This leaf mold will also retain large volumes of water from melting snow or rain, giving it off slowly to feed brooks and streams, and yet assuring an adequate water supply to the forest trees.

The trees challenge you! In the following pages lies the key to a most absorbing hobby.

The authors wish to thank the National Herbarium for the use of their specimens in preparing sections on the southern and western trees.

EXPLANATIONS AND SUGGESTIONS

1. *The floral regions*, as treated in this guide, are shown in the map below. The area marked A represents the

northeastern region; B indicates the southern region; and C designates the western region. Some trees are found in only a small section of these areas. In such cases their distribution is indicated after the description of the tree. A few shrubs that every one wishes to know are included also.

2. *The names of trees* vary in different sections of the country. Frequently a tree is burdened with several names; or, still worse, the same name is applied to entirely different trees. The American Committee on Horticultural Names has tried to remedy this confusion by selecting the most appropriate name for each kind of tree. Their selections have been used in this guide. Following the name of a tree is the Latin name in parentheses, thus: Silver Maple (*Acer saccharinum* L.). The letter or letters after the Latin name stand for the author's name; in this case Linnæus. The Latin name is introduced so that one can refer to the more extended books in which the Latin names are used in preference to the English.

It will be noticed that the name of a tree sometimes appears in more than one place in the key. This is due to their wide variations. For instance, the oaks are a large group and have a great variety of leaves. Again a tree is "keyed out" in two places if the statements by which it is identified may be differently interpreted.

3. *Where fruits are used in the key* for identifying a tree, these with very few exceptions can be found at any time of the year either on the tree or on the ground.

4. *Buds are frequently not satisfactorily developed* until after midsummer. When you are keying out a tree in the early summer and bud characters are required to identify it, you can generally find well-developed buds on a twig that has died the previous winter. However, if no buds are available, you will notice that in the key one of the divisions under bud characters includes but two or three trees. A glance at the illustrations will show you whether they include the specimen that you are examining.

5. *A few words are defined on page 315.* These are common English words but may not as yet be familiar to all who use this guide. No strictly technical words are used. Illustrations of the shapes of leaves are also given in this connection.

6. *No two leaves of a tree are exactly alike.* This is the cause, in part, of the attractiveness of the tree. But each

tree has a definite leaf-shape or pattern, which can be found by making a careful examination of the various forms and picking out the one that is most representative. This is not always an easy thing to do. If two or more persons are engaged in the task there is sure to be an argument. This difference of opinion is most helpful in developing judgment and power of observation, and it is sure to result in the selection of a representative type of leaf.

The person who cannot observe these precautions must abandon the work, for he will make no progress in this line of study—or indeed in any other. If he is not willing to do more than examine the first leaf within reach, let him close the book and go home—or to the movies.

7. *If the leaf is irregular or lobed* the form of the leaf can best be understood by finding out which of the figures on page 315 most nearly completely covers it. This figure will then represent the form or shape of the leaf.

8. *To make a proper selection,* choose a leaf from a tree or branch as mature and well sunned as possible. Young shoots and shaded branches rarely bear typical leaves. Remember also that young leaves may be quite different from mature ones. The descriptions of leaves in the following pages are based on full-grown leaves.

9. *In examining the bark,* you will note that young trees have nearly smooth bark, but in the majority of mature trees the bark becomes cracked into scales or ridges that are characteristic of each kind of tree. Therefore you must examine the trunk of an old tree, best seen two or three feet from the ground, to find the kind of bark mentioned in the key. In the younger growth of an old tree, that is, in the upper part of the trunk or branches, you will, of course, find smooth bark like that of a young tree.

The color of the twigs also assists in identifying a tree. The color varies with the life of the twig, being often quite different in the spring, summer, and fall, as well as with its later growth.

10. *From the variations of leaves and bark* you are not to conclude that you cannot arrive at an exact knowledge

of the trees. You will come to know them and their peculiarities much more certainly than the identity of your friends.

11. *The dimensions given in this book* of a leaf, fruit, or tree represent averages. They give you a general idea of the size, not exact size, for there is no such thing.

12. *If a twig must be removed* from a tree, remove it with a clean cut of a sharp knife. Never tear off a twig or branch.

13. *A pocket magnifying glass* is of the greatest assistance in observing many features about leaves, buds, and other parts of the tree. It also reveals many interesting and beautiful things that cannot be seen with the naked eye.

14. *Many people are poisoned* by touching two plants mentioned on pages 146-47. So before beginning the field work, study these plants and learn to avoid them.

SUPPOSE THAT YOU have selected a leaf from a northeastern tree (as directed on page 9) which is like the one shown in the figure below (Fig. 1). To find the name of this tree turn to the key on page 13. If you do not know the meaning of a word in the key, turn to definitions, page 315.

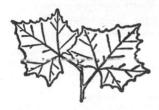

Fig. 1

You will find in the key three main groups: I, The Cone-Bearing Trees, leaves *needle-like* or *scale-like* (Figs. 2, 3, 4); II, The Broad-Leaved Trees, leaves *broad* and *flat* (Figs. 5, 6, 7); and III, The Monocots, leaves *long* and *narrow*, or *fan-shaped* (Figs. 8, 9). Comparing your leaf with these three statements and the figures under them, you see that your leaf belongs to the Broad-Leaved Trees. You are directed to page 16 where the Broad-Leaved Trees are keyed out. All your work with the key will be of this nature: you are asked to choose between two or more statements. Contrasting statements always begin at the same distance from the margin of the page, and if they are widely separated from each other by intervening lines they are lettered (*a, aa; b, bb, etc.*) so as to point them out more clearly. Read both statements in order to make a correct choice.

On page 16, under The Broad-Leaved Trees, you find

again two headings: A, Leaves *opposite* (Fig. 11) and B, Leaves *not opposite* but *alternating* (Fig. 12). Here, from the figures and your specimen you know that your tree has alternating leaves, and you turn to page 18. You now choose between the two statements: 1, Leaves *simple* (Fig. 18) and 2, Leaves *not simple* but *compound* (Fig. 17). The illustrations tell you that your leaf is simple, and you are directed to look below. Here you read: 1a, Leaf *margin smooth* (Fig. 18) and 1b, Leaf *margin toothed* (Fig. 19). The figures cause you to select "Leaf margin toothed," and you are directed to page 22. Here you choose between *Juice milky* and *Juice not milky*. By cutting a twig you learn that your specimen has watery juice (not milky). Under "Juice not milky" you have to decide between a, Branches *with spines* and aa, Branches *without spines*. You must examine the branches carefully, for in some trees there are sometimes only a few spines developed. In the case of your tree there are no spines; and under the heading "Branches of tree without spines" you choose between b, *Large veins spreading from the petiole* (Fig. 24) and bb, *Large veins mostly spreading from the middle vein* (Fig. 26). The figures in the key lead you to the first statement, and under this you find two headings: c, Leaves *with lobes* (Fig. 24) and cc, Leaves *without lobes* (Fig. 25). Your leaf is clearly lobed, and under this heading you have three statements describing three kinds of leaves. You see that the second one corresponds with your leaf, and this brings you to the Sycamore. You are now directed to page 125, where you read the full description and find that it agrees with the tree that you are examining. You have become acquainted with your first tree.

GENERAL KEY TO THE NORTHEASTERN AND SOUTHERN TREES[1]

Before attempting to use the key read pages 7 to 12.

---

[1] A general key to the western trees will be found on p. 30.

THE THREE MAIN GROUPS OF TREES

I. The Cone-Bearing Trees

Leaves needle-like or scale-like. Fruit a cone or rarely a bluish berry. See Figs. 2, 3, 4. See below and p. 30.

Fig. 2   Fig. 3   Fig. 4

II. The Broad-Leaved Trees

Leaves broad and flat. See Figs. 5, 6, 7. See pp. 16 and 31.

Fig. 5   Fig. 6   Fig. 7

III. The Monocots

Leaves long and narrow, or fan-shaped. See Figs. 8, 9. See p. 29.

Fig. 8   Fig. 9

I. The Cone-Bearing Trees

A. *Leaves mostly clustered at ends of short twigs; soft slim needles.* See Fig. 10. *Larch.* p. 47.

Fig. 10

15

B. *Leaves not clustered at ends of short twigs but scattered along the branchlets.* See Figs. 2, 3, and 4.

a. Leaves projecting from the twigs; not opposite or whorled. See Figs. 2 and 3.

    b. Leaves long slender needles in groups of 2, 3, or 5. See Fig. 2. *Pine.* pp. 39, 189.

    bb. Leaves short needles; not in groups. See Fig. 3.

        c. Leaf with short stem, twig rough after leaf-fall.
           Leaf flat, blunt, notched at end. *Hemlock.* p. 51.
           Leaf four-sided, sharp at end. *Spruce.* p. 48.

        cc. Leaf without stem, twig smooth after leaf-fall.
           Bark grayish, nearly smooth. *Fir.* p. 52.
           Bark reddish brown, slightly ridged. *Bald-cypress.* pp. 53, 191.

aa. Leaves usually pressed against twigs; opposite or three in a whorl. See Fig. 4.

    b. Twigs flattish.
        Cone cylindrical, twigs strongly flattened. *Arbor Vitae.* p. 54.
        Cone roundish, twigs slightly flattened. *White Cedar.* pp. 55, 191.

    bb. Twigs square or rounded, fruit berry-like. *Juniper.* pp. 55, 191.

II. The Broad-Leaved Trees

A. *Leaves opposite.* See Fig. 11. See p. 17.
B. *Leaves not opposite but alternating.* See Fig. 12. See p. 18.

Fig. 11

Fig. 12

A. LEAVES OPPOSITE

1. *Leaves simple, not composed of several leaflets.* See Fig. 13. See below.
2. *Leaves not simple but composed of several leaflets (compound).* See Fig. 14. See p. 18.

Fig. 13

Fig. 14

1. Leaves simple

Leaves with large veins spreading from the petiole. See Fig. 15.
Leaves lobed. *Maple.* See Fig. 15. See pp. 153, 229.
Leaves not lobed. *Catalpa and Paulownia.* pp. 180, 245.

Fig. 15

Fig. 16

Leaves with large veins mostly spreading from the middle vein. See Fig. 16.
  a. Leaf margin smooth (toothless). See Fig. 13.
    Leaves pale and mostly whitish on lower surface. *Dogwood.* pp. 165, 237.
    Leaves not whitish below.
      Tips of leaves mostly indented.
        Margin of leaf curled under. *Red Ironwood.* p. 232.
        Margin of leaf not curled under. *Black Ironwood.* p. 233.
      Tips of leaves blunt or sharp-pointed, not indented.
        Leaves with black dots; fragrant. *Eugenia.* p. 236.
        Leaves not as above.
          Midrib exceptionally broad. *Mangrove.* p. 234.
          Midrib otherwise.

   Leaves ovate to lanceolate, 2-6 inches long.
    Buttonbush. pp. 181, 246.
   Leaves usually elliptical or obovate.
    Leaves mostly blunt-pointed, leathery, rusty
     beneath. *Viburnum.* p. 184.
    Leaves sharp-pointed.
     Leaves 1-2 inches long. *Privet.* p. 178.
     Leaves 3-4 inches long. *Fiddlewood.* p.
      245.
     Leaves 4-8 inches long. *Fringetree.* pp.
      178, 244.

aa. Leaf margin toothed. See Fig. 16.

  Leaves ovate, obovate or rounded. *Viburnum.* pp. 182,
   246.

  Leaves elliptical.

   Leaves fine-toothed, hairy beneath. *Burningbush.* p.
    152.

   Leaves blunt-toothed, smooth beneath. *Adelia.* pp.
    178, 244.

2. *Leaves not simple but composed of several leaflets (compound)*

Leaves with large veins extending to the teeth.
 Leaf composed of 5-7 leaflets. *Buckeye.* pp. 159, 230.
 Leaf composed of 3-5 leaflets. *Box Elder.* p. 154.

Leaves with large veins not extending to the teeth but branch-
  ing and uniting within the margin.
 Teeth rounded or nearly lacking. *Ash.* pp. 174, 241.
 Teeth sharp.
  Leaf of 3 leaflets. *Bladdernut.* p. 152.
  Leaf of 5-11 leaflets. *Elderberry.* p. 181.

B. LEAVES NOT OPPOSITE BUT ALTERNATING

1. *Leaves simple (not composed of several leaflets).* See Fig.
 18. See p. 19.

2. *Leaves not simple but composed of several leaflets (compound).* See Fig. 17. See p. 27.

Fig. 17   Fig. 18   Fig. 19

1. Leaves simple

1a. Leaf margin smooth (toothless). See Fig. 18. See below.
1b. Leaf margin toothed. See Fig. 19; also p. 22.

1a. Leaf margin smooth

Branchlets surrounded by transparent sheath above attachment of leaf. *Pigeon Plum.* p. 214.

Branchlets without transparent sheath.

  a Branchlets spiny.

      Pith orange colored. *Osage Orange.* pp. 118, 213.

      Pith not orange colored. *Bumelia.* pp. 171, 238.

  aa. Branchlets not spiny.

      b. Juice milky or gummy, *Bumelia.* pp. 171, 238.

      bb. Juice not milky.

          c. Twigs and leaves spicy.

             Twigs shining green. *Sassafras.* pp. 123, 216.

             Twigs brownish. *Spicebush.* p. 124.

          cc. Twigs and leaves not spicy.

             d. Buds not covered with overlapping scales. See Fig. 20.

                Leaves long and narrow, buds flattened against twigs. *Willow.* pp. 65, 193.

                Leaves oblong, leathery, evergreen. *Persea.* p. 216.

                Leaves large and broad, buds not flattened against twigs.

                   Leaf with broad notch at end. *Tulip Tree.* pp. 121, 215.

Leaf pointed at end. *Magnolia*. pp. 118, 214.

dd. Buds covered with overlapping scales. See Fig. 21.

Fig. 20

Fig. 21

e. Large veins mostly spreading from petiole. See Fig. 22.

Leaf with 5 large veins. *Redbud*. pp. 140, 221.

Leaf with 3 large veins. *Sugarberry*. pp. 115, 213.

ee. Large veins mostly spreading from middle vein. See Fig. 23.

f. Leaves with sharp tip.

Leaves ovate to elliptical, 2-4 inches long. *Dogwood*. pp. 165, 237.

Leaves lanceolate to elliptical, 4-6 inches long. *Corkwood*. p. 194.

Leaves oblong, obovate to oblanceolate.

Fig. 22

Fig. 23

g. *B a r k   o f   t r u n k rough*. Bark scaly or ridged; fruit an acorn. *Oak*. pp. 95, 202.

Bark ridged in angular plates; fruit cherry-like. *Tupelo.* pp. 164, 236.

gg. *Bark of trunk smoothish.*

Large trees; fruit an acorn. *Oak.* pp. 95, 202.

S m a l l tree or shrubs. Leaf thin, 10-12 i n c h e s long. *Pawpaw.* pp. 122, 216.

Leaf thick and leathery.

Leaf 3-4 inches long. *Laurel.* p. 169.

Leaf 4-12 inches l o n g. *Rhododendron.* p. 168.

ff. Leaves with blunt or rounded tip.

Juice resinous, unpleasant o d o r. *S m o k e t r e e.* p. 145.

Juice watery.

Fruit a small, woody pod; leaf roundish. *Witch-hazel.* pp. 124, 216.

Fruit an acorn, leaf not r o u n d i s h. *Oak.* pp. 95, 202.

1b. Leaf margin toothed

Juice milky.

Leaves 1-2 feet long, deeply 5-7 lobed, the upper lobes again deeply incised. *Papaya*. p. 235.

Leaves smaller; lobed or not lobed.

Leaves smooth or roughish above. *Mulberry*. pp. 116, 213.

Leaves harshly rough above. *Paper Mulberry*. pp. 117, 213.

Juice not milky.

a. Branches of tree or some of them with spines.

Thorns on sides of long branches. *Thorn*. pp. 132, 217.

Thorns at ends of short, rough twigs.

Teeth of leaf blunt or lacking. *Buckthorn*. pp. 161, 233.

Teeth of leaf sharp.

Buds blunt, often hairy. *Pear. Apple*. p. 127.

Buds pointed, smooth, *Plum*. pp. 134, 218.

aa. Branches of tree without spines.

b. Large veins spreading from petiole. See Fig. 24.

Fig. 24

Fig. 25

Fig. 26

c. Leaves with lobes. See Fig. 24.

Lobes narrow; fine-toothed; leaf starlike. *Sweet Gum*. pp. 125, 217.

Lobes broad; coarse-toothed; leaf roundish. *Sycamore*. pp. 125, 217.

Lobes short; blunt-toothed; leaf ovate. *Poplar*. pp. 58, 193.

cc. Leaves without lobes. See Fig. 25.

d. Leaves broadly ovate, roundish or triangular.

Leaves thin, sharp-toothed. *Linden*. pp. 162, 233.

Leaves firm, blunt-toothed. *Poplar*. pp. 58, 193.

dd. Leaves ovate.

Fine-toothed, even at base. *Jersey-tea*. p. 162.

Coarse-toothed or smooth, usually uneven at base. *Hackberry*. pp. 115, 213.

bb. Large veins mostly spreading from middle vein. See Fig. 26.

c. Buds not covered with overlapping scales. See Fig. 20.

Leaves usually long and narrow. *Willow*. pp. 65, 193.

Leaves lanceolate to oblong, tapering to base. *Gordonia*. p. 234.

Leaves broad-ovate to obovate. *Alder*. p. 91.

cc. Buds covered with overlapping scales. See Fig. 21.

d. Leaves with large veins extending to the teeth. See Fig. 19.

e. Bark of trunk smooth (not ridged, sometimes cracking).

f. *Small trees or shrubs.*

Leaf very uneven at base. *W i t c h-hazel*. pp. 124, 216.

Celtis. pp. 114, 213.

Leaf even at base or nearly so.

Leaves aromatic. *Myrica*. pp. 75, 194.

Leaves not aromatic. Bark slate-gray with muscle-like swell-

ings. *Hornbeam.*
pp. 85, 200.
Bark russet to dark
brown.
Leaf base heart-
shaped. *Hazel-
nut.* p. 87.
Leaf base narrow
o r rounded.
Clethra. p. 167.

ff. *Large trees.*
Bark light steel-gray.
Beech. pp. 93, 201.
Bark red-brown, yellow-
ish or white. *Birch.*
pp. 88, 201.
Bark brown or greenish
b r o w n ; fruit an
acorn. *Oak.* pp. 95,
202.

ee. Bark of trunk rough (scaly,
warty or ridged).
f. *Large branches ending
in coarse, stiff twigs.*
Buds several at end of
twig; fruit an acorn.
Oak. pp. 95, 202.
Buds one at end of twig.
Leaves o b l o n g to
lanceolate. *Chestnut.*
pp. 94, 201.
Leaves ovate to round-
ish. *Linden.* pp. 162,
233.

ff. *Large branches ending
in slender twigs.*
Bark ridged or warty.
Fruit winged nutlet.

Elm. pp. 110, 212.

Fruit cherry-like. *Celtis.* pp. 114, 213.

Bark in thin large scales. *Water Elm.* pp. 114, 213.

Bark in thin narrow scales. *H o p Hornbeam.* pp. 86, 200.

Bark in papery strips or coarse plates. *Birch.* pp. 88, 201.

dd. Leaves with large veins not extending to the teeth, but branching and uniting within the leaf margin. See Fig. 27.

Fig. 27

e. Leaves broadly ovate, triangular or roundish. *Poplar.* pp. 58, 193.

ee. Leaves elliptical, lanceolate, oblong or obovate.

f. Bark of trunk smooth (or slightly ridged but n o t scaly ridged).

g. *Bark smooth.*

Bark with vertical stripes. *Shadblow.* p. 131.

Bark with horizontal stripes. *Cherry Plum. P e a c h.* pp. 133, 134, 218.

Bark w i t h o u t
stripes, some-
times minutely
warty.

Teeth of leaf
few or indis-
tinct or lack-
ing. *Ilex*. pp.
149, 227.

Teeth of leaf nu-
merous, fine,
sharp. *Choke-
berry*. p. 130.

See here also
certain forms
of *Shadblow*.
p. 131.

gg. *Bark s l i g h t l y
ridged*.

Bark r e d d i s h
brown w i t h
tan - colored
v e r t i c a l
stripes. *Silver-
bell*. pp. 172,
239.

Bark light gray
or brown.

Bark with ridges
widely s e p a-
r a t e d; leaf
s w e e t i s h.
Sweetleaf. pp.
173, 241.

B a r k o f t e n
b l a c k -
b l o t c h e d.
Buckthorn. pp.
161, 233.

ff. Bark of trunk rough ridged.

Ridges deep, rounded; leaf sour. *Sourwood.* pp. 170, 237.

Ridges shallow, broad, flat. *Silverbell.* pp. 172, 239.

Ridges narrow, scaly, or smooth. *Shadblow.* p. 131.

See here also certain f o r m s of *Crab Apple.* p. 127.

fff. Bark of trunk in rough scales or plates.

g. B a r k in thick, squarish blocks. *Persimmon.* pp. 172, 239.

gg. Bark in irregular or oblong thin scales or plates. Trees of wet soil. *Farkleb e r r y.* pp. 170, 238.

Trees of drier soil. *P e a r. A p p l e.* p. 127.

ggg. Bark in coarse plates or outturned scales; h o r i z o n-tal lines on b r a n c h e s. *Peach. Plum. C h e r r y.* pp. 133, 134, 218.

2. *Leaves not simple but composed of several leaflets*
(*compound*)

Branches and twigs generally spiny.
  Spines at base of petiole.
    Leaflets broad (oval or oblong); ½-2 inches long.
      4 leaflets. *Cat's Claw.* p. 222.
      7-9 leaflets. *Locust.* pp. 143, 225.
    Leaflets narrow (linear); or if broad, then less than ½ inch long.
    Leaflets arranged along one main stalk of leaf. *Wild Lime.* p. 227.
    Leaflets arranged on secondary stalks branching from the main stalk of the leaf.
    Leaf mostly with 2 leaflet-bearing stalks. *Mesquite.* p. 224.
    Lcaf mostly with 6 or more leaflet-bearing stalks. *Pithecolobium.* p. 222.
  Spines scattered on stems and branchlets.
    Spines large. *Honeylocust.* pp. 140, 222.
    Spines small.
      Leaflet ovate to oblong; teeth few. *Prickly Ash.* pp. 144, 226.
      Leaflet ovate; teeth many. *Aralia.* pp. 164, 234.
Branches and twigs not spiny.
  Leaves composed of 3 leaflets. { *Poison Ivy.* p. 147. / *Hoptree.* pp. 144, 227. }
  Leaves composed of more than 3 leaflets.
    Juice milky. *Sumac.* pp. 146, 227.
    Juice not milky.
      Leaves aromatic when crushed.
        Pith chambered. *Walnut.* See Fig. 28; pp. 77, 194.
        Pith solid. *Hickory.* See Fig. 29; pp. 79, 194.

Fig. 28

Fig. 29

Leaves not aromatic when crushed.
Leaf margin smooth.
Leaflets opposite.
Shrubs. *Shining Sumac.* p. 148.
Large trees.
Leaves pinnate, *i.e.,* with leaflets attached to main stalk of leaf.
Leaflets with distinct petiolules. *Jamaica Dogwood.* p. 226.
Leaflets without petiolules, or nearly so. *Sapindus.* p. 231.
Leaves bipinnate, *i.e.,* with leaflets attached to branches of the main stalk of the leaf.
Leaflets ovate, about 2½ inches long. *Coffeetree.* pp. 141, 222.
Leaflets linear, about ½ inch long. *Albizzia.* p. 225.
Leaflets mostly alternate.
Leaflets curved; unequal on the two sides of the midrib. *Sapindus.* p. 231.
Leaflets not curved; equal on the two sides of the midvein. *Yellow-wood.* p. 142.
Leaf margin toothed.
Leaflet toothed only at base. *Ailanthus.* p. 145.
Leaflet toothed at upper end. *Mountain Ash.* pp. 126, 243.

III. The Monocots

Leaves sword-like, not lobed or divided, 1½-3 feet long. *Spanish Bayonet.* p. 247.
Leaves fan-shaped, lobed, 5-6 feet long. *Sabal Palmetto.* p. 247.

GENERAL KEY TO THE WESTERN TREES

I. The Cone-Bearing Trees

A. Leaves 1-1¾ inches long, mostly clustered at end of short twigs. *Larch*. p. 259.

B. Leaves not clustered at ends of short twigs, but scattered along the branchlets.

  a. Leaves projecting from the twigs, not opposite or whorled.

    b. Leaves in groups of 2, 3, 4, or 5, surrounded by papery scales at base. *Pine*. p. 251.

    bb. Leaves not in groups, but attached singly to stem.

      c. Leaves decurrent, *i.e.*, base of leaf appears to extend down the stem.

        d. Petiole not distinct; cone made up of dry, woody scales. *Redwood*. p. 270.

        dd. Petiole distinct, thin, yellow; cone fleshy, red. *Yew*. p. 274.

        ddd. Leaves abruptly narrowed at base and apex, cone fleshy, green, often purple tinged. *California Nutmeg*. p. 274.

      cc. Leaves not decurrent.

        d. Twigs smooth after leaf-fall.

          e. Buds pointed, not resinous; cones hanging. *Douglas Fir*. p. 263.

          ee. Buds not pointed; resinous; cones erect. *Fir*. p. 264.

        dd. Twigs rough after leaf-fall, cones pendant.

          e. Leaves not stalked, four-sided, not in two ranks. *Spruce*. p. 260.

          ee. Leaves short stalked, flat, becoming two-ranked. *Hemlock*. p. 262.

  aa. Leaves scale-like, usually pressed against twigs, mostly opposite or 3 in a whorl.
  b. Twigs flat.
    c. Scale-leaves usually opposite (sometimes 3 in a whorl) overlapping one another.
      d. Branchlets very flat, cone elongate. *Arbor Vitae.* p. 268.
      dd. Branchlets only slightly flattened, cone roundish. *"Cypress."* p. 268.
    cc. Scale-leaves 4 in a whorl, not overlapping. *Incense Cedar.* p. 268.
    bb. Twigs not flat.
  c. Scales scattered spirally. *Sequoia.* p. 270.
  cc. Scales in pairs or threes.
    d. Branchlets disposed in one plane, cone with thickened scales. *Cypress.* p. 270.
    dd. Branchlets not in one plane, cone berry-like. *Juniper.* p. 272.

II. The Broad-Leaved Trees

A. Leaves very large, 5-6 feet long, fan-shaped; trunk unbranched. *Fan Palm.* p. 275.

AA. Leaves thick, lanceolate, sharp-pointed, greatly broadened at base, about 8 inches long. *Joshua Tree.* p. 274.

AAA. Leaves absent or much reduced, stems prickly, succulent, columnar or jointed. *The Cacti.* p. 308.

AAAA. Leaves absent most of the year, or inconspicuous, stems spiny or unarmed, but not succulent, usually much branched.
  a. Twigs zigzag, olive green, with thin prickles ¼ inch long. *Palo Verde.* p. 301.
  aa. Twigs straight, branchlets ending in spines, light green.
    b. Branchlets stout, ending abruptly in a sharp point. *Koeberlinia.* p. 307.

    bb. Branchlets slender.
       c. Covered with fine hairs for one or two years. *Smoke-tree.* p. 301.
       cc. Woolly when young, slightly hairy for one or two years; covered with scales of undeveloped buds. *Male Palo Verde.* p. 300.
AAAAA. Leaves not as above.
B. *Leaves opposite.* See below.
BB. *Leaves not opposite, but alternate.* See p. 33.

B. LEAVES OPPOSITE

1. *Leaves simple, not composed of several leaflets.* See below.
2. *Leaves not simple, but composed of several leaflets (compound).* See below.

1. Leaves simple

Leaves palmately lobed. *Maple.* p. 302.
Leaves not lobed.
    a. Leaves very narrow (linear-lanceolate), petiole short or absent. *Desert Willow.* p. 313.
    aa. Leaves broad, petiole long.
       b. Leaves 1½-2 inches long. *Single-leaf Ash.* p. 310.
       bb. Leaves usually 4-5 inches long. *Dogwood.* p. 309.

2. Leaves compound

Leaves with large veins extending to the teeth.
    a. Leaf composed of 5 leaflets (palmate). *Buckeye.* p. 305.
    aa. Leaf composed of 3 leaflets (if 5, pinnately arranged). *Box Elder.* p. 305.
Leaves with large veins not extending to teeth, but branching and uniting within margin.
    a. Teeth rounded or nearly lacking, fruit winged, dry. *Ash.* p. 310.
    aa. Teeth sharp, fruit a small berry. *Elderberry.* p. 314.

BB. LEAVES NOT OPPOSITE BUT ALTERNATE

1. *Leaves simple* (*not composed of several leaflets*). See below.
2. *Leaves not simple, but composed of several leaflets* (*compound*). See p. 35.

1. Leaves simple

Leaves lobed,

   a. Palmately lobed (with larger veins branching from base).

   b. Leaves small (about 1½ inches long). *Flannel Bush.* p. 307.

  bb. Leaves large (6-10 inches long). *Sycamore.* p. 293.

  aa. Pinnately lobed (with larger veins branching from midrib).

   b. Lobes shallow, saw-toothed. *Alder.* p. 283.

  bb. Lobes usually deep, not saw-toothed. *Oak.* p. 284.

Leaves not lobed.

   a. Margin entire (toothless).

   b. Leaves yellow or golden on lower surface. *Golden-leaved Chestnut.* p. 284.

  bb. Leaves otherwise.

    c. Leaves very narrow (linear-lanceolate). *Desert Willow.* p. 313.

   cc. Leaves broader.

     d. Fruit an acorn (nut enclosed at base by a scaly cup). Leaves of various shapes. *Oak.* p. 284.

    dd. Fruit fleshy, leaves tapering at both ends, aromatic. *California Laurel.* p. 293.

    ddd. Fruit fleshy, warty, twigs red, leaves oval or oblong. *Madroña.* p. 309.

    dddd. Fruit dry, 3-lobed; leaves with 1 or 3 main veins. *Ceanothus.* p. 306.

    ddddd. Fruit dry, narrow-cylindrical, topped by a

very long, bearded style; leaves about 1 inch long. *Mountain Mahogany*. p. 295.

aa. Margin toothed or spiny.

b. Leaves few (scattered) and small (1 inch long), branches spiny. *Smoketree*. p. 301.

bb. Leaves abundant and mostly larger.

c. Leaves unequal at base. *Hackberry*. p. 292.

cc. Leaves equal at base.

d. Margins doubly saw-toothed (with 2 series of teeth, the smaller inserted among the larger).

e. Short spur shoots present, bearing 2 leaves; buds not stalked, covered with numerous scales. *Birch*. p. 282.

ee. Spur-shoots absent, buds stalked, apparently covered by 2 scales grown together. *Alder*. p. 283.

dd. Margin not doubly serrate (teeth of more or less uniform size).

e. Lower portion of leaf without teeth.

f. Leaves crowded on spur shoots. *Mountain Mahogany*. p. 295.

ff. Leaves scattered on elongate branchlets.

g. Leaves ovate, large teeth on upper part of leaf; fruit bluish, fleshy. *Service Berry*. p. 295.

gg. Leaves ovate, teeth mostly large and rounded, present except at base; fruit dry, seeds with long hairs. *Poplar*. p. 276.

ggg. Leaves mostly ovate with sharp-pointed teeth or spines, fruit an acorn. *Oak*. p. 284.

gggg. Leaves oblanceolate, tapering gradually to base, fragrant; fruit small, roundish, purple, covered with white wax. *Wax-myrtle*. p. 280.

ee. Teeth present at base of leaf also.

    f. Leaves with 3 main veins extending to upper part of leaf, joining at base; teeth minute. *Ceanothus.* p. 306.

    ff. Leaves with one main vein extending to tip; other veins joining it along its length.

      g. Teeth very fine, closely set; fruit not an acorn.

        h. Fruit fleshy.

          i. Buds without scales, fruit black, "cherry-like," with 2 or 3 stones. *Buckthorn.* p. 306.

          ii. Buds covered with overlapping scales; fruit red or blue, with 1 stone (1 or more glands usually present at base of leaf). *Plums & Cherries.* p. 296.

          iii. Buds covered with overlapping scales; fruit on spur-shoots, small apples; teeth of leaf with minute glands. *Apple.* p. 294.

        hh. Fruit dry, small, containing long hairy seeds.

          Leaves narrow, linear, or lancoelate. *Willow.* p. 279.

          Leaves mostly broader. *Poplar.* p. 276.

      g. Teeth larger, more distinct from one another; fruit an acorn.

        h. Leaves rusty woolly below (smooth and white with age). *Tanbark Oak.* p. 285.

        hh. Leaves not rusty, woolly, *Oak.* p. 284.

2. Leaves compound

A. *Leaves bipinnate.* See p. 36.

B. *Leaves pinnate.* See p. 36.

A. Leaves bipinnate

a. Leaves with 6 or more pinnae (leaflet-bearing stalks).
  b. Branches armed with prickles. *Acacia*. p. 298.
  bb. Branches not armed with prickles. *Mimosa*. p. 298.
aa. Leaves with usually 2, occasionally 4, pinnae.
  b. Leaves small (1-1½ inches long), falling soon after their appearance.
    c. Leaflets 4-8 per pinna, branches zigzag. *Palo Verde*. p. 301.
    cc. Leaflets 8-12 per pinna, branches straight. *Male Palo Verde*. p. 300.
  bb. Leaves larger, not short-lived.
    c. Leaflets 50-60 per pinna, gradually diminishing in size toward tip, petiole very short or lacking, stalk of pinnae flattened. *Horse Bean*. p. 299.
    cc. Leaflets 10-22 per pinna, petiole not short, stalk of pinnae not flattened. *Mesquite*. p. 299.

B. Leaves pinnate

a. Leaflets large (2-4 inches long).
  b. Leaflets very unequal at base, wider on upper side of midvein and curved; fruit a berry. *Wild China Tree*. p. 306.
  bb. Leaflets only slightly, if at all unequal or curved; fruit with husk enclosing nut. *Walnut*. p. 281.
aa. Leaflets smaller, ½-1½ inches long.
  b. Leaves small (1-1½ inches long), falling soon after 301.
  bb. Leaves small (1-2½ inches long). *Ironwood*. p. 301.

TREES OF THE NORTHEASTERN REGION

THE CONE-BEARING TREES

Pine (*Pinus* L.)

THIS EXTENSIVE group includes some of our largest and most valuable forest trees, and no other group contains so many attractive forms. They are characterized in most cases by their straight stems, large spreading branches (short as compared with the length of the stem) and resinous juice. The bark is usually thick and scaly-ridged. The leaves are long, slim needles arranged in clusters of two to five. Each cluster is surrounded at the base, for a time at least, with minute thin scales. The flowers are of two kinds, arranged in cones. The pollen-bearing cones are small and are composed of overlapping scales. They are grouped at the end of the twigs (see No. 3, below) and appear in the spring, dropping off after a few weeks. The seed-bearing cones are solitary or in clusters of two or more, and have thicker overlapping scales. These cones in the spring are very small but continue to grow, becoming large brownish cones with thick woody scales that are often spine-tipped. In some kinds this development requires only a year; in other varieties two or even three years. A scale of the cone usually covers two winged seeds (see No. 1, below). The scales curve outwards when the seeds are shed, making the cones much larger. There are in our range eight varieties of Pines.

Key to the Species of Pines.

Leaves in clusters of five.   1. White Pine.
Leaves in clusters of three.
    Leaf 6-10 inches long.   2. Loblolly Pine.
    Leaf 2-5 inches long.   3. Pitch Pine.
Leaves in clusters of three and two.   4. Yellow Pine.
Leaves in clusters of two.

Cones curved, leaf about 1 inch long.   5. Jack Pine.
Cones straight.
   Scales of cone without spines.   Leaf 4-6 inches long.
                                       6. Red Pine.
   Scales of cones with spines.   Leaf 1½-3 inches long.
      Spines of cone slender.   7. Scrub Pine.
      Spines of cone stout.   8. Table Mountain Pine.

1. WHITE PINE (*P. Strobus* L.). This is the finest northern pine. The stem is frequently 100 feet high and occasionally

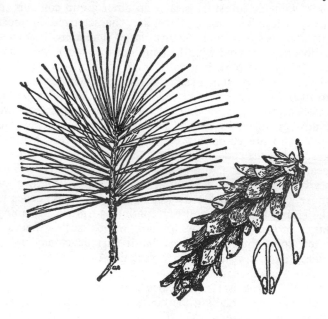

over 200 feet. The plume-like branches are arranged in regular whorls on the trunk, and sweep upwards in graceful curves forming a somewhat cylindrical top. The young twigs are slightly hairy, becoming smooth and greenish with yellow-brown tinge. The bark on young stems is smooth, greenish red; on old trunks it cracks into broad reddish or grayish-brown scaly ridges. The leaves are in clusters of five; slender, flexible, angled, light or dark bluish green, 3-5 inches long. The cones are cylindrical, 4-8 inches long, scales thin at tip, spineless. Its range is from Canada southward, along the Alleghenies to Georgia and westward to Iowa.

The White Pine is the finest timber tree in the world. It once formed vast forests from New Brunswick through Canada and the Lake States to Minnesota. These are now destroyed and will not perhaps be used for extensive forest planting because of the danger from the White Pine Blister.

2. LOBLOLLY PINE (*P. taeda* L.). This is a tree 80-100 feet high, with wide-spreading branches forming a some-

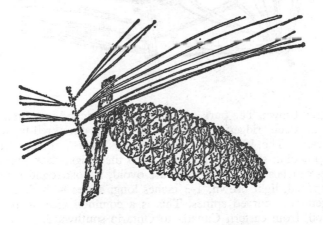

what roundish top. The twigs are smooth and brownish yellow. The bark on old trunks is broken into shallow, broad, flat, red-brown, scaly ridges or plates. The leaves are in clusters of three (rarely two) slender, stiff, three-sided and often twisted, light green, 6-10 inches long. The cone is long-ovoid, reddish brown, 2-6 inches long; scales tipped with short, straight or curved spines. Its range is from southern New Jersey southward. It grows rapidly and will be used in reforestation.

3. PITCH PINE (*P. rigida* Mill.). A small tree 40-60 feet high with short trunk. The branches are coarse, rough, often twisted and beset with many old cones. The twigs are bright green, changing to yellow-brown and finally to

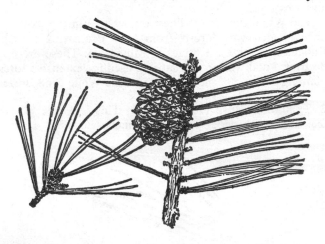

gray-brown. The bark on old trunks is cracked into broad, flat, deep ridges, covered with thick, dark red-brown scales. The leaves are in clusters of three, three-sided, spreading stiffly at right angles to the twigs; dark green, 2-5 inches long. The cones are ovoid, almost round when opened, light brown, 1-3 inches long; scales with slender, generally curved spines. This is a common tree on poor soil, from eastern Canada to Ontario southward.

4. YELLOW PINE (*P. echinata* Mill.). A somewhat round-topped tree, 80-100 feet high. The branchlets and twigs are very brittle; at first greenish violet and covered with a waxy coating, becoming dark red-brown. The bark on the branches cracks into large scales and on old trunks is broken into large irregular scaly plates of a reddish or grayish color. The leaves are in clusters of two and three, slender, dark blue-green, 3-5 inches long. The cones are generally in clusters, dull brown and about 2 inches long;

the scales tipped with nearly straight spines that soon drop off. It is a valuable timber tree, ranging from southern New York to Illinois and southward.

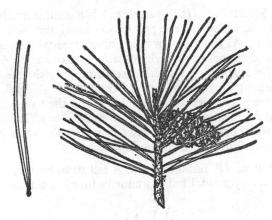

5. JACK PINE (*P. Banksiana* Lamb.). A small northern tree, with wide-spreading slender branches forming an open symmetrical top. It often becomes stunted, however, and very irregular. The twigs are yellow green, becoming dark purplish brown. The bark on old trunks cracks into a shaggy network of thick, scaled ridges or plates, of a dark

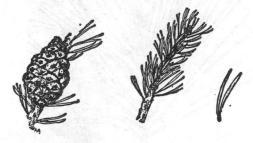

brown or slightly reddish color. The leaves are two in a cluster, generally growing in bunches at intervals along the twigs. They are stiff, flattish, dark green, and about 1 inch long. The cones are uneven at the base and generally curved, shining yellow-brown, 1-2 inches long. The scale is usually spineless and much thickened at the tip. It is found from northern Maine throughout Canada and the Lake States.

The Scotch Pine (*P. sylvestris* L.) is a similar much cultivated tree which has escaped locally along the New England coast. As usually seen it is a small tree with irregular trunk and branches, though sometimes growing to 60-80 feet. The twigs are yellowish, becoming grayish; the bark brownish or grayish and on old trunks scaly-ridged. The leaves are in clusters of two, thickly set on the twigs, bluish or grayish green, often twisted, 2-5 inches long. The cones are mostly curved and dull gray in color; the scale has a thick, squarish, curved tip without spine.

6. RED PINE (*P. resinosa* Ait.). A tall straight tree, at first somewhat pyramidal but at maturity forming a round top.

The twigs are yellowish becoming light reddish brown. The bark on old trunks cracks into shallow, irregular ridges covered by thin, loose, light red-brown scales. The leaves are thickly set at the end of the twigs, two in a cluster, slender, flexible, shining dark green, 4-6 inches long. The cone is ovoid, shining light brown, growing at right angles to the branchlet, about 2 inches long. The scale of the cone is thickened at the tip and without spine. This is a valuable timber tree of dry woods, ranging from eastern Canada to Manitoba, and southward to northern Minnesota and Pennsylvania.

The extensively cultivated Austrian Pine (*P. austriaca* Hoess.) is a beautiful tree and similar to the Red Pine. The twigs are brownish or yellow-brown, thickly set with stiff and very dark green needles. The bark on old trunks cracks into coarse irregular flat plates covered with grayish brown, or nearly black, thin scales. The scales of the cone are tipped with a short spine.

7. Scrub Pine (*P. virginiana* Mill.). A short-stemmed tree with long, widely separated branches forming a somewhat flattened pyramidal top. It often has irregular branch-

ing which makes it more attractive. The twigs are purplish with whitish coating, becoming gray-brown. The bark on old trunks is cracked into shallow flat ridges with thin dark-brown scaly surfaces. The leaves are two in a cluster, stout, flattish, deep green (sometimes with grayish tinge), and twisted, 1½-3 inches long. The cone is narrow ovoid, dark red-brown, 2-3 inches long. The scales are tipped with slender, generally curved spines. It is a tree of sandy, gravelly soils, ranging from Long Island to southern Indiana southward.

8. TABLE MOUNTAIN PINE (*P. pungens* Lamb.). A slender tree with rounded top rarely over 40 feet high. The

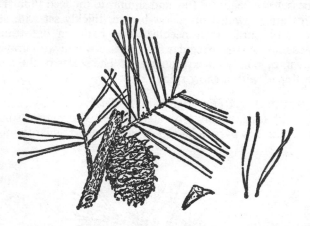

twigs are light orange in color, becoming dark brown. The bark on the old branches cracks into thin loose scales, and on old trunks breaks into large scaly plates of a red-brown color. The leaves are crowded on the twigs, usually two in a cluster, and twisted, bluish green in color, 1-3 inches long. The cones are uneven at the base and often in clusters of three or more, shining, light brown, 2-4 inches long; the scales of cone tipped with stout curved spine. It is found in the Appalachian Mountains from New Jersey southward.

American Larch. Tamarack
(*Larix laricina* Koch.)

This is a slender, graceful tree, often spire-like, with small horizontal or drooping branches. The twigs are smooth, orange-brown, becoming darker with age. The bark is smooth, cracking into thin, roundish, reddish-brown scales. The leaves borne in dense clusters at the end

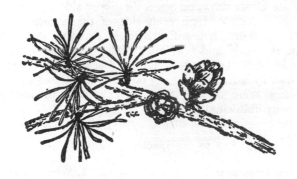

of very short twigs; soft, bright green, about 1 inch long. On vigorous branchlets the leaves are not clustered but borne singly. This tree and the Bald Cypress are the only American Cone-Bearing Trees that shed their leaves in the fall. In the spring the delicate green leaves together with the young reddish cones give the Larches a charm that is equalled by few trees. The cones are ovoid, less than 1 inch long, with thin roundish scales. This tree is found mostly in swamps throughout Canada, southward to Maryland, northern Indiana, Illinois and Minnesota.

The familiar cultivated European Larch (*L. decidua* Mill.) is sometimes found in a wild state in the New England States. It has longer leaves and cones; the branches generally drooping, with yellowish twigs.

Spruce (*Picea* Link.)

The Spruces are the most common representatives of the Cone-Bearing Trees in Canada and the northern United States. The stems are tall, the tops spire-like, and the slender branches are arranged in whorls. The wood is resinous, valuable as lumber, and the principal source at present of wood pulp. The leaves are arranged in spirals around the branchlets, but often become twisted so that they are either crowded upon the upper side or separated into two rows, one on each side of the branchlet. The leaves are four-sided, stiff, with a very minute stem which becomes woody and remains standing out from the twigs after leaf-fall. The bark is thin and scaly. The cones are ovoid or cylindrical and hang down from the twigs. Within our range there are only three native spruces, though there are many cultivated forms.

Key to the Species of Spruces.

Twigs smooth, scales of cone flexible.   1. White Spruce.
Twigs hairy, scales of cone firm.
   Cones falling in early winter.   2. Red Spruce.
   Cones hanging on twigs for years.   3. Black Spruce.

1. WHITE SPRUCE (*P. canadensis* BSP.). A handsome tree, frequently 50-70 feet high. The twigs are stout, smooth, light yellow-brown, becoming grayish brown. The bark on young trees is nearly smooth but on old trunks it cracks into thin, light gray or brownish irregular scales. The leaves have an unpleasant odor when crushed; they are squarish, somewhat curved, sharp-tipped, and bent upward so that they lie on the upper side of the branchlet; at first pale bluish and silvery, becoming blue-green, 1/3-1 inch long. The cones are cylindrical, greenish, becoming

light brown and shining, soft and papery, 2-3 inches long, with very thin and flexible roundish scales. The cones fre-

quently almost cover up the top of the tree. It is found throughout Canada, southward to southern Maine, and westward through the Lake States.

2. RED SPRUCE (*P. rubra* Link.). This is also a splendid and valuable tree, though somewhat smaller than the

White Spruce. The twigs are hairy and yellowish green or reddish brown, becoming smooth and dark brown with age; on old branches often drooping. The bark on old trunks cracks into thin irregular red-brown or grayish scales. The leaves often spread from all sides of the twigs;

they are squarish, curved, somewhat blunt-pointed; color greenish, with tinge of yellow, becoming deep green and very shining, ⅓-1 inch long. The cones are ovoid, reddish green, becoming light reddish brown, usually less than 2 inches long, with firm roundish scales. Before the Wrigley habit became established among adults in America the resinous juice of this tree furnished the spruce chewing gum for children. Its range is from eastern Canada along the St. Lawrence to New York and southward in the mountainous districts of North Carolina and Tennessee.

The familiar Norway Spruce (*P. Abies* Karst.) is an introduced shade tree, reported as established in Connecticut. It is recognized by its long drooping branchlets; the twigs are brownish and usually smooth. The bark is coarsely scaly and red- or gray-brown. The leaves are slender, dark green, shining. The cones are very large and cylindrical, 4-6 inches long.

3. BLACK or BOG SPRUCE (*P. mariana* BSP.). A small slender tree of bogs and cold rocky slopes. It is very similar to the Red Spruce. The young twigs are rusty hairy and

light yellow-brown in color, becoming brownish and smooth with age. The bark is scaly and gray-brown. The leaves are nearly straight, spreading from all sides of the twigs; pale or dark bluish green with whitish coating; rarely ½ inch long. The cones are purplish brown, about 1 inch long, and remain on the branches for years. The scales of the cone are often slightly toothed. It is found from central Pennsylvania northward, in the mountains, along the Great Lakes and throughout Canada.

Hemlock (*Tsuga* Carr.)

CANADIAN HEMLOCK (*T. canadensis* Carr.). This is a large forest tree usually found on rocky ridges, steep sides of ravines, and mountain slopes. The branches are long and slender, with somewhat drooping branchlets. The twigs are delicate, light yellow-brown, becoming dark reddish brown. The bark on old trunks cracks into deep, coarse, gray-brown ridges, covered with thick scales that

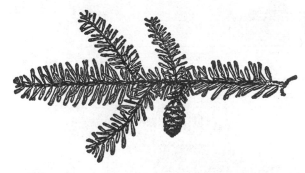

have a red under-surface. The leaves are short, flat, blunt, usually in two rows, shining dark yellow-green above with a silvery stripe beneath; ⅓-½ inch long with a minute petiole which stays on the twig after leaf-fall. The foliage of the Hemlock is perhaps the most delicate and graceful of any of our Cone-Bearing Trees, and is especially striking, in the spring. The cones are ovoid, brownish, ½-1 inch long, with thin roundish scales. It is found in eastern Canada, through the States and Provinces bordering on the Great Lakes, and southward through the Appalachian Mountains.

CAROLINA HEMLOCK (*T. caroliniana* Engl.) is a small tree, rarely 60 feet. It closely resembles the Canadian Hemlock but differs in its longer shining deep green leaves (⅗-⅘ inch) and longer cones (1-1½ inches), the scales of the cone being oblong. Its range is from the mountains of Virginia, through the Blue Ridge to Georgia.

Firs (*Abies* Link.)

BALSAM FIR (*A. balsamea* Mill.). This tree is the most popular of our evergreens. The regular spreading branches, forming a spire-like top, and the fragrant silvery foliage make a familiar sight during the Christmas season. Unfortunately the country can ill afford at present to sacrifice annually the millions of trees that are used in this way.

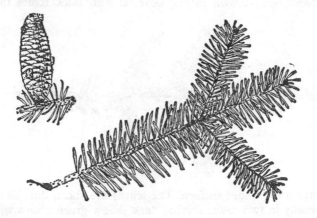

When an adequate forestry policy is established it will be possible to meet this need without harm. In the meantime it would be a good plan to adopt the excellent suggestion recently advanced to plant each year a Christmas tree for the birds, about the house, school or parks. Here is an opportunity to do something worth while and to experience a pleasure that few realize.

This tree attains a height of 40-60 feet; the branches are arranged in whorls of four to six. The twigs are at first hairy, yellowish or brownish green, becoming smooth, grayish red or purplish. The bark is gray-brown, nearly smooth; generally with resinous blisters, and on old trunks sometimes cracking into scaly plates. The leaves are usually in two rows, flat, generally blunt-pointed, shining dark green above, silvery beneath, ½-1 inch long. There is no petiole; therefore the twigs are smooth after leaf-fall.

The cones are erect, cylindrical, sticky with resin, purplish, 2-4 inches long. The scales of the cone are oblong and fall off while the cone is attached to the tree. It is found throughout Canada, northern New England, and the Appalachian Mountains to Virginia, and westward through the Lake States to northern Iowa.

FRASER FIR (*A. fraseri* Lind.) is a small tree of the Alleghenies which occurs from southwestern Virginia to Tennessee. The bark is smooth, cracking on old trunks into thin brownish or grayish scales. The leaves are usually notched at the tips and are generally less than an inch long. The cones are usually over two inches long, with their scales partly covered by a downward-turning leaflet.

Common Bald Cypress (*Taxodium distichum* Rich.)

A lofty tree, frequently 100 feet high, with spreading branches forming a flat roundish top. It grows in swamps,

frequently in standing water, with the base of the trunk greatly enlarged. Oddly shaped corky outgrowths, called "knees," develop from the roots and reach up into the air, sometimes to a height of several feet. The twigs are delicate, and usually spread out in two rows on the branchlets, giving a feathery appearance. They are light yellow-green, becoming reddish brown with age. The bark cracks into broad, flat, red-brown ridges, covered with thin fibrous scales. The leaves are usually in two rows, narrow-oblong and flat, but on some branchlets they are sharp-pointed overlapping scales. They are light green, ½-⅘ inch long, and in the fall are cast off together with some of the twigs. The cones are roundish, rough, of a brownish color, about 1 inch broad. It is found from southern New Jersey, and from southern Indiana and Illinois southward. It is one of our very valuable timber trees and often planted north of its range.

American Arbor Vitae (*Thuja occidentalis* L.)

The spire-like top and compact bright green foliage have made this tree a favorite, and it is now cultivated in many

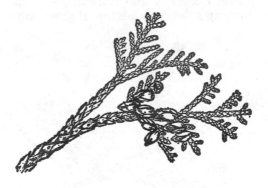

forms. The branchlets are divided at their ends into fan-like clusters of flattish twigs which are yellowish green, becoming after leaf-fall smooth, shining, and reddish brown. The bark is light brown, cracking into narrow, flat ridges that are somewhat fibrous and often spirally twisted. The leaves are small overlapping scales arranged in four rows, ⅛-⅓ inch long. Both wood and leaves are aromatic. The cones are small, pale brown, ½ inch long or less, with thin oblong scales. It is found on rocky banks of streams and in swampy ground, throughout Canada and the bordering States, and along through the mountains to Tennessee.

White Cedar (*Chamaecyparis thyoides* BSP.)

This is a tall tree with spire-like top. The branches are slender, nearly horizontal, and divided into fan-like clusters of slightly flattened twigs, greenish in color, becoming

reddish brown. The bark on young trees cracks into papery scales and on old trunks divides into narrow, flat, fibrous ridges, often with a spiral twist. The leaves are very small, scale-like, or awl-shaped, in 4 rows, dull blue-green (reddish in winter), strongly scented when crushed; about ⅛ inch long. The cones are minute, smooth, round, purplish to dark red-brown, ⅕-⅖ inch broad. The scales of the cone are flat-topped and provided with a minute point in the center. The White Cedar grows in swamps from southern Maine and New Hampshire, southward along the coast. Forms of this tree, the so-called Retinosporas, are perhaps the most extensively cultivated evergreens.

Juniper (*Juniperus*)

1. COMMON JUNIPER (*J. communis* L.). A small shrubby tree, rarely exceeding 20 feet in height, with erect branches

forming an irregular, open top. Other forms are recognized, as *var. depressa* Pursh., a shrub with branches spreading out from the center and forming mats 10-20 feet broad and only two or three feet high. Another form (*var. montana* Ait.) has stems creeping over the ground. The branchlets of the common Juniper are smooth, yellowish, becoming red-brown. The bark is thin, dark reddish brown, and cracks into thin scales. The leaves grow three in a whorl and stand out nearly at right angles to the twig. They are thin, needle-pointed, dark green above and grayish white-striped beneath; ⅓-⅖ inch long. The cones,

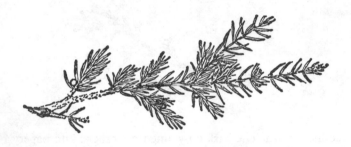

found at the base of the leaves, are berry-like (the scales having become fleshy and grown together); they are at first green, becoming blue with a whitish coating; about ⅓ inch broad. It is found in poor dry soils nearly throughout our range to southern Pennsylvania and Missouri.

2. RED CEDAR (*J. virginiana* L.). This shrub or small tree is among the most widely distributed of our trees, and it is cultivated in several forms. It develops a spire-like or rounded top and in exposed situations often forms mat-like growths. The wood is fine-grained and fragrant, and is used for lead pencils, cedar chests, etc. The twigs are squarish, slender, green, becoming dark red-brown and rounded after leaf-fall. The bark is light reddish or grayish brown and cracks into long narrow strips on old trunks. The leaves are aromatic, and of two kinds: scale-like and

pressed close against the twigs, or needle-like and spreading out from the twigs. They are usually developed in four rows on the twigs; are dark blue-green (often reddish in

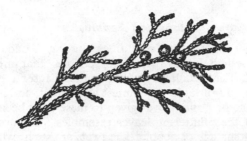

winter), and less than ⅛ inch long. The cones are berry-like, bluish with white coating, and borne on short, erect stems. It is common on dry hills or low ground throughout our range, northward to southern Nova Scotia, Ontario and North Dakota.

THE BROAD-LEAVED TREES

Poplar. Aspen. Cottonwood (*Populus* L.)

THIS IS A GROUP of large trees, having broad usually coarse-toothed leaves with long petioles that are often flattened. This peculiarity of the petiole causes the leaves to flutter and rustle in the faintest air current; and it is said that the name *Populus* was given to these trees because the music of their fluttering leaves resembles the murmurings of an assemblage of people. The twigs are stout, with large resinous buds at their tips. The bark is light colored, and on old trunks ridged. The soft wood of these rapidly growing trees will be extensively used in the future for wood pulp. The flowers are of two kinds and borne on different trees. They appear in the spring in drooping clusters before the leaves are developed. The pollen-producing flowers are reddish or purple, growing in thick fringe-like clusters (see No. 1, below). The seed-bearing flowers are in larger and narrower tassels. The minute seeds are formed in large numbers, in flask-shaped pods, each seed being surrounded by fine hairs (see No. 2 below). When the pods split open, the seeds escape in cottony masses, thus accounting for the name Cottonwood, applied to certain poplars. The hairy seeds are carried by the wind in enormous numbers to great distances, which explains the sudden appearance of poplars in freshly cleared or burned lands. There are eight kinds of poplars within our range.

Key to the Species of Poplars.

Petiole strongly flattened.
    Leaf roundish or ovate.
        Leaf-margin smooth or fine blunt-toothed.
                    1. Quaking Aspen.
        Leaf-margin coarse blunt-toothed. 2. Large-toothed
                                    Aspen.

Leaf triangular or kidney-shaped.
Branches spreading. 3. Southern Cottonwood.
Branches erect. 4. Lombardy Poplar.
Petiole rounded or slightly flattened.
Leaf white felty beneath. 5. White Poplar.
Leaf smooth or slightly hairy beneath.
Leaf blunt-pointed. 6. Swamp Cottonwood.
Leaf narrow-pointed.
Leaf pale or brown beneath. 7. Balsam Poplar.
Leaf green beneath. 8. Balm of Gilead Poplar.

1. QUAKING ASPEN (*P. tremuloides* Michx.). An attractive round-topped tree, 20-50 feet high, usually with

crooked branches drooping at the ends. The twigs are greenish, becoming shining red-brown, and finally dark gray. The bark on young stems is thin, smooth, yellowish green or brown, sometimes greenish white, often roughened by horizontal bands. At the base of old trunks the bark is sometimes ridged and nearly black. The leaves are ovate or round heart-shaped, short-pointed, margins with fine teeth, smooth (downy when young), 1½-4 inches long; petioles strongly flattened near the leaf. See if you can ever catch this tree with motionless leaves. It is found on sandy and gravelly soils throughout Canada southward to Pennsylvania and Missouri.

2. LARGE-TOOTHED ASPEN (*P. grandidentata* Michx.). A large tree 40-70 feet high with slender rigid branches forming a narrow rounded top. The twigs are at first very hairy, becoming smooth, shining, dark red-brown or dark orange-colored, and finally gray with tinge of orange. The bark on young stems is smooth, light gray-green becoming at the base of old trunks dark brown, broken into broad flat ridges. The leaves are round-ovate with few

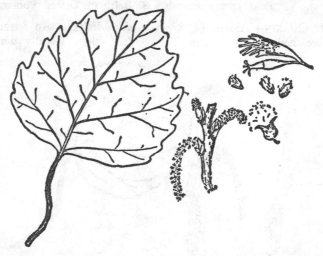

coarse blunt teeth, smooth, white-woolly when young and on vigorous young sprouts remaining so, 2-5 inches long. It is found in rich woods and on borders of streams and swamps, from eastern Canada to the mountains of North Carolina and westward to Iowa and Ontario.

3. SOUTHERN COTTONWOOD (*P. deltoides* Marsh.). A large tree 50-125 feet high with massive branches spreading evenly upwards, forming a graceful, open top. The twigs are smooth, yellow-green, shining, becoming gray-green. The bark is smooth, light yellow, tinged with green, becoming green-brown, and on old trunks broken into deep, broad ridges of a gray or brown color. The leaves are triangular or broadly ovate, abruptly narrow-pointed,

teeth numerous and rounded, shining, smooth, slightly hairy when young, 4-6 inches long. It grows along the borders of waterways from Quebec westward and southward; is less abundant east of the Alleghenies.

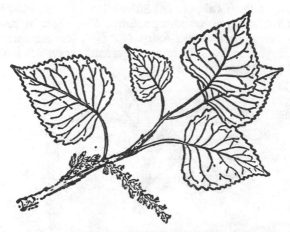

4. LOMBARDY POPLAR (*P. nigra* L.). A spire-like tree covered from top to bottom with short, ascending branches,

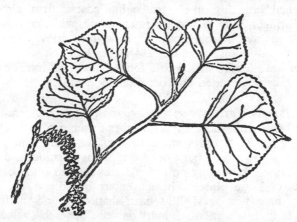

height 30-70 feet. The twigs are olive-green becoming gray. The bark is gray or brown and ridged on old trunks.

The leaves are triangular, ovate, usually broader than long, 1½-4 inches. This Poplar was formerly much planted and is a frequent escape.

5. WHITE POPLAR. ABELE. SILVER POPLAR (*P. alba* L.). A wide-branching round-topped tree 40-60 feet high. The twigs are densely white-hairy (felty), becoming smooth and gray. The bark is smooth, greenish gray, often dark

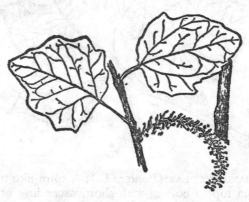

blotched, breaking on old trunks into coarse, firm, almost black ridges. The leaves are round-ovate, with irregularly lobed or wavy margins; smooth, dark green above, usually silvery and woolly beneath, 1-4 inches long. Some of the forms have leaves with 3 to 5 lobes. This is an introduced tree, much cultivated and occasionally escaping.

6. SWAMP COTTONWOOD (*P. heterophylla* L.). A tree of 40-90 feet with short large branches forming a somewhat narrow top. The twigs are mostly coarse, hairy and pale brown or gray. The bark on young stems is smooth, dark gray-brown, becoming on older trunks broken into coarse ridges of loose plates. The leaves are broadly ovate, tip blunt, base flat or slightly heart-shaped, round-toothed, smooth though sometimes hairy on veins beneath (velvety-hairy when young). It is found in borders of swamps from Connecticut southward; also from Ohio and southern Illinois through the Mississippi Valley.

7. BALSAM POPLAR (*P. balsamifera* L.). A straight-stemmed tree, 30-90 feet high, with a few spreading

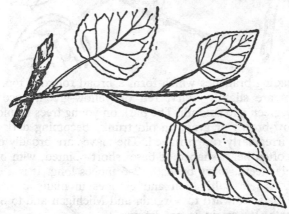

branches forming a narrowed top. The coarse twigs are yellow-brown, smooth, shining, becoming red-brown or gray with very sticky, fragrant buds. The bark on young trees is smooth, light red-brown, becoming later dark gray and broken into coarse ridges. The leaves are ovate to lanceolate, somewhat long taper-pointed, finely blunt-toothed, smooth, dark green above, pale or brownish beneath, 3-5 inches long. It grows along the borders of swamps and rivers throughout Canada, southward to New England and westward to northern Iowa. It is cultivated in several forms.

8. BALM OF GILEAD POPLAR (*P. candicans* Ait.). A form resembling the Balsam Poplar but having more wide-

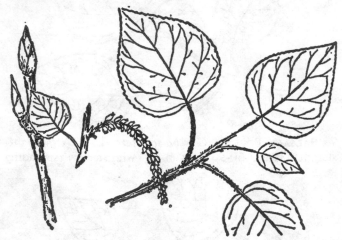

spreading branches which form a broad rounded top. The twigs are slightly hairy, red or yellow-green, becoming gray-green and smooth. The bark on young trees is smooth, yellow-brown or gray; on old trunks becoming dark gray and irregularly rough ridged. The leaves are broadly ovate and often heart-shaped at base, short-pointed, with blunt, regular teeth, hairy beneath, 2-6 inches long. It is a common tree in cultivation and escapes in many places, in Canada southward to Virginia and Michigan and to South Dakota. Its origin is not known.

Willow (*Salix* L.)

This is a large group. Most of them are shrubby, though a few attain the height of large trees. They demand only light and moisture. To start a tree you need only to stick a branch into moist ground. No other care is necessary and they grow very rapidly. No swamp or low river bank would be complete without the decoration of willows. The tree forms of those plants have for the most part irregular, crooked trunks, with the bark broken into dark gray or brown ridges. Their slender twigs bear small buds, usually flattened against the twig, and narrow, fine-toothed leaves with short petiole. There are two small leaflets (stipules) at the base of the petiole. These may fall off early or remain through the season. The flowers are of two kinds and borne on different plants. They are very small and densely grouped in erect or slightly drooping clusters. When they first appear in the early winter they are in small, silvery, hairy clusters—the so-called pussy willow stage. Early in the spring they grow longer, and the pollen-bearing ones take on a yellow or purple color (see No. 3, below). The seed-bearing clusters usually become greenish and produce many small, hairy seeds in each of the flask-like pods of the cluster. When the pods open the seeds are set free in cottony masses (see No. 1, below). There are 13 tree-like willows in our range, besides many cultivated forms.

Key to the Tree Forms of Willows.

Length of leaf more than 5 times the breadth.
　Leaf margin smooth. 1. Common Osier.
　Leaf margin with few narrow-tipped teeth.
　　　　　　　　　　　　　　　2. Longleaf Willow.
　Leaf margin with many fine teeth.
　　Leaf silky hairy, pale above and beneath (see
　　　　　　　　exception). 3. White Willow
　　Leaf smooth, dull green above, pale beneath.
　　　　　　　　　4. Babylon Weeping Willow.
　Leaf green above and beneath. 5. Black Willow.
Length of leaf less than 5 times the breadth.
　Leaf broadest below the middle.
　　Teeth irregular or few or lacking.
　　　Leaf green beneath, twigs very brittle at base.
　　　　　　　　　　6. Brittle Willow.

Leaf pale and usually hairy beneath.

7. Beak Willow.

Leaf whitish and smooth beneath.

8. Pussy Willow.

Teeth regular and fine.

Teeth gland-tipped.

Twigs smooth, crushed leaves spicy.

11. Balsam Willow.

Twigs hairy. 12. Missouri Willow.

Teeth not gland-tipped.

Leaf very shining, dark green, leathery.

9. Shining Willow.

Leaf dark green, thin and firm.

10. Peachleaf Willow.

Leaf pale green with silky hairs (see exc.).

3. White Willow.

Leaf broadest above the middle.

Leaf usually less than 3 inches long.

Leaf very smooth. 13. Purple Osier.

Leaf hairy, especially on veins beneath.

7. Beak Willow.

Leaf usually more than 3 inches long.

Tip of leaf short, teeth coarse or lacking.

8. Pussy Willow.

Tip of leaf long, narrow, teeth fine.

12. Missouri Willow.

1. COMMON OSIER (*S. viminalis* L.). A shrubby tree,

rarely over 15 feet high, the branches long, wand-like, yellow-green. The bark is nearly smooth and pale brown. The leaves are narrow lanceolate, smooth and dull-green above, silvery silky beneath, 3-6 inches long. It was introduced for wicker work, and is an occasional escape from Newfoundland to Pennsylvania.

2. LONGLEAF or SANDBAR WILLOW (*S. interior* Rowl.). A shrub or rarely a slender tree, spreading readily by

branches from the roots and often forming thickets. The branches are erect, with slender, smooth, yellowish or purple-red branchlets. The bark is nearly smooth, dark brown tinged with red. The leaves are narrow lanceolate, rather short-pointed, narrowed at each end, teeth widely separated, and often sharp-tipped; smooth and green on both sides but silky when young, 2-5 inches long. The petiole is very short. This willow is found on sandbars and low wet banks from eastern Quebec throughout our range, though it is rare in the Atlantic States.

3. WHITE WILLOW (*S. alba* L.). A large tree 60-90 feet high with large wide-spreading branches. The twigs are green and smooth. The bark is dull brown and coarsely ridged on old trunks. The leaves are lanceolate, with long

narrow tips, fine-toothed, silky hairy on both sides, 2-5 inches long. It is an introduced tree, much cultivated but rarely escaping.

The Golden Willow (*var. vitellina* Koch.) is a very common form of the White Willow. It is cultivated nearly throughout our range and escapes readily, so that it is the most familiar of our willows. The twigs are brilliant yellow in the spring, becoming red-brown with age. The bark is dark gray or brown, and cracked on old trunks into coarse, scaly ridges. The leaves are silky-hairy when young, but later become smooth and green above and whitish (sometimes slightly hairy) beneath. Another form of the White Willow is the cultivated Cricketbat Willow (*var. cærulea* Koch.) with leaves bluish green above and nearly white beneath. It rarely escapes.

4. BABYLON WEEPING WILLOW (*S. babylonica* L.). A tree rarely over 60 feet high with long, gracefully drooping

branches. The twigs are delicate, smooth, yellow-green, becoming brown and shining. The bark on young stems is smooth and gray, but on old trunks breaks into a network of shallow ridges. The leaves are narrow lanceolate with very long, narrow tips; fine-toothed, smooth but hairy when young, bright green above and pale beneath, 2-6 inches long. It is extensively cultivated and escapes locally from Connecticut to Virginia and Michigan.

5. BLACK WILLOW (*S. nigra* Marsh.). A shrub or a tree with clustered stems 20-60 feet high. The branching is irregular, forming an uneven open top. The twigs are red-

dish or grayish brown, becoming darker with age. The bark is dark brown or nearly black and divided into broad flat ridges that become shaggy on old trunks. The leaves are narrow-lanceolate with very long and often curved tips, bright green and smooth above, slightly hairy on veins beneath, 2-6 inches long. This is one of the most common of our native willows. No low river bank or lake shore would seem complete without these picturesque trees with their crooked black trunks and graceful foliage. It is found from southern Canada throughout our range. A form (*var. falcata* Torr.) with narrow curved leaves is common from Massachusetts southward.

6. BRITTLE WILLOW (*S. fragilis* L.). A graceful tree often 50 feet high, with rounded top of upward-spreading

branches. The twigs are yellow-green often with tinge of red, becoming shining brown with age. They separate from the branchlets with a cracking sound, by a slight pressure of the finger at the base of the twig. The winds often bring down a shower of these twigs, and if they are carried away by rains or a stream and landed in a moist place, they take root and develop into trees. Several of the willows are spread in this way. The bark is smooth and

gray on young stems, becoming dull brown and broken into irregular, scaly ridges on old trunks. The leaves are lanceolate with narrow tips, fine-toothed, or irregularly wavy-toothed, smooth and green on both sides though slightly paler beneath; 3-6 inches long. This tree was introduced into New England before the Revolutionary War for basket manufacture, and is now distributed from Newfoundland to Quebec and southward to Kentucky.

7. BEAK WILLOW (*S. Bebbiana* Sarg.). A shrub or small bushy tree, sometimes 25 feet high. The twigs are hairy, becoming smooth, purplish or brown. The bark is thin, reddish-green or gray, and becomes divided into plate-like scales. The leaves are elliptic-lanceolate to obovate, firm, wrinkled, the teeth being few, coarse, often blunt and irregular, rarely lacking. The leaves are usually hairy; dull green above and whitish blue-green beneath, 1-4 inches long. This is a willow that frequently wades out of the marshes into drier ground. It is found from Canada south-

ward to New Jersey and Pennsylvania; westward to Nebraska.

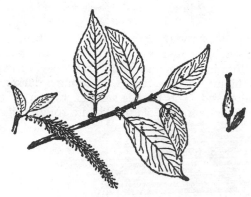

8. Pussy Willow (*S. discolor* Muhl.). A shrub or small tree, frequently 10-20 feet high. The twigs are stout and hairy, becoming smooth and red-purple. The bark is smooth and light brown, cracking into thin, oblong scales.

The leaves are lanceolate to elliptical, teeth blunt and irregularly placed, bright green above, whitish and often silvery beneath, smooth on both sides though hairy when young, 2-5 inches long. It is found throughout our range south to Delaware and Illinois. A related form (*S. erioce-phala* Michx.) has very hairy twigs. Leaves often permanently rusty-hairy beneath and coarsely toothed.

9. SHINING WILLOW (*S. lucida* Muhl.). A shrub or small tree, rarely 25 feet high with short trunk and many erect branches forming a round symmetrical top. The twigs are smooth, shining, orange-brown, becoming darker, often with tinge of red. The bark is smooth, brown or reddish brown, breaking on very old trunks into rough ridges. The

leaves are ovate-lanceolate with long narrow tips, fine-toothed, leathery, very shining dark green, smooth but hairy when young, 2-6 inches long. It is found throughout our range to Virginia, Kentucky, and Nebraska; sometimes cultivated. Forms with very narrow leaves or with leaves hairy beneath are found in the northeastern part of our range.

10. PEACHLEAF WILLOW (*S. amygdaloides* Anders). A small tree, though some attain a height of 40-60 feet, with straight ascending branches forming a rather narrow round top. The twigs are slender, dark orange or red-brown and shining, becoming orange-brown. The bark is brown, often with reddish tinge and broken on old trunks into irregular, flat ridges. The leaves are ovate-lanceolate with long, very narrow tips often curved, fine-toothed, shining green

above, pale or silvery beneath, 2-6 inches long. It is found on borders of waterways, from western Quebec westward

along the Great Lake Provinces; southward to New Jersey, Kentucky and Nebraska; not common in the East.

11. BALSAM WILLOW (*S. balsamifera* Barr.). A shrub—occasionally a small tree—with slender, erect stems. The twigs are shining, light red-brown becoming yellow-green. The bark is thin, smooth, dull brown-gray. The young

leaves are aromatic, elliptical, short-pointed, fine- or sometimes coarse-toothed, thin and firm, dark green above, pale or silvery beneath, smooth but hairy when young, 2-4 inches long. Found in bogs and lowland thickets, from Canada to northern New England and westward to Minnesota and South Dakota.

12. MISSOURI WILLOW (*S. missouriensis* Bebb.). A tree 30-50 feet high with straight trunk and slender, upright or slightly spreading branches. The twigs are velvety-hairy and light green during their first year, becoming brownish

or reddish brown and usually smooth. The bark is thin, smooth, light gray, becoming darker on old trunks and broken into plate-like scales. The leaves are lanceolate to obovate, fine-toothed, smooth, dull green above, pale green or whitish beneath; sometimes slightly hairy (hairy on both sides when young); 3-6 inches long. Found in the sandy river bottoms of the tributaries of the Mississippi and Missouri rivers, from Kentucky to Illinois and Nebraska.

13. PURPLE OSIER (*S. purpurea* L.). A shrub, or sometimes a slender tree 30-50 feet high, with long slender

branches. The twigs are long, wand-like and purple. The leaves are placed nearly opposite on the twigs; oblance-olate, slightly toothed, very smooth on both sides, dull green above, pale or whitish beneath, 1-3 inches long. Introduced for basket rods and ornament, and now escaped locally in the Middle and Eastern States.

Bayberry. Wax-Myrtle (*Myrica* L.)

These plants are shrubs or small trees with gray, smoothish bark and scaly buds. The leaves in some species are evergreen, toothed and resinous-glandular. The flowers are very minute and in compact clusters. They are of two kinds and usually borne on different trees. The pollen-bearing flowers are cone-like and become drooping clusters when the pollen is being shed. The seed-bearing clusters consist of a few flowers and form bunches of nutlets which are usually covered with a paraffine-like wax.

1. WAX-MYRTLE (*M. cerifera* L.). This is a shrub or small tree of 20-40 feet. The stem is often crooked; the branches

slender and nearly erect. The twigs are rusty hairy, becoming bright red or gray-brown, smooth and shining, darker with age. The bark nearly smooth, light gray. The leaves evergreen, aromatic, oblanceolate, thick and firm, margins smooth or with a few coarse teeth towards the apex; dotted on both sides with glands; 1-3 inches long. The small nutlets are closely clustered on short twigs and covered with a bluish-white wax. Flourishes in moist, sandy soil, from southern New Jersey southward along the coast.

2. BAYBERRY (*M. carolinensis* Mill.). A small plant, rarely exceeding 10 feet in height, often forming large colonies in poor dry soils. The twigs are at first slightly hairy, becoming smooth and brownish gray. The leaves are aromatic; oblong, narrowed at the base, blunt-pointed,

smooth, dark green, dotted above and beneath with yellow glands, teeth few and blunt or lacking; 2-4 inches long. The nutlets are in crowded clusters on the branchlets and covered with a grayish-white wax. The wax from these fruits and that of the preceding species was used by the early settlers for candles. This plant is of common occurrence from eastern Canada southward along the Atlantic States; also on the shores of Lake Erie. There are two other common shrubs in this group: The Sweet Gale (*M. Gale* L.) with erect, dark brown stems, leaves wedge-shaped and sharp-toothed at tip, dark green above, pale beneath, smooth, 1-3 inches long; nutlets in small cone-like clusters; found on borders of swamps from Canada and Great Lake States, in the mountains to Virginia; and the Sweet Fern (*M. asplenifolia* L.), a fragrant, attractive little shrub, rarely exceeding 2 feet in height and forming extensive patches on dry uplands. The leaves are long and narrow with scalloped margins, 3-5 inches long. The fruit is small, burr-like. Found from Canada southward to North Carolina and Indiana.

Walnut (*Juglans* L.)

This is a group of large trees valuable for timber and also for their nuts. The branches are coarse and wide-spreading; the bark ridged; the large terminal buds have two pairs of opposite scales. The pith of the twigs is chambered (in thin plates separated by cavities). The leaves are large, aromatic and composed of numerous hairy, toothed leaflets. The flowers are very minute, of two kinds, and borne on the same tree. The pollen-bearing flowers appear in the spring in long drooping clusters. The seed-bearing clusters are few-flowered and develop into ridged nuts covered with a fleshy rind.

1. BUTTERNUT (*J. cinera* L.). A tree 40-80 feet high with short trunk and heavy spreading branches forming a broad

and rather irregular top. The twigs are coarse, at first sticky and rusty-hairy, greenish, becoming smooth, yellow, or red-brown. The bark on young stems is smooth and grayish, becoming cracked into flat ridges of a brownish gray color. The leaf is 1-2 feet long, composed of 7-14 oblong-lanccolate leaflets. They are yellow-green, rough above, hairy beneath, sticky when young, sharp-toothed, 2-4 inches long. The fruit is usually in clusters of 3-5 cylindrical nuts, greenish-hairy, becoming brown, 2-4 inches long. The brown shell of the nut has sharply notched ridges. A yellow-brown dye used by the early settlers for dyeing their homespun was obtained from the rind of the nut and from the fresh bark. Found in rich woods and pastures from eastern Canada and Ontario southward throughout our range.

2. BLACK WALNUT (*J. nigra* L.). This is a handsome tree frequently 100 feet high, with straight trunk, stout, spread-

ing branches, and beautiful foliage. The twigs are velvety brown, becoming nearly smooth and light brown. The bark on young stems is smooth, brownish, becoming scaly, and on old trunks, breaking into prominent ridges covered with thick, dark brown scales. The leaves are 1-2 feet long and composed of 11-23 ovate-lanceolate leaflets; the leaflets smooth, bright green, shining above, hairy beneath, sharp-toothed, about 3 inches long. The fruit usually solitary or in pairs, roundish, dull green becoming brown, 1-2 inches broad. The nut is dark brown with irregular, smooth ridges. One of our most valuable timber trees; found in rich soils from western Massachusetts to Ontario and Minnesota southward.

Hickory (*Hicoria* Raf.)

These trees are found only in eastern North America with the exception of one species in Mexico and one in China. They are large trees with somewhat narrowed tops. The wood is very strong and elastic. The twigs have a solid pith (not chambered) and scaly buds. The leaves are composed of several leaflets, often aromatic, toothed, thick and firm. The flowers are of two kinds, very small, borne on the same tree. The pollen-bearing flowers appear in the spring in long drooping clusters. The seed-bearing flowers are in small clusters. They develop into solitary or few-clustered, roundish fruits with a firm husk (rind) that splits open at maturity exposing a smoothish nut. There are eight hickories within our range and the majority of them are valuable trees.

Key to the Species of Hickories.

Bud scales opposite (see No. 2 below).
    Leaflets 9 to 17. 1. Pecan.
    Leaflets 5 to 9. 2. Bitternut.
Bud scales overlapping (see No. 5 below).
  Bark firm, rough or ridged.
    Leaves smooth or nearly so.
      Fruit roundish; husk splitting to base.
          3. Small-fruited Hickory.
      Fruit pear-shaped; husk not splitting to base.
          4. Pignut.
    Leaves hairy.
      Nut brownish, narrowed at end. 5. Mockernut.
      Nut white; rounded at end. 6. Pale Hickory.
  Bark in long loose plates; husk of nut thick, splitting
          to base.
    Leaflets 3 to 5. 7. Shagbark Hickory.
    Leaflets 7 to 9. 8. Shellbark Hickory.
  Bark scaly, husk thin, splitting to base of nut.
          3. Small-fruited Hickory.

1. PECAN (*H. pecan* Britt.). A splendid tree, occasionally 180 feet high, with stout branches that, given room, spread

out into a broad, rounded top. The twigs are hairy, becoming smooth and red-brown. The bark is reddish brown, breaking on old trunks into a network of thick scaled ridges. The leaves are 12-18 inches long and composed of

9 to 17 lanceolate leaflets, often curved, coarsely toothed, dark green above, pale beneath, 4-8 inches long. The fruit is oblong with thin husk splitting nearly to the base, 1-2 inches long. The nut is brown, smooth, pointed at each end; seed sweet. Grows in river bottoms from eastern Indiana and Iowa southward. Now cultivated for its nuts and in several varieties.

2. BITTERNUT (*H. cordiformis* Britt.). A slender tree sometimes 100 feet high with spreading branches and at-

tractive foliage. The slender twigs are greenish and hairy, becoming reddish or yellowish brown and smooth, finally

gray. The buds at the ends of the twigs are very characteristic, flattened and bright yellow. The bark is gray and
smooth on young stems, becoming cracked into a network
of shallow, firm, flat ridges. The leaves are 6-12 inches
long and composed of 5 to 11 (generally 9) leaflets which
are lanceolate, coarse-toothed, yellow-green and smooth
above, pale and hairy beneath. The fruit is roundish, covered with yellowish scales, having four ridges or wings at
top. The husk is thin and splits part way to the base. The
nut is gray or red-brown with thin shell and very bitter
seed. Found in swampy ground and also in uplands; distributed from southern Maine, Quebec, and Ontario to
Minnesota and southward.

3. SMALL-FRUITED HICKORY (*H. microcarpa* Britt.). A
tree occasionally 100 feet high with slender branches form-

ing a somewhat narrow top. The twigs are greenish, hairy,
becoming smooth, red-brown and shining; buds greenish
becoming red-brown and smooth. The bark is grayish and
smooth on young stems, later becoming cracked into ridges
and finally broken into narrow, plate-like scales, thus
giving a shaggy appearance. The leaves are 8-12 inches
long and composed of 5-7 oblong or ovate leaflets, long,
narrow-pointed, teeth sharp and short, light green, shining
and smooth above, 2-6 inches long. The fruit is roundish,
slightly hairy or minutely scaly; husk thin, splitting to the
base, about 1 inch long. The nut is light-colored, somewhat
flattened, thin-shelled, seed sweet. An exceedingly variable

species, found in rich uplands, from southeast Ontario and Massachusetts to Michigan and Iowa southward.

4. PIGNUT (*H. glabra* Britt.). This tree resembles the Small-fruited Hickory. The branches are rather slender and drooping, forming a more open top. The twigs are nearly smooth, greenish, becoming tinged with red and

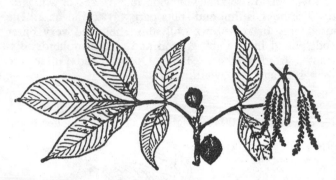

finally gray-brown. The buds are greenish or grayish and smooth. The bark is smooth, light gray on young stems, becoming dark on old trunks and cracked into rough, flattish ridges that are sometimes scaly. The leaves are 6-12 inches long, composed usually of 5 or 7 lanceolate or oblanceolate leaflets, sharp-toothed, yellow-green and smooth above, 2-6 inches long. The fruit is usually pear-shaped, smooth, with thin husk that generally splits part way to base, sometimes remaining closed, or again separating almost to the base; 1-2 inches long. The nut is light brown with thick or thin shell; the seed sometimes sweet or again bitter. The Pignut flourishes in dry uplands from New Hampshire to southern Ontario, Illinois and Kansas, southward to Virginia and along the Appalachian Mountains to North Carolina. The Pignut and Small-fruited Hickory will be found growing together and will be recognized by the fruit and bark characters mentioned above. However, there are also puzzling forms that show characters intermediate between these two species.

5. MOCKERNUT (*H. alba* Britt.). This handsome tree has a height of 50-90 feet. The branches are comparatively short, forming an oblong top. The abundant fragrant foliage is attractive alike in summer and fall. The twigs are stout, hairy, brownish, becoming nearly smooth, often tinged with red, and finally gray. The bark is gray; breaks into a network of shallow, firm ridges, on old trunks the ridges becoming deep and rough. The large, fragrant leaves are 8-15 inches long and composed of 5 to 9 obovate to oblong-lanceolate leaflets, fine or coarse-toothed, shining dark yellow-green above, paler and hairy beneath, 3-8

inches long. The fruit is roundish, 1-2 inches long, with very thick husk, splitting nearly to the base; the nut, light red-brown, four-angled, pointed at top, rounded at base, very thick shell, seed sweet; a fine looking nut but a joke when you crack it and discover the size of the seed. The Mockernut generally grows on rich, dry ridges; is found from eastern Massachusetts to southern Ontario, Michigan to Nebraska southward.

6. PALE HICKORY (*H. pallida* Ash.). This tree rarely exceeds 50 feet in height. The twigs are slender, reddish brown and sometimes hairy, with buds that become brownish and scurfy-hairy in the fall. The bark is grayish brown, smooth, becoming slightly ridged or sometimes broken into very rough, deep ridges, almost black. The leaves are 6-15 inches long and composed usually of 7 lanceolate leaflets, fragrant, fine-toothed, dark green above, pale and often

yellowish beneath, silvery-scaly when young. The fruit is roundish, usually hairy, husk usually splitting nearly to base, 1-2 inches broad. The nut white, thick-shelled, seed

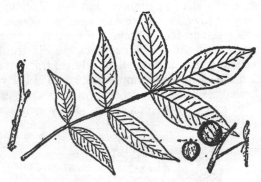

sweet. It is found usually in sandy soils from southern New Jersey and Pennsylvania southward.

7. SHAGBARK HICKORY (*H. ovata* Britt.). This is the best known hickory in the North because of its fine nuts. It is a handsome tree, often 80-90 feet high, with lustrous, clean foliage. The twigs are stout, at first brown hairy, becoming

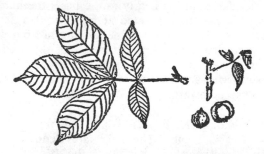

smooth, shining, red-brown, finally gray. The bark is smooth, brownish gray on young stems, cracking into shallow, firm ridges, and on old trunks breaking into thick plates sometimes a foot or more long. These plates are often attached to the trunk at the middle, and the ends turn outward, giving the trunk a shaggy appearance. The leaves are 8-14 inches long, composed usually of 5 obovate or oblong-lanceolate leaflets, fine-toothed, dark yellow-green and smooth above, shining and smooth or slightly hairy beneath, 4-7 inches long. The fruit is roundish with thick husk, separating completely into four parts, 1-2 inches long. The nut is whitish, usually thin-shelled, somewhat wrinkled, and ridged, seed sweet. It prefers low hillsides and river bottoms, and is found from southern Quebec and Ontario nearly throughout our range.

8. SHELLBARK HICKORY, KING NUT (*H. lacinosa* Sarg.). This fine tree is suggestive of the Shagbark Hickory in many respects; the twigs are, however, yellowish and hairy at first and finally grayish. The old bark is sometimes broken into enormous plates (3-4 feet long) that do not curve out as much as in the Shagbark. The leaves are 1-2 feet long and composed usually of 7 leaflets, shining dark green above, paler and soft-hairy beneath. The fruit is larger, 2-3 inches, and the nut is dull yellowish white, or brownish, thick-shelled, pointed at each end. It prefers moister soils than the Shagbark, and is found from central New York southward along the Appalachian Mountains to Tennessee and from southeast Ontario through Michigan, Indiana, Illinois to southern Iowa, Nebraska and Kansas southward.

Hornbeam, Blue Beech (*Carpinus caroliniana* Walt.)

This is a small bushy tree rarely 40 feet high with stout, spreading, crooked branches forming a flat top. The twigs are very slender, pale green and hairy, becoming smooth, shining dark red and finally dull reddish gray. The short trunk is uneven as though having muscles under its smooth, slate-gray bark. The leaves are long ovate, the base rounded, often unequally, sharply double-toothed (the teeth spreading out from the margin), dull green above, light yellow-green and hairy on veins beneath, 2-4 inches long. The flowers are minute, in cone-like clusters and of two kinds on the same tree. The pollen-bearing cones become long drooping clusters in the spring when shedding

their pollen. The seed-bearing cones develop into long clusters of three-lobed leaflets having a small nutlet at the base of each leaflet. These leaflets are green in the summer, becoming brown in the fall. They are blown away in early winter. The Hornbeam is found along streams from Nova Scotia to western Ontario southward.

American Hop Hornbeam. Ironwood (*Ostrya virginiana* Koch.)

An elegant tree, sometimes 60 feet high, with slender branches forming a very symmetrical ovoid top. It is closely

related to the Blue Beech, but the dull brown bark becomes cracked on old trunks into narrow, oblong, plate-like scales. The ovate or oblong-ovate leaves have sharp double teeth that curve in towards the tip of the leaf. The flowers are also similar, but the nutlets are inclosed in a papery flattened sac and arranged in hop-like clusters. It prefers drier soils than the Blue Beech and is found from Nova Scotia to Manitoba and North Dakota southward.

Hazelnut (*Corylus*)

AMERICAN HAZELNUT (*C. americana* Walt.). A shrub or small bushy tree usually forming thickets. You should

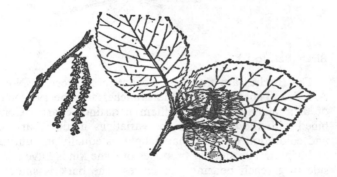

know these thickets because they will furnish nearly every year a crop of hazelnuts, though the squirrels may reach them first. The twigs and buds are stiff-hairy, russet brown, becoming dark brown and smooth. The leaves are thin, roundish-heart-shaped, coarsely double-toothed, roughish above and hairy beneath, 3-5 inches long. The flowers resemble those of the Blue Beech, but the seed-bearing flowers are in very small cones and form large nuts surrounded by stiff curled leaves. Found from Maine to Saskatchewan and southward.

BEAKED HAZELNUT (*C. rostrata* Ait.) is a more northern form, having almost smooth twigs and ovate oblong leaves that are somewhat lobed. The leaves about the nut are united and prolonged into a densely bristly tube.

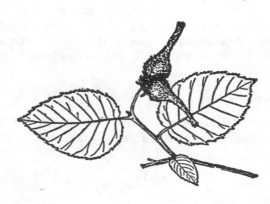

Birch (*Betula* L.)

The Birches are the most elegant forest trees of North America. The delicacy of the branches and the symmetry of their arrangement give them a distinct charm. Combined with these features are variations in the character and coloration of bark that delight us equally in summer and winter. The slender branches of some kinds have short side twigs each bearing two leaves. The bark is smooth, resinous (therefore burning readily), marked with horizontal lines, sometimes cracking into papery sheets, or on old trees of some species, breaking into thick plates or coarse ridges. The leaves are ovate or triangular, often uneven at the base, sharp-toothed, rarely lobed. The flowers are of two kinds. The pollen-producing flowers grow in slender, erect, cone-like clusters of overlapping scales, the clusters becoming long drooping tassels when the pollen is shed in the spring (Nos. 1, 4). The seed-producing flowers are in shorter, thicker cones. The fruit is a minute, winged nutlet containing a single seed, each one covered by a scale of the cone. Fruit and scales are shed in the winter. (Nos. 2, 4.) There are many cultivated varieties of Birches in addition to the native (wild) forms mentioned below.

Key to the Species of Birches.

Branchlets with wintergreen taste.
>Bark dark brown, not cracking into papery layers.
>>1. Sweet Birch.
>Bark yellowish or silvery, cracking into papery layers.
>>2. Yellow Birch.

Branchlets without wintergreen taste.
>Bark light reddish brown, cracking into papery layers.
>>3. River Birch.
>Bark creamy white, cracking into papery layers.
>>4. Canoe Birch
>Bark dull-white, not separating easily into layers.
>>5. Gray Birch.

1. SWEET or CHERRY BIRCH (*B. lenta* L.). A forest tree occasionally 80 feet high. Bark smooth, shining, resembling that of the cultivated cherry, dark brown tinged with red, marked by horizontal lines; on old trees broken into thick, irregular grayish plates. Branches slender, the lower ones nearly horizontal and often drooping at the ends. Twig with sweet wintergreen taste. Leaf ovate, base often uneven, heart-shaped or rounded, sharp double teeth, dark green above, paler and slightly hairy in angle of veins beneath, silky-hairy when young, 2-6 inches long.

Sweet or Cherry Birch   Yellow Birch

2. YELLOW BIRCH (*B. lutea* Michx.). Differs from the Sweet Birch in its very shining yellow or silver-gray bark,

which cracks into loose, ribbon-like strips, curling at the ends. On old trees the bark often cracks into thick, rough, brownish or grayish plates. Branches coarser and twigs with slight wintergreen taste. Leaf less heart-shaped, more hairy on veins beneath, 2-4 inches long. From Canada to Massachusetts, Tennessee, and Illinois.

3. RIVER BIRCH (*B. nigra* L.). A beautiful tree of river banks and swamps. Bark shining, reddish or grayish brown, cracking into thin papery scales that cover the trunk and large branches with a shaggy coat; bark of old trees cracked into dark brown thick plates. Twigs reddish. Leaves narrow at base, irregularly sharp-toothed, sometimes lobed, deep green, shining, very hairy when young, 1-3 inches long. New Hampshire to Minnesota southward.

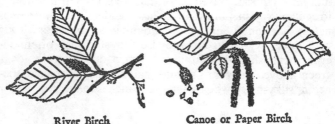

River Birch   Canoe or Paper Birch

4. CANOE or PAPER BIRCH (*B. papyrifera* Marsh.). This attractive forest tree is recognized by its creamy white bark (rarely bronze-colored), which peels off readily into papery layers; inner bark in shades of orange. There are several varieties; the common one has ovate leaves narrowed or rounded at the base, irregularly toothed, dull green, usually smooth above, slightly hairy in angles of veins beneath, hairy and resinous when young, 1-4 inches long. Canada, southward to Pennsylvania, Indiana, Iowa, and Nebraska.

A small tree or shrub (var. *cordifolia* Fern.) with

broadly ovate, heart-shaped leaves, is found from Canada to New England and the Great Lakes.

5. GRAY or POPLAR BIRCH (*B. populifolia* Marsh.). A small tree, rarely 35 feet high, found on poor soil and

swamp margins. Bark dull, chalky-white, not peeling readily; marked with black triangular spots below each branch. Bark of young trees and of branches bright reddish brown. Leaf triangular, with long, narrow tip, base flat or slightly heart-shaped, coarse-toothed, dark green, smooth and shining; resinous when young, 2-3 inches long. From eastern Canada to New York, southward to West Virginia and Delaware.

The Blue Birch (*B. cærulea* Blanch.) differs from the Gray Birch in its more ovate, dull, bluish-green leaves, narrowed at base; also in its shining, creamy or pinkish-white bark.

Alder (*Alnus* L.)

The Alders are shrubs, or small trees, commonly with crooked stems and branches forming tangled thickets in wet ground and along streams. The bark is smooth and brownish. The leaves ovate-elliptical or obovate and sharp-toothed. The flowers very minute, in cone-like clusters; of two kinds and borne on the same tree. The pollen-bearing cones become long drooping tassels in the early spring when the pollen is being shed. The seed-producing flowers are in small green cones that grow larger during the summer. In the fall they have become woody and crack into hard scales, thus liberating the minute winged nutlets. Three of our alders are distinguished as follows:

1. THE HAZEL ALDER (*A. rugosa* Spreng.) is recognized by its smooth, brown bark, and obovate leaves narrowed at

the base, with sharp, nearly regular teeth; dark green above and slightly hairy beneath. It is found from Maine southward (mostly along the coast, rarely inland) to Minnesota.

2. THE SPECKLED ALDER (*A. incana* Moench.) has a smooth gray-brown bark, with small, whitish, horizontal spots. The leaf is elliptical to ovate, rounded at the base,

double-toothed and downy beneath. This is the common alder throughout Canada and southward to Pennsylvania, Iowa, and Nebraska.

3. THE EUROPEAN ALDER (*A. rotundifolia* Mill.) is a cultivated tree often 60 feet high. The leaves are roundish and sticky, at least when young. It has escaped from eastern Canada to New Jersey and Pennsylvania.

American Beech (*Fagus grandifolia* Ehrh.)

A tree of unusual charm both in summer and winter. In the forest the trunk is tall and slim with slender branches forming a narrow top, but in the open the trunk is short with wide-spreading branches. The twigs are slender, light

green, hairy, becoming smooth, yellow, and finally changing to reddish brown and gray. The bark is smooth, light steel-gray, often blotched with lighter or darker patches. The leaves are in two rows on the long twigs at the end of the branchlets, but on older parts they are clustered at the ends of short twigs; they are long-ovate, narrowed at each end, coarsely toothed, bluish-green above, shining yellow-green beneath, silky-hairy when young, 1-5 inches long. The flowers are small, in dense round clusters. The fruit consists of two three-angled nuts in a prickly bur that splits open when frosted. There are several cultivated forms, notably the European Beech with very dark leaves, the Copper Beech with purplish leaves, and the Weeping

Beech with drooping branches. In the north the beech is found on rich uplands but in its southern range in moist places from Nova Scotia and Ontario to Wisconsin and southward.

Chestnut. Chinquapin (*Castanea* Adans.)

1. CHESTNUT (*Castanea dentata* Borkh.). The Chestnut has been perhaps the most familiar of our trees because everyone enjoys gathering chestnuts in the fall. It is a stately tree, 40-100 feet high, with large wide-spreading branches forming an ovoid top. The attractive foliage,

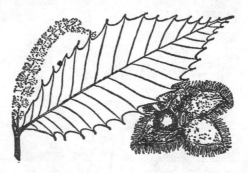

especially when the tree is in flower, presents a picture scarcely equalled in beauty by any other tree. The twigs are shining yellow-green, often tinged with red or brown, and finally dark brown. The bark is gray-brown, cracking on old trunks into shallow, broad, flat ridges. The leaves are thin, oblong-lanceolate, narrowed at each end, teeth coarse and regular, smooth, dull green above, paler beneath, hairy when young, 3-8 inches long. The flowers are small, appearing in long erect white clusters in July. The fruit, one or more brownish nuts in a pricky bur that splits open when frosted; seed of nut very sweet. This was one of our most abundant and valuable trees, now largely destroyed in the east by a fungal disease. It will be reëstablished after the pest has spent itself. Found in rocky woods from southern Maine to Ontario and Michigan southward.

2. THE CHINQUAPIN (*C. pumilia* Mill.) is a shrub or small tree with thick small leaves, densely silvery-hairy beneath.

It is found in dry woods and upland thickets from New Jersey to Indiana southward.

Oak (*Quercus* L.)

The Oaks form our largest and most common tree group and are among the most valuable of our timber trees. They are generally large trees with coarse branches and stiff twigs; buds covered with overlapping scales; the largest in clusters of two or more at the ends of the twigs. The bark is grayish or brownish, cracked on old trunks into scales or ridges. The leaves are variable in form but usually lobed or toothed; hairy when young. The flowers are minute and of two kinds. The pollen-bearing clusters appear in the spring as long, drooping tassels. The seed-producing flowers are in small compact clusters, each flower surrounded by numerous small scales. These scales become the cup and partly cover the acorn (see No. 1, below). There are 21 oaks within our range.

There are two main groups of oaks which can be recognized by their leaves. If the leaves or their lobes end in sharp points (bristle-tipped) they belong to the Red or Black Oak group; if without bristle tips they belong to the White Oak group.

Key to the Oaks:

a. Leaves or their lobes bristle-tipped. Bark dark, usually ridged. The Black or Red Oaks.
  b. Leaf distinctly lobed.
    c. Leaf green beneath.
      d. Cup of acorn shallow or saucer-shaped.
        e. Mouth of cup over ⅔ inch wide.
            Lobes of leaf usually contracting towards their tips. 1. Red Oak.
            Lobes of leaf usually broadening towards their tips. 2. Southern Red Oak.
        ee. Mouth of cup less than ⅔ inch wide.
            Acorn about as long as thick. 3. Pin Oak.
            Acorn decidedly longer than thick. 2. Southern Red Oak.
      dd. Cup of acorn top-shaped.
        Scales of cup smooth. 4. Scarlet Oak.
        Scales of cup hairy.
          Inner bark bright orange 5. Black Oak.
          Inner bark yellowish. 6. Northern Pin Oak.
    cc. Leaf gray or white-hairy beneath.
      Large trees. Lobes of leaf lanceolate. 7. Spanish Oak.
      Small trees or shrubs. Lobes of leaf short-triangular. 8. Scrub Oak.
  bb. Leaf slightly lobed at top, or not lobed.
    Leaf strongly widened at top.
      Leaf brown-hairy beneath. Cup top-shaped. 9. Blackjack Oak.
      Leaf smooth beneath. Cup saucer-shaped. 10. Water Oak.
    Leaf not strongly widened at top.
      Leaf smooth beneath. 11. Willow Oak.
      Leaf hairy beneath. 12 Shingle Oak.
aa. Leaves or their lobes not bristle-tipped. Bark usually

gray and scaly; rarely dark ridged. The White Oaks.
b. Leaf with short rounded lobes or coarsely toothed.
   c. Stem of acorn lacking or very short.
      Tall trees. Leaf with 16 or more teeth.
          13. Chestnut Oak.
     Small trees or shrubs. Leaf with 14 or less teeth.   14. Scrub Chestnut Oak.
   cc. Stem of acorn conspicuous.
     d. Stem of acorn equaling or shorter than petiole of leaf.
      Bark whitish; flaky. 15. Basket Oak.
      Bark dark, ridged and firm.
         16. Rock Chestnut Oak.
     dd. Stem of acorn much longer than petiole of leaf.
         17. Swamp White Oak.
bb. Leaves with deep lobes.
   c. Leaf hairy on veins beneath.
     Mouth of cup fringed. 18. Mossycup Oak.
     Mouth of cup not fringed.
      Acorn nearly covered by cup.
         19. Overcup Oak.
      Acorn half or less covered by cup.
         20. Post Oak.
   cc. Leaf smooth and pale beneath.
         21. White Oak.

1. RED OAK (*Q. rubra* L.). This is the most stately of our northern oaks, 50-150 feet high with few, stout, spreading

branches forming a narrow rounded top. The twigs are shining and at first green, becoming reddish and finally dark brown. The bark, smooth gray-brown on young stems, later cracking into shallow, broad, flat ridges. The leaves thin with 5-11 triangular lobes pointing sharply upwards; each lobe having usually two or more bristle-tipped teeth; dull green above, paler and smooth beneath; 4-9 inches long. The acorn brownish red ½-1 inch long, cup saucer-shaped, flattish, with small, smooth, tightly fitting scales. The Northern Red Oak (*var. borealis*) differs in its larger and less deeply lobed leaves. The leaves remain green later in the fall and the bark remains smooth much longer. The acorn cup is deeper with coarser scales. The Red Oak is found from eastern Canada through south Quebec and Ontario to Minnesota and Kansas and southward.

2. SOUTHERN or TEXAN RED OAK (*Q. schnecki* Britt.). This tree of the Middle West and South sometimes quite equals the Red Oak in size. The twigs are hairy, green, be-

coming smooth, with red or yellow tinge, finally brown or gray. The bark, smooth and gray on young stems; on old trunks broken into reddish-brown, plate-like ridges. Leaves bright green, shining above, paler and hairy in angle of veins beneath; lobes 5-9, broadening slightly towards their tips, each lobe with about three bristle-tipped teeth; 3-8 inches long. The acorn cup deeper than that of the Red Oak, with light brown or gray, woolly scales. Found mostly in bottom lands from North Carolina to Indiana and Iowa southward.

3. PIN or SWAMP OAK (*Q. palustris* Du Roy). A fine

forest tree 40-100 feet high, easily recognized by the numerous slender lower branches often drooping nearly to the ground. These remain on the tree for years after they are dead and were used by the pioneers as staples (pins) in the construction of their buildings. The twigs are hairy and dark red, later smooth, shining green, finally gray-brown. Bark smooth, gray-brown often with reddish tinge, on old trunks sometimes cracking into shallow, firm ridges. Leaf resembles the Southern Oak but smaller; lobes deep, 5-7 in number, sometimes broadening strongly toward

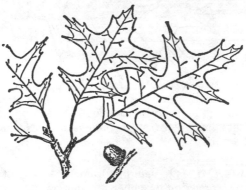

their tips, having two or more bristle-tipped teeth; shining deep green above, hairy in angle of veins beneath; 2-5 inches long. Acorn nearly round, about ½ inch thick, often with dark stripes. Found in low, wet ground from Massachusetts to Iowa, south to Virginia, Tennessee and Kansas.

4. SCARLET OAK (*Q. coccinia* Muench.). A fine forest tree 60-80 feet high with foliage that almost glistens in the sunlight, and in the fall showing more brilliant colors than the other oaks. The twigs are scurfy-hairy, soon becoming smooth and shining, light green, often with tinge of red or yellow, finally light brown. The bark, smooth and brown, cracking on old trunks into irregular, shallow, dark brown ridges (inner bark reddish). The leaves shining, bright green above, paler sometimes hairy in angles of veins be-

neath (very hairy when young), with 5-7 long, narrow lobes, some of which broaden strongly towards their tips and are provided with several bristle-tipped teeth; 3-8 inches long. The acorn ovoid and about half-covered by the top-shaped cup; the scale coarse, brown and smooth.

Found in light, dry soils from southern Maine to Ontario, Minnesota, and Nebraska, southward to North Carolina and Missouri.

5. BLACK OAK (*Q. velutina* Lam.). A large forest tree with wide-spreading branches forming an oblong, or in the open a rounded top. The twigs are at first scurfy-hairy, becoming smooth, dull or reddish brown, finally dark brown.

The bark, smooth and brown on young stems, later cracking into rough, rounded ridges, sometimes nearly black and granular; inner bark bright orange. The leaves somewhat thick and leathery, lobes commonly long and broad with bristle-tipped teeth, middle pair usually with parallel sides; dark green and smooth above, dull yellow-green or brown, usually with rusty hairs in angle of veins beneath (very hairy when young), 4-12 inches long. The fruit resembles that of the Scarlet Oak but the scales are usually hairy and turned outward at the mouth of the cup (when dry). Found in dry, gravelly uplands from southern Maine and Ontario to Iowa and southward.

6. NORTHERN PIN OAK (*Q. ellipsoidalis* Hill.). A small western tree rarely exceeding 50 feet and sometimes shrubby. Resembles the Pin Oak in some respects but is related to the Black Oak in its fruit characters. Twigs at first reddish-brown and covered with matted hairs, later smooth and dark gray or brown. The bark nearly smooth, dull gray or brown, later becoming cracked into thin plates; inner bark light yellow. The leaves as in Pin Oak. The acorn somewhat cylindrical or roundish, ½-⅔ inch long; cup top-shaped with hairy, pale brown scales. Found on dry uplands from southern Michigan to Manitoba, southward to Iowa.

7. SPANISH OAK (*Q. digitata* Sudw.). A tree of 20-80 feet with stout spreading branches forming an open top. The

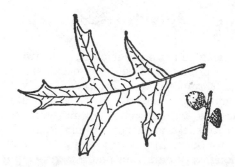

twigs are very rusty or yellow-hairy becoming red-brown or light gray. Bark pale or dark brown, cracking on old trunks into shallow, broad, scaly ridges. Leaves exceedingly variable but often with 3 5 long, narrow, tapering lobes, the terminal one generally longest and often curved. The leaves shining dark green above, densely gray or rusty-hairy beneath, teeth few; 3-8 inches long. The acorn roundish, about ½ inch broad; cup flattish top-shaped, scales oblong, reddish with pale hairs. Found on poor, dry soils from southern Pennsylvania and New Jersey southward along the Atlantic States, and from southern Indiana and Illinois southward. The Swamp Spanish Oak (*Q. pagodaefolia* Asche.) is a smaller tree with leaves 5-13 lobed. Found in wet river bottoms from southern Indiana and Illinois southward.

8. Scrub Oak (*Q. ilicifolia* Wang.). A shrub or small tree, rarely 20 feet high with crooked stems and branches,

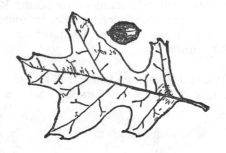

often forming impassable thickets. The twigs are hairy, dark green, often tinged with red, becoming red-brown or gray, finally smooth, dark brown or nearly black. Bark smooth and dark, cracking on old stems into thin small scales. Leaves leathery, obovate, narrowed at base, with 3-7 short, bristle-tipped lobes, shining, dark green above, silvery-hairy beneath, 2-5 inches long. Acorn ovoid, about ½ inch long, very numerous on the twigs. Cup top-shaped, scales slightly hairy. Found on rocky hills and sandy barrens from eastern Maine to Ohio and southward to North Carolina and Kentucky.

9. BLACKJACK OAK (*Q. marilandica* Muench.). A small tree, 20-40 feet with short, twisted branches forming a compact and sometimes irregular top. The twigs scurfy-hairy, light brown, becoming reddish-brown, finally

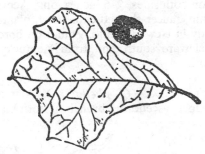

smooth, brown or gray. The bark becomes very dark and cracks on old trunks into squarish plates. Leaves somewhat leathery, clustered at ends of twigs, broadly wedge-shaped, with 3 (rarely 5) short, bristle-tipped lobes or teeth towards the top; shining above, rusty-hairy beneath, 4-10 inches long. Acorn roundish or oblong, and about half covered by the top-shaped, thick-rimmed cup, its scales rusty-hairy. Found in sand and clay soils from Long Island to southern Minnesota and Nebraska southward.

10. WATER OAK (*Q. nigra* L.). An attractive tree 60-80 feet high with numerous slender branches forming a

rounded top. The twigs are slender, smooth, reddish, becoming gray or brown. Bark nearly smooth, grayish, becoming darker and cracking into shallow, smooth ridges of firmly attached scales. Leaves variable but generally obovate with long tapering base and wavy margin or slightly 3-lobed, bristle-tipped at top; frequently evergreen, shining on both sides, 2-6 inches long. Acorn small, roundish, in thin, saucer-shaped cup. Much planted in the South and hardy in New England. Found on borders of swamps from Delaware south and from Kentucky and Missouri southward.

11. WILLOW OAK (*Q. phellos* L.). A tree of 60-80 feet with slender ascending branches, forming a round top.

Twigs smooth, red-brown, becoming dark brown or gray-brown. Bark nearly smooth, reddish brown; on old trunks breaking into very shallow ridges. The leaves somewhat leathery, narrow-lanceolate, narrowed at each end, bristle-tipped, margin slightly wavy, shining, smooth on both sides, sometimes hairy beneath, 2-5 inches long. Acorn roundish, cup thin, flattish, with hairy scales. Found in low ground from Long Island and from Kentucky and Missouri southward. Sometimes planted and several hybrids are recorded.

The Laurel Oak (*var. laurifolia*) has larger and broader leaves; elliptical or oblong, sometimes lobed at top. Found from New Jersey southward.

12. SHINGLE OAK (*Q. imbricaria* Michx.). An attractive forest tree with long symmetrical trunk and slender, horizontal, or rather pendulous branches, forming a narrow, rounded or irregular top. The twigs, at first hairy and dark

green, become smooth and red-brown, finally dark brown. Bark nearly smooth, light brown and shining on young stems, becoming darker and cracking into shallow, firm

ridges. Leaves elliptical to lanceolate, margin smooth but sometimes wavy, rarely somewhat 3-lobed, bristle-tipped, very shining dark green above, hairy beneath, 2-6 inches long. Acorn roundish, cup shallow and slightly top-shaped, scales slightly hairy and close-pressed. Found in rich woods and bottom lands from Pennsylvania westward to southern Wisconsin, eastern Nebraska; southward through the Appalachians.

13. CHESTNUT or YELLOW OAK (*Q. Muhlenbergi* Engl.). A handsome tree occasionally 160 feet high with very

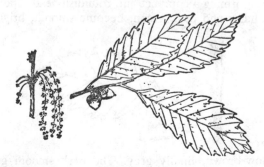

broad base, tall, straight trunk and round top. The twigs slender, at first hairy and green, become smooth, reddish, often with tinge of yellow, and finally gray or brown. The bark grayish, cracking into thin, silvery gray or white scales. Leaves elliptical, teeth regular and usually sharp-pointed, shining bright green above, pale and generally hairy beneath, 2-8 inches long. The acorn roundish, less than 1 inch long, about half covered by a cup of small, hairy scales; seed sweet. Found mostly in limestone soils from Vermont to Minnesota and southward.

14. SCRUB CHESTNUT OAK (*Q. prinoides* Willd.). This is a shrub or small bushy tree, rarely 15 feet high. Closely

resembles the Chestnut Oak but the leaves are obovate and smaller, the margins wavy-toothed; densely hairy beneath. Found in poor soils from Maine to Minnesota and southward.

15. BASKET or COW OAK (*Q. Michauxi* Nutt.). An attractive tree sometimes 100 feet high, with stout ascending branches forming a compact and roundish head. The twigs, at first hairy and dark green, become smooth, bright red

or yellow-brown, finally gray. The bark smooth grayish on young stems, cracking into thin silvery or reddish gray scales on old trunks. Leaves long-obovate with regular roundish teeth, dark green above, pale to silvery-woolly beneath, 4-8 inches long. Acorn usually 1 inch or more long, cup deep saucer-shaped with hairy scales; seed edible. Found in borders of streams and swamps from southern New Jersey southward and from Indiana and Illinois southward.

16. ROCK CHESTNUT OAK (*Q. prinus* L.). A short-stemmed tree with coarse, widely spreading branches forming an irregular top. The twigs are greenish purple becoming yellow or red-brown and finally dark brown. Bark

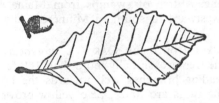

smooth, brownish, somewhat shining on young stems, later cracked into deep, hard ridges, dark brown, almost black. Leaves thick, obovate to lanceolate, margins scalloped with somewhat irregular teeth, dark green with yellow tinge above, pale and slightly hairy beneath, 4-8 inches long. Acorn less than 1½ inches long and about half covered by a firm cup with thickened, hairy scales; seed slightly sweetish. A common, rugged tree of rocky ridges from southern Maine to Ontario southward to Delaware and along the mountains.

17. SWAMP WHITE OAK (*Q. bicolor* Wild.). A tree of 50-70 feet with coarse, wide-spreading, often crooked branches forming a broad irregular top. The twigs shining green becoming light yellow- or red-brown, finally brown, often with purple tinge. Bark smooth reddish-brown, on young stems and branches often peeling off in large thin plates; on old trunks broken into coarse, flat ridges covered

by grayish-brown scales. Leaves obovate with coarse, blunt, short teeth or sometimes lobed, dark green above, usually pale and silvery-hairy beneath, 2-8 inches long.

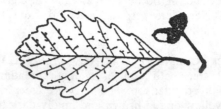

Acorn oblong, about 1 inch long, cup hairy with stem 1-4 inches long. A tree of swamps from Maine and western Quebec westward to southern Minnesota and southward.

18. MOSSYCUP or BURR OAK (*Q. macrocarpa* Michx.). A valuable tree occasionally more than 160 feet high, with wide-spreading branches well towards the top of a long trunk. The twigs are hairy, pale yellow-brown, becoming

light gray or brown and sometimes with corky wings. The bark smooth gray or brown, later cracking into deep ridges covered with irregular scale-like plates of a reddish-brown color. The leaves obovate, the upper portion wavy-margined and separated from the lower lobed portion by a deep sinus that sometimes nearly reaches the middle vein. Occasionally the margins are not lobed but wavy. Leaves shining green above, usually downy beneath, 5-12 inches long. The acorn 1½-2 inches long, the cup hairy and more or less fringed at the mouth. Flourishes in rich bottom lands from Nova Scotia to Manitoba, southward to western Massachusetts and Kentucky.

19. OVERCUP or SWAMP POST OAK (*Q. lyrata* Walt.). A tree usually with short trunk and small branches forming a symmetrical round top. The twigs hairy, slender, green,

often red-tinged, becoming smooth, yellowish or gray-brown. Bark smooth, gray or brown, breaking into thick plates, covered with thin, light gray or reddish scales. Leaves obovate with 7-9 irregular, triangular, or oblong lobes, with or without teeth; dark green above, white-woolly beneath (rarely smooth), 5-12 inches long. Acorn roundish, 1-2 inches broad, nearly covered by cup. Grows in river swamps from southern New Jersey to Indiana and Missouri southward.

20. POST OAK (*Q. stellata* Wang.). A tree sometimes 90 feet high but usually much smaller, sometimes shrubby;

with stout, spreading branches forming a close rounded top. The twigs woolly, brownish, becoming smooth and darker. The bark brownish, cracking into deep, broad, oblong plates. Leaves leathery, with 3-7 irregular lobes, the upper ones much larger, often flattened and notched at their tips, dark green and rough above, grayish- or brownish-hairy beneath, 4-8 inches long. Acorn ovoid, 1 inch or less long, cup flat or top-shaped, scales usually hairy. This is an exceedingly variable tree and several forms are reported. It is found in dry, rocky or sandy districts from Massachusetts to Pennsylvania and Nebraska southward.

21. WHITE OAK (*Q. alba* L.). One of our finest and most valuable trees. This oak with its short trunk and large, wide-spreading branches is a familiar sight in the open country. The twigs are hairy, light reddish-green, becom-

ing smooth, bright red and finally light gray. The bark is gray or brown on young stems, cracking into thin gray or whitish scales, and on old trunks broken into shallow ridges covered by flat, oblong scales. Leaves obovate and usually deeply divided into 3-9 coarse oblong lobes, some of them often having smaller lobes at their tips; bluish green above, pale beneath, 4-9 inches long. Acorn less than 1 inch long in a cup of hairy, united scales. The leaves of this oak are variable and the numerous hybrids add to the difficulty. Found in a variety of situations from Maine to Ontario and Minnesota southward.

Elm (*Ulmus* L.)

The elms are for the most part trees with straight trunks and slender branches, wide-spreading and sometimes drooping. The bark is rough, light brown or grayish; the buds chestnut brown, scaly, smooth or hairy. The leaves are in two rows on the twigs, elliptical to obovate, often unequal at base, and toothed. The flowers are minute, in small clusters. The fruit is a small, winged nutlet (see No. 5, below). There are many cultivated varieties of elms.

Key to the Elms

Twigs smooth or nearly so.
    Branches without corky wings.   1. American Elm.
    Branches often with corky wings.
        Leaf ovate to lanceolate.   2. Winged Elm.
        Leaf elliptical to obovate.   3. September Elm.
Twigs hairy.
    Branches often with corky wings.   4. Rock Elm.
    Branches without corky wings.   5. Slippery Elm.

1. AMERICAN or WHITE ELM (*U. americana* L.). This familiar tree with straight trunk and wide-spreading and

drooping branches sometimes attains a height of 150 feet. The twigs are slender, green, smooth (sometimes hairy), soon becoming reddish brown. The bark grayish, cracking into broad, flat, scaly ridges. The leaves obovate to elliptical, abruptly narrowed to a sharp tip, usually unequal at the base, often double-toothed, smooth or roughish above, pale and sometimes hairy beneath, 2-6 inches long. Margin of wing of nutlet hairy. Prefers moist soil and is found from Newfoundland to Manitoba and southward.

The English Elm (*U. campestris* L.) resembles the American Elm but has irregular, non-drooping branchlets; the leaves are also rougher on the upper side.

2. WINGED ELM, WAHOO (*U. alata* Michx.). A small tree with short, straight branches forming a narrow, rounded

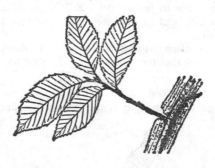

top. The twigs are green, smooth or slightly hairy, soon becoming reddish brown or gray and developing two thin, corky wings. The bark thin, light reddish brown, becoming cracked into shallow, irregular, flat, scaly ridges. Leaves leathery, ovate-oblong, double-toothed, smooth above, hairy beneath, 1-3 inches long. Fruit hairy. Usually found in dry uplands from Virginia to southern Indiana, Illinois, and Kansas southward.

3. SEPTEMBER or SOUTHERN ELM (*U. serotina* Sarg.). A tree 40-60 feet high with small, spreading branches forming a broad, symmetrical top. The twigs usually smooth, reddish-brown, becoming gray-brown and often developing 2-3 thick, corky wings. Bark light brown, slightly ridged and scaly. Leaves elliptical to narrowly obovate, shining light green above, hairy on veins beneath, 2-3

inches long. Fruit fringed with long, white hairs. Flowers appear in September. Found locally on hills and river banks; eastern Kansas and Tennessee southward.

4. ROCK ELM (*U. thomasi* Sarg.). The trunk is tall and straight with short, stout branches forming a narrow top. The twigs stiff, velvety, becoming smooth, red-brown,

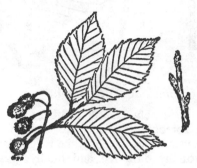

finally brown or gray. They often develop three or four irregular, thick, corky wings. Bark gray or gray-brown, cracking on old trunks into coarse, irregular, scaly ridges. Leaves obovate to elliptical, double-toothed, shining dark green above, paler and soft-hairy on the simple straight veins beneath, 2-4 inches long. Fruit is hairy. Found on gravelly and clay uplands and rocky river banks, from western Quebec through Ontario to Michigan and Wisconsin, south to Connecticut and northern New Jersey, west to Missouri and Nebraska.

5. SLIPPERY ELM (*U. fulva* Michx.). A tree 40-70 feet high with short trunk and spreading branches forming a flat and rather irregular top. The twigs are rough, hairy, green, becoming brown or gray, often with tinge of yellow or red. Bark dark or red-brown, becoming cracked into rough ridges; inner bark white and very mucilaginous. Leaves ovate-oblong, pale, rusty-green, very rough above, hairy and often rough beneath, fragrant when dried, 1-7 inches long. Fruit with smooth wing and hairy center.

Grows on rocky hillsides and river banks from Quebec to North Dakota and southward.

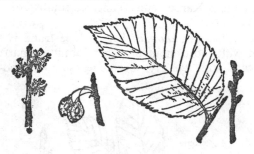

Water Elm (*Planera aquatica* Gmel.)

A small tree rarely exceeding 30 feet with short trunk and slender spreading branches forming a broad, flat top. It is very suggestive of the elms; the twigs slender, reddish-brown, becoming dark red and finally gray. Bark thin,

light brown or gray; cracks into large loose scales, exposing the red-brown inner bark. The leaves resemble those of the elms, being nearly smooth, dark green above, paler beneath, 1-3 inches long. Flowers as in the elm, but the fruit consists of an elongated nutlet with irregular, soft outgrowths. Found in swamps from Indiana and Illinois southward.

Hackberry. Sugarberry (*Celtis* L.)

1. HACKBERRY (*Celtis occidentalis* L.). A shrub or small tree though sometimes 60-80 feet high. The trunk is short with numerous slender branches, horizontal or slightly drooping, which form a wide, flattened top. Twigs slender, usually smooth, light green becoming reddish-brown. Bark

smoothish, light brown, becoming warty or coarse-ridged. Leaves ovate, usually uneven at base, teeth sharp, sometimes lacking, light green and usually smooth above, paler and somewhat hairy beneath, 2-4 inches long. Flowers, small, greenish, solitary or few-clustered. Fruit cherry-like, on long stem, dark purple, sweet, lasting through the winter, ⅖ inch broad. This tree is variable in nearly all its characters. Found on rocky hills and river banks from western Quebec to North Dakota and southward.

Several forms are recognized, as: *C. crassifolia* Lam., with hairy twigs and harsh, often heart-shaped leaves, and *C. canina* Raf., with leaves narrowed at the base and with long, narrow tips.

2. SUGARBERRY (*C. mississippiensis* Spach.). This small tree resembles the Hackberry, but the leaves are lanceolate

with long, narrow tips and rounded or narrowed bases. They are also thin, smooth, and without teeth as a rule. The fruit is dark orange-red. Found from southern Indiana and Illinois southward.

Mulberry (*Morus* L.)

The Mulberries are small trees with wide-spreading branches, rough, gray or brown bark, and milky juice. The leaves are coarsely toothed. The flowers are small and appear in the late spring in long, drooping clusters. The fruit is sweet, white or purple, in blackberry-like clusters.

1. RED MULBERRY (*M. rubra* L.). A tree of 20-40 feet with short trunk and smooth, spreading branches forming

a dense, broad, rounded top. The twigs are usually hairy, greenish gray, often with tinge of red or yellow, becoming smooth and brownish. Bark reddish-brown becoming ridged on old trunks and broken into irregular, long, scaly plates. Leaves ovate, base usually heart-shaped, margins coarsely toothed, sometimes 2-7 lobed, dark green above and usually roughish, hairy beneath, 3-8 inches long. Fruit dark purple. Found in river valleys and on low hills, from western New England to Ontario, North Dakota and southward. It is much cultivated.

2. WHITE MULBERRY (*M. alba* L.). An introduced tree escaped from cultivation from New England and Ontario southward. It resembles the Red Mulberry, but the bark is

light brown and broken on old trunks into coarse ridges. The leaves are smooth and shining, light green, sometimes lobed, 2-5 inches long. Fruit white or pinkish.

Paper Mulberry (*Broussonetia papyrifera* Vent.)

A small tree with short trunk, broad, round top, and milky juice. The twigs are stout, hairy and green, becom-

ing gray. Bark smooth, gray-brown, cracking into a network of firm and often twisted ridges. Leaves ovate, thin, coarsely blunt-toothed, sometimes with two or many lobes, harshly rough above, pale and hairy beneath, 4-8 inches long. The pollen-bearing flowers appear in the late spring in long, drooping clusters. The seed-bearing flowers are in small, round clusters and form a reddish, hairy fruit 1 inch or less broad. This is a cultivated tree but has escaped from New York southward.

Osage Orange (*Maclura pomifera* Sch.)

A tree of 40-60 feet with stout, erect, spreading branches forming a rounded, open top. The twigs are hairy, green,

becoming smooth, light brown with yellow tinge, and often developing sharp spines. The bark is broken into deep, irregular ridges of an orange-brown or dark-gray color. Leaves ovate-lanceolate, toothless, shining, dark green, 2-6 inches long. The pollen-bearing flowers are in long, drooping clusters; the seed-bearing flowers in round clusters; they form a yellowish-green orange-like fruit 6 inches or less broad. Often planted and escaped in many localities, especially in the East.

Magnolia (*Magnolia* L.)

Trees with smooth, grayish or brownish bark sometimes becoming scaly or ridged. The leaves are large, toothless, sometimes with two lobes at base. The flowers are very large, white or pinkish, solitary at the end of stiff branchlets. Fruit cone-like, fleshy and reddish. Cultivated in many varieties.

Key to the Magnolias.

Leaves without lobes at base.
    Leaf 2-6 inches long. 1. Sweetbay.
    Leaf 6-8 inches long. 2. Cucumbertree.
    Leaf 8-24 inches long. 3. Umbrella Magnolia.
Leaves with ear-like lobes at base.
    Leaf white beneath. 4. Bigleaf Magnolia.
    Leaf light green beneath 5. Fraser Magnolia.

1. SWEETBAY, SWAMP MAGNOLIA (*M. virginiana* L.). A small tree or shrub with small, erect, somewhat spreading branches forming a narrow, rounded top. The twigs hairy,

bright green becoming smooth, red-brown and finally gray. Bark usually smooth, light gray or nearly white, becoming gray and sometimes wrinkled or scaly on old trunks. Leaves oblong to elliptical, shining green above, pale or whitish beneath (silky-hairy when young), 2-6 inches long. Flowers white, very fragrant, roundish, 3 inches or less broad. Fruit red, smooth, 2 inches or less long. Found in swamps from eastern Massachusetts southward along the coast and extending into Pennsylvania and central North Carolina.

2. CUCUMBERTREE (*M. acuminata* L.). A slender forest tree sometimes 90 feet high with spreading branches forming a pyramidal top. The twigs are bright reddish brown becoming gray. Bark grayish brown to dark brown, broken on old trunks into scaly ridges. Leaves thin, oblong-ovate,

slightly hairy beneath (very hairy when young), 6-8 inches long. Flowers greenish yellow, bell-shaped, about 2 inches

long. Fruit red, cucumber-like, 2½ inches long or less. Found near streams from western New York and Ontario to Illinois southward.

3. UMBRELLA MAGNOLIA (*M. tripetala* L.). A small tree often with inclined trunk and stout, twisted branches forming an irregular open top. Twigs shining, greenish, smooth, becoming reddish-brown, and finally gray. Bark smooth, light gray, roughened by small sharp projections. Leaves in umbrella-like clusters at the tips of twigs, ob-

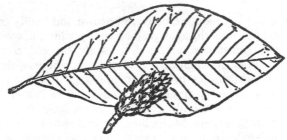

lanceolate, thin, smooth (velvety when young), 8-24 inches long. Flowers white, cup-shaped, unpleasant odor. Fruit rose-colored, 4 inches long or less. A tree much cultivated and found wild in ravines and swamps from southern Pennsylvania along the Appalachian Mountains.

4. BIGLEAF MAGNOLIA (*M. macrophylla* Michx.). This small tree differs from the Umbrella Magnolia in that its

smooth, light gray bark breaks into small scales and the huge leaves, clustered at the ends of twigs, have two ear-like lobes at the base, white-hairy beneath, 1-3 feet long. Flowers creamy white, purple at base, fragrant, 8-12

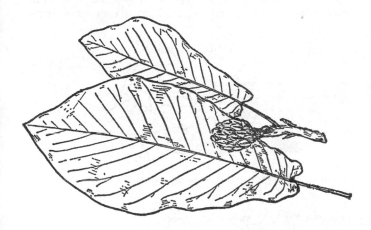

inches broad. Fruit roundish, bright rose, 2-6 inches long. A tree unsurpassed in our range in the size of leaf and flower. Found in wooded valleys from central North Carolina and Kentucky southward.

5. FRASER or MOUNTAIN MAGNOLIA (*M. fraseri* Walt.). This small tree differs from No. 4 in that its leaves are smooth, pale green beneath (not white-hairy), 8-18 inches long; flowers cream-white, fragrant, 5-10 inches broad. Fruit cylindrical, rose-red, 5 inches long or less. Found along mountain streams from northeastern Kentucky and West Virginia through the mountains southward.

Tulip Tree. Yellow Poplar. Whitewood (*Liriodendron tulipifera* L.)

Perhaps the most stately tree of our range, sometimes reaching a height of 200 feet with a stem as regular as though turned on a lathe and frequently showing 50-100 feet of trunk without a branch. The twigs are stout, yellow-green, becoming shining red-brown and finally gray. The bark is smooth, brownish gray, becoming cracked into a regular network of shallow, firm ridges; on old trunks broken into deep, rough ridges. Leaves very smooth and

shining with a broad notch at the tip, usually 4-lobed, 2-8 inches long. Flowers tulip-like, green-orange, 1-3 inches deep. Fruit cone-like, hanging on through the year, 2-3 inches long. This magnificent tree is found in rich woods from Massachusetts westward to Ontario and Wisconsin and southward.

American Pawpaw (*Asimina triloba* Dunal.)

A small tree or shrub with short stem and straight, spreading branches. Twigs smooth or rusty-hairy, light red-brown. Bark dark gray or brown, smooth, sometimes slightly ridged and often white-blotched. Leaves thin, obovate, evenly narrowed to base, smooth (hairy when young), 4-12 inches long. Flowers green, hairy, becoming dull red, about 2 inches broad. Fruit banana-like, greenish yellow to dark brown, 2-6 inches long, sometimes edible. Grows in moist soil, often forming dense thickets, from

New Jersey to southern Ontario westward to Nebraska and southward.

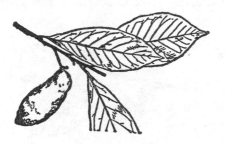

Sassafras (*Sassafras variifolium* Ktze.)

A small tree, though occasionally 100 feet high, with stout, crooked branches forming a flat top. The twigs are spicy, at first hairy, yellow-green, soon becoming bright green, shining and often tinged with red, finally reddish

brown. Bark shallow-ridged on young stems becoming broken on old trunks into deep, rough ridges. Leaves ovate to obovate, lobed or unlobed, smooth (very hairy when young), 2-6 inches long. Flowers small, greenish yellow, in loose, drooping clusters. Fruit small, cherry-like, dark blue. Grows in rich well-drained soils from southern Maine and Ontario to Kansas and southward.

Spicebush (*Benzoin aestivale Nees.*)

A spicy shrub or small bushy tree found in moist soil and along streams. Bark smooth and light brown on the

twigs; dark brown and nearly smooth on the stems. Leaves thin, obovate, smooth, pale beneath, 2-5 inches long. Flowers minute, bright yellow, in dense clusters, appearing before the leaves. Fruit a small brilliant red berry.

Witch-Hazel (*Hamamelis virginiana L.*)

A shrub or small tree with short stem and crooked, spreading branches forming a broad, open top. Twigs

hairy becoming smooth, light yellow-brown, finally brown. Bark light brown, nearly smooth, becoming scaly on old trunks. Leaves obovate to roundish, unequal at base, margin irregularly wavy or coarsely toothed, usually smooth above, hairy on veins beneath, 2-6 inches long. Flowers in yellow clusters, appearing as leaves begin to fall. Fruit a woody, hairy pod, splitting into two parts when the flowers appear. Common in moist woods and borders of woodlands from Nova Scotia and Ontario to Minnesota and southward.

Sweet Gum (*Liquidambar styraciflua* L.)

A straight-stemmed tree, 40-80 feet, with regular-spreading branches forming a narrow top. Twigs hairy, becoming smooth, light yellow or reddish brown, some-

times developing one or more corky wings. Bark dark gray becoming deep scaly-ridged on old trunks. Leaves star-like with 5-7 regular, narrow lobes, 2-6 inches broad. Flowers greenish and very small; the pollen-bearing ones in erect clusters 2-3 inches long, the seed-bearing ones in round clusters on a long, drooping stem. Fruit a prickly ball 1 inch or more broad, often hanging on the tree during the winter. Found in wet soils from southern Connecticut to Illinois and southward.

Planetree. Sycamore (*Platanus occidentalis* L.)

One of our largest trees, 50-80 feet high, sometimes 175 feet. The massive, wide-spreading branches form a very broad and irregular top. Twigs green, hairy, becoming dark yellow-brown, smooth and finally gray. Bark reddish brown or gray, cracking off on young stems and large branches in large, irregular, thin patches, thus showing the inner bark in white, greenish or yellow-gray colors. On old trunks the bark breaks into coarse, scaly ridges of a dark brown color. The leaves roundish with rather heart-shaped base, margins with 3-5 short, sharp-pointed lobes,

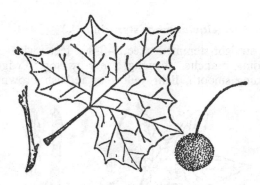

usually with a few teeth, 4-9 inches wide. Flowers in round clusters on long stem. Fruit a round, green ball, becoming brown, 1 inch or less broad. Found along borders of waterways from southern Maine and Ontario to Nebraska and southward.

American Mountain Ash (*Sorbus americana* Marsh.)

One of our most attractive small trees with slender, spreading branches forming a narrow, rounded top. The twigs stout, hairy, red-brown, becoming smooth and dark brown. Bark smooth, gray-brown, breaking into plate-like scales on old trunks; inner bark fragrant. Leaves 6-9 inches long, composed of 9-17 elliptical leaflets, smooth, fine-toothed, above middle, 1-3 inches long. Flowers white, in flat clusters, 3-5 inches broad. Fruit berry-like, brilliant coral red, hangs on during the winter. Found in moist, rocky woods and swamp borders from eastern Canada to Maine, southward to Iowa, and in the mountains to North Carolina. Often cultivated.

The cultivated Rowan or European Mountain Ash (*S.*

Aucuparia L.) has 9-15 blunt leaflets, hairy, especially beneath. It sometimes escapes.

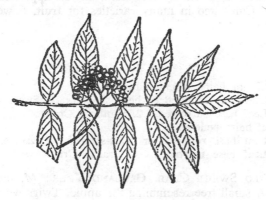

Pear (*Pyrus communis* L.)

A small, pyramidal tree that often escapes from cultivation. Twigs short, sometimes ending in spines. Bark smooth, reddish brown, cracking on old trunks into gray-

brown oblong scales. Leaves ovate-elliptical to obovate, teeth very fine or lacking; smooth above and beneath (downy when young); petiole equal to or longer than leaf-blade. Flowers white, in showy clusters on short branches. Fruit a pear with gritty flesh.

Apple. Crab (*Malus* Hill.)

Small trees with rather crooked, spreading branches. Bark smooth, brownish, becoming scaly. Twigs sometimes ending in spines. Leaves mostly ovate, generally toothed.

Petiole usually shorter than leaf-blade. Flowers white or rose-colored, in showy clusters. Fruit an apple; flesh not gritty. Cultivated in many varieties for fruit, flowers and foliage.

Key to the Species of Apple.

Leaf not hairy when mature.
    Leaf base rounded or heart-shaped. 1. Sweet Crab.
    Leaf base narrowed. 2. Southern Crab.
Leaf hairy beneath.
    Leaf base rounded or heart-shaped. 3. Apple.
    Leaf base narrowed. 4. Prairie Crab.

1. WILD SWEET CRAB. GARLAND TREE (*M. coronaria* L.). A small tree resembling the apple. Twigs woolly and

white, becoming smooth, gray or red-brown, somewhat spiny. Bark light reddish brown, cracks into shallow, flat, scaly ridges. Leaves ovate, thin, sharp-toothed, often with several small lobes smooth beneath (velvety when young), 1-4 inches long. Flowers fragrant, rose-colored. Fruit greenish yellow, waxy, fragrant, 1-2 inches broad. Found in thickets and open woods from Ontario to Nebraska and southward.

2. SOUTHERN or NARROWLEAVED CRAB (*M. angustifolia* Michx.). An attractive tree rarely exceeding 25 feet, with

stiff, spreading branches forming a broad, open top. Twigs hairy, becoming smooth and brownish, with spine-like outgrowths. Bark gray or red-brown, broken into narrow, flat, scaly ridges on old trunks. Leaves elliptical-oblong, rather

leathery, with or without teeth, shining, 1-2 inches long. Flowers pink, very fragrant. Fruit yellow-green, fragrant, 1 inch or less broad. Found in river thickets from New Jersey to Illinois and Kansas southward.

3. APPLE (*M. Malus* Britt.). This is the cultivated apple. The twigs are hairy, becoming reddish brown and finally smooth, gray-brown, often with spines. Bark smooth, gray-brown, cracking on old trunks into irregular, thin scales. Leaves ovate-oblong, base rounded or heart-shaped, toothed, hairy beneath, 1-2 inches long. Flowers white or pinkish, in showy clusters. Often escaping.

4. PRAIRIE CRAB (*M. ioensis* Britt.). A small tree resembling the Sweet Crab but the leaves are mostly oblong, thick, narrowed at base, blunt-toothed and often lobed, white-woolly beneath. Found from Minnesota and Wisconsin southward .

The Soulard Crab (*M. soulardi* Britt.) is found with the Prairie Crab and is supposed to be a hybrid of it and some other form. Its leaves are wrinkled, irregularly scallop-toothed. Often cultivated.

Chokeberry (*Aronia* Med.)

A group of shrubs or small trees of common occurrence in swamps and moist soil; beautiful in flower, fruit, and autumn coloration. They are upright plants with slender, dark brown stems and branches. Leaves ovate to obovate, fine-toothed. Flowers small, white or reddish, like the apple blossoms, in flat clusters. Fruit small, red, purple, or black, berry-like. Found from eastern Canada to Wisconsin, Minnesota, and southward.

1. RED CHOKEBERRY (*A. arbutifolia* Ell.) has elliptical to obovate leaves, usually very hairy beneath, 1-3 inches

long. Fruit usually pear-shaped, red, about ⅓ inch broad, 9 or more in a cluster.

2. PURPLE CHOKEBERRY (*A. atropurpurea* Britt.) is similar, but the fruit is roundish, dark purple to black, about ⅖ inch broad and 9 or less in a cluster.

3. BLACK CHOKEBERRY (*A. melanocarpa* Britt.) has smooth leaves, fruit essentially black, usually shining.

Shadblow (*Amelanchier* Med.)

Very attractive small trees or shrubs with slender, spreading branches forming a narrow or broad top. Bark smooth, sometimes scaly or ridged on old trunks. Flowers

white in loose, dropping clusters, appearing from March to April. Fruit berry-like, red to dark purple.

1. DOWNY SHADBLOW. SHADBUSH (*A. canadensis* Med.). A handsome shrub or tree, rarely 50 feet high, with numerous branches forming a narrow top. Twigs slender, light green, becoming red-brown (very hairy when young). Bark smooth, gray, becoming striped with reddish brown or nearly black, irregular vertical lines; on old trunks sometimes breaking into narrow, smooth or scaly ridges. Leaves ovate to obovate, base heart-shaped or rounded, fine sharp-toothed, hairy on veins beneath (woolly when young), 1-4 inches long. Fruit dry, bright

red to dark purple. Grows on dry, open hills and woodlands from New England to Nebraska and southward.

2. ALLEGHANY SHADBLOW. SERVICEBERRY (*A. laevis* Wieg.). A similar tree, but the leaves are rounded at base, rarely heart-shaped, teeth coarse, smooth beneath (somewhat hairy when young), 1-3 inches long. Fruit juicy, sweet. Found in moister localities from Newfoundland to Quebec and Wisconsin southward along the mountains.

3. ROUNDLEAF SHADBLOW (*A. sanguinea* Lind.). A shrub or small, slim tree with smooth, light-colored bark. Leaves broadly elliptical or roundish, teeth coarse and incurved, smooth above and beneath, 1-3 inches long. Fruit large, dark purple, juicy, sweet. Found from eastern Canada to Ontario and Minnesota and southward along the mountains.

Hawthorn. Thorn. Haw (*Crataegus L.*)

A group of very attractive plants; shrubs or small trees; rather flat-topped, with branches usually crooked and thorny. Bark smooth brown or gray, becoming scaly. Leaves commonly ovate, toothed and often lobed. The flowers appear in early summer, in flat, showy clusters, generally white. Fruit resembles a small apple but with dry or mealy flesh and containing 1-5 nutlets; in shades of green, red, purple, yellow, blue and black. These plants belong largely to eastern North America and some 200 forms have been described. They are distinguished by the number and color of their stamens (the pollen organs), the number and markings of the nutlets, and the character of the leaves. To the beginner, at least, the majority of them present a hopelessly intergrading group. Excellent keys and description of the species will be found in the books mentioned on page 318. Four of these plants are shown below, illustrating their variations. 1. Frosted Hawthorn. 2. Downy Hawthorn. 3. English Hawthorn. 4. Roundleaf Hawthorn.

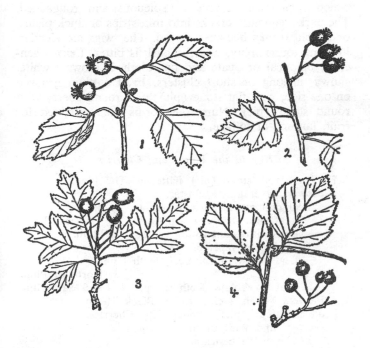

Peach (*Amygdalus* L.)

A small, low-branching tree with smooth, greenish twigs soon becoming reddish purple and finally gray-brown. Bark smooth, dark brown with short horizontal lines, becoming on old trunks rough-scaly. Leaves lanceolate, long taper-pointed, sharply toothed, shining light green, rather drooping, 4 inches long or less. Flowers in small clusters, pink, fragrant. The velvety skin of the fruit distinguishes the Peach from the next group. Escaped from cultivation in many localities.

Plum and Cherry (*Prunus* L.)

A large group of small trees or shrubs, mostly with brownish red, smooth bark marked with horizontal lines which sometimes become conspicuous and roughened. The bark frequently cracks into thin strips or thick plates. or on old trunks becomes ridged. The twigs are slender, in some forms spiny, and the bark is bitter. Leaves generally elliptical or ovate and fine-toothed. Flowers white, showy, in long or short clusters. Fruit a plum grooved on one side, with flat stone (pit); or a round cherry with round stone (pit). Numerous forms are cultivated for fruit, flowers, or foilage.

Key to the Plums and Cherries.

Fruit grooved, stone (pit) flattened. The Plums.
  Flowers several in a cluster.
    Leaf dull green, abruptly pointed at tip.
      Leaf with slender sharp teeth. 1. American Plum.
      Leaf with blunt teeth. 2. Canada Plum.
    Leaf shining, taper pointed.
      Leaf ovate to elliptical, teeth blunt.
                        3. Hortulan Plum.
      Leaf lanceolate, teeth sharp. 4. Chickasaw Plum.
  Flowers 1-3 in a cluster. 5. Black Thorn.
Fruit and stone (pit) rounded. The Cherries.
  Flowers and fruit in short clusters.
    Leaf smooth beneath.
      Leaf ovate to obovate. 6. Sour Cherry.
      Leaf roundish, fragrant. 7. Mahaleb Cherry.
      Leaf lanceolate, shining. 8. Pin Cherry.
    Leaf hairy beneath. 9. Mazzard Cherry.
  Flowers and fruit in long clusters.
    Leaf with fine sharp teeth. 10. Choke Cherry.
    Leaf with fine blunt teeth. 11. Black Cherry.

1. AMERICAN PLUM (*P. americana* Marsh.). A small tree or shrub with short trunk and wide-spreading, scrubby branches that are often spiny and drooping. Twigs smooth or hairy, bright green becoming yellow-

brown and finally red-brown. Bark smooth, light or dark brown, cracking into thin, long scales. Leaves obovate or elliptical, abruptly narrow-pointed, sharply toothed, dull green, somewhat rough above, nearly smooth

beneath, 2-4 inches long. Fruit orange to bright red, less than 1 inch broad, ripening in mid-summer or later. Found in thickets and on river banks from Connecticut to Montana and southward. Cultivated in several forms.

The Alleghany Plum, American Sloe (*P. alleghaniensis* Port.) is a straggling shrub or small tree with loose scaly bark and lanceolate leaves. Fruit dark purple with whitish coatings, ½ inch broad. Found in the mountains from central Pennsylvania to Virginia and North Carolina and also in southern Connecticut.

2. CANADA PLUM (*P. nigra* Ait.). A broad round-topped tree with twisted spiny branches, rarely 25 feet

high. Twigs smooth or hairy, bright green becoming light or dark red-brown. Bark gray-brown, smooth, cracking into thick curved plates composed of papery layers and becoming very rough on old trunks. Leaves broadly ovate, abruptly narrow-pointed, blunt-toothed, 2-5 inches long. Fruit orange-red or yellow, 1 inch or more broad. Grows on river banks and waste lands from Newfoundland through southern Canada to Minnesota, southward to Iowa, Pennsylvania, and southern New England. Cultivated in several varieties.

3. HORTULAN PLUM (*P. hortulana* Bly.). A small tree or shrub suggesting Nos. 1 and 2, but the twigs are usually without spines and the dark brown bark cracks

into large thin scales or plates. Leaves ovate to elliptical with long, slender tips, fine, incurved, blunt teeth, shining green, 2-6 inches long. Fruit deep red, rarely yellow, 1 inch or less broad, ripening in the fall. Found in low, moist soil from Indiana to Iowa southward. Several of the best plums have been derived from this plant.

4. CHICKASAW PLUM (*P. angustifolia* Marsh.). Differs from the Hortulan Plum in its usually spiny branches and narrow lanceolate leaves, minutely sharp-toothed, 1-3 inches long. Fruit red or yellow, about ½ inch broad, ripening in summer. Found in sandy soil from New Jersey west to Kansas and southward.

5. BLACK THORN (*P. spinosa* L.). This is an introduced plant found in waste places from the New England States to Pennsylvania and New Jersey. Branches spiny, bark

smooth and nearly black; leaves obovate, sharp-toothed, downy beneath, 2 inches long or less. Fruit black with whitish coating.

Three of the following species are introduced cherries which often escape from cultivation. (See Nos. 6, 7, 9.)

6. SOUR or MORELLO CHERRY (*P. Cerasus* L.). A small, low-branching tree recognized by its smooth red-brown

bark, marked with horizontal lines. On old trunks the bark cracks into out-turned gray-brown scales, becoming rough. Leaves thin, ovate to obovate, fine-toothed, smooth above and beneath (resinous when young), 1-4 inches long. Fruit red, sour.

7. MAHALEB or PERFUMED CHERRY (*P. Mahaleb* L.). A shrub or small tree. Bark nearly smooth and light

brown. Leaves roundish with very fine blunt teeth, smooth, fragrant, 1-2 inches long. Fruit shining, black, bitter.

8. PIN, RED, or BIRD CHERRY (*P. pennsylvanica* L.). A small tree with slender, horizontal branches forming a rather narrow top. Twigs shining, bright red becoming brownish. Bark thin, smooth, red-brown, with horizontal

marks, cracking horizontally into papery strips. Leaves thin, oblong-lanceolate, fine incurved teeth, shining, smooth, 3-6 inches long. Fruit light red, very sour, ⅕ inch broad, ripens in August and September. Found in open woods and clearings throughout Canada, south to Iowa, Pennsylvania and along the mountains to North Carolina and Tennessee.

9. MAZZARD. SWEET CHERRY (*P. Avium* L.). This is a large, rather pyramidal tree. Bark deep red-brown with

conspicuous horizontal lines, cracking horizontally on old trunks into thick curled strips and finally becoming somewhat ridged. Leaves thick, obovate, abruptly narrow-pointed, coarsely toothed, hairy on veins beneath, 2-5 inches long. Fruit dark red, rarely yellow, sweet.

10. CHOKE CHERRY (*P. virginiana* L.). A shrub or small tree common throughout our range. Twigs smooth, shining, light brown or reddish brown. Bark smooth, dull

brown or grayish, becoming cracked on old trunks into irregular curved scales; inner bark with unpleasant odor. Leaves thin, obovate to ovate, abruptly pointed, sharp slender teeth, smooth above and beneath, 2-4 inches long. Fruit in drooping clusters, yellowish to nearly black, about ⅓ inch broad, puckery, sweeter after frost.

11. BLACK CHERRY (*P. serotina* Ehrh.). This is the most valuable of our native cherries and the largest, sometimes

exceeding 100 feet. Twigs greenish with tinge of yellow, becoming bright red, finally red brown. Bark smooth, reddish brown with horizontal markings, cracking on old trunks into thick, irregular, scaly plates, dark reddish brown or grayish. Leaves rather leathery, ovate, oblong to elliptical, taper-pointed, fine, incurved, blunt teeth, smooth and shining above, 2-6 inches long. Fruit in long clusters, dark red to black, sweetish, ⅖ inch broad or less. Flourishes from Nova Scotia to North Dakota and southward.

Redbud. Judas Tree (*Cercis canadensis* L.)

A small, highly ornamental tree with rather irregular branches forming a flat top. Twigs slender, shining, light

brown becoming dull gray-brown. Bark smooth, light brown or gray, cracking later into oblong, red-brown scaly plates. Leaves roundish, heart-shaped, dark green and smooth above, paler and sometimes hairy on veins beneath, 2-5 inches long. Flowers pinkish, pea-like, in small clusters on the trunk and branches before the leaves appear. Fruit a pod, 2-3 inches long. Found in rich soil from Ontario to Minnesota southward. Often cultivated.

Honeylocust. Waterlocust (*Gleditsia* L.)

1. HONEYLOCUST (*G. triacanthos* L.). A large tree, sometimes 100 feet, the branches and trunk often armed with large branched thorns. The branches usually divide into

slender, somewhat pendulous branchlets, forming a broad top. Twigs smooth, shining, greenish red becoming brown. Bark smooth, dark gray-brown, cracking on old trunks into coarse ridges, covered with firm curved scales. Leaves 6-8 inches long, composed of many long-ovate leaflets which are smooth, dark green above, often hairy beneath (hairy when young), slightly toothed, ½-1 inch long.

Flowers minute, greenish, in drooping clusters. Fruit a leathery, flat, many-seeded pod, brown, often twisted, contains a sweetish pulp between the seeds, 8-18 inches long. Found in rich woods from Ontario to Nebraska and southward. Often cultivated.

2. WATERLOCUST (*G. aquatica* Marsh.). A low-branching tree with stout, often crooked, branches. Bark smooth, gray or red-brown becoming roughened and sometimes scaly. The thorns are more frequently flattened and unbranched, and the fruit is small, usually one seed without pulp, 1-2 inches long. Found in swamps from southern Indiana and Illinois to North Carolina and southward.

Kentucky Coffeetree (*Gymnocladus dioicus* Koch.)

A large forest tree with coarse branches developed near the ground or at a height of 50-80 feet. Twigs slightly hairy, stout, very crooked and blunt-tipped, greenish brown. Bark gray or brown, cracking into coarse, flat ridges covered with thick firm scales. Leaves 1-3 feet long, composed of many ovate leaflets 1-2 inches long. Flowers whitish, in clusters. Fruit a woody pod with sweet pulp

about the seeds, 4-10 inches long, hanging in clusters during the winter. Found in rich soil from southern Ontario to Minnesota southward. Often cultivated.

Yellow-Wood (*Cladrastis lutea* Koch.)

A beautiful, small tree with wide-spreading branches (slightly drooping) forming a broad top. Twigs slender,

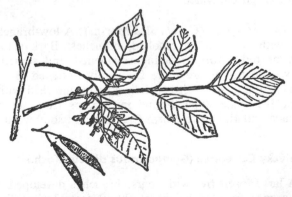

hairy, green-brown, becoming shining, red-brown, finally darker brown. Bark smooth, gray or light brown often blotched and on old trunks wrinkled. Leaves 8-11 inches long, composed of 5-11 ovate to roundish leaflets, thin, nearly smooth, 3-4 inches long. Fruit a smooth pod 2-4 inches long. Flowers white, fragrant, pea-like, in drooping clusters, 4-20 inches long. Found in rich woods from western North Carolina through Tennessee and Kentucky to Missouri. Often planted.

Common Locust. Black Locust (Robinia L.)

1. COMMON LOCUST (*Robinia pseudoacacia* L.). A tall, slender tree with erect, rather crooked branches, forming a narrow cylindrical top. Twigs hairy, green, becoming smooth and red-brown. The smooth, brownish bark of

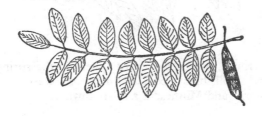

young trees becomes broken into a coarse network of deep ridges on old trunks. Leaves 6-14 inches long, composed of 7-21 leaflets, elliptical or ovate, thin, nearly smooth, 1-2 inches long. The petiole has two bristles at its base which often persist for years and develop into hard spines. Flowers white, very fragrant, pea-like, in drooping clusters, 4-8 inches long. Fruit a small, flat pod, 2-4 inches long. Found from Pennsylvania southward along the mountains; also in the Ozark Mountains.

2. CLAMMY LOCUST (*R. viscosa* Vent.) is a small tree, having sticky twigs and petioles. Flowers pink, nearly odorless; pod roughish. Both of these forms are cultivated and several forms have been derived from them.

Common Prickly Ash (*Xanthoxylum americanum* Mill.)

A shrub or small tree with prickly stem and branches. Twigs gray with bluish tinge. Bark gray, nearly smooth. Leaves composed of 5-11 ovate-lanceolate, deep green leaflets, 1-2 inches long. Flowers minute green-yellow, in

small groups, before the leaves appear in the spring. Fruit a very small black pod. Found from western Quebec to Ontario and Minnesota and southward.

Hoptree (*Ptelea trifoliata* L.)

A shrub or small tree with slender trunk and spreading branches. Twigs hairy, soon becoming smooth or somewhat roughened and brown. Bark nearly smooth, dark gray. Leaf usually composed of three dark green ovate leaflets with smooth or fine-toothed margins, 4-6 inches long. Flowers small in branching clusters. Fruit flat, about 1 inch broad, with broad-winged margin. Found in rocky places from Long Island to Ontario and Minnesota southward. Often cultivated.

Ailanthus (*Ailanthus glandulosa* Desf.)

A handsome tree with large, wide-spreading branches. Twigs coarse, hairy, yellow-green becoming smooth, reddish brown. Bark grayish and nearly smooth, becoming

marked with vertical, light-colored cracks and on old trunks broken into diamond-shaped spaces. Leaves 1-3 feet long, composed of 11-41 leaflets, long-ovate, generally with few blunt teeth at base of leaflet. Flowers very small but in large, branching clusters. Fruit in large, showy clusters, each one having two twisted wings; sometimes has unpleasant odor. An introduced tree, now common in many sections.

American Smoketree (*Cotinus americanus* Nutt.)

An attractive shrub or small tree with widely spreading branches. Twigs smooth, at first purplish, later passing through shades of green to red or orange-brown. Bark smooth, gray, cracking into long, thin scales. Leaves elliptical to obovate, smooth, dark green, 3-6 inches long. The flowers and fruit are minute, in large, loose clusters, the stalks long and hairy, giving a feathery or smoky appear-

ance to the clusters. Found on rocky banks of streams from Tennessee to Kansas and southward. Resembles the cultivated European Smoketree which has smaller, rounded, leathery leaves.

Sumac (*Rhus* L.)

Shrubs or small trees with foliage attractive in summer and (in some forms) scarcely rivalled in the fall for richness of coloration. They usually have milky or resinous juice and some species are very poisonous. Leaves large, composed of many lanceolate or ovate leaflets, margins usually toothed and sometimes lobed. Flowers minute, greenish white, in compact or loose clusters. Fruit in reddish, cone-shaped clusters or in loose clusters of cream-white nutlets. There are several cultivated varieties.

Key to the Sumacs.

The first two species are poisonous.
    Leaf composed of three leaflets. 1. Poison Ivy.
    Leaf composed of several leaflets.
        Leaf toothless or with few teeth.
            Leaf not winged between leaflets. 2. Poison Sumac.
            Leaf winged between leaflets. 3. Shining Sumac.
        Leaf toothed.
            Twigs brown, hairy. 4. Staghorn Sumac.
            Twigs whitish, smooth. 5. Smooth Sumac.

1. POISON IVY (*R. toxicodendron* L.). A vine climbing over fences or about trees. Sometimes a low, bushy shrub. Leaf composed of three ovate leaflets, usually toothless but sometimes toothed or lobed. Flowers very small in

long clusters. Fruit roundish, cream-white nutlets about ⅕ inch broad, in loose clusters. A common plant from Nova Scotia to Minneapolis southward.

2. POISON SUMAC (*R. vernix* L.). A shrub or small, low-branching tree. Twigs reddish brown changing to orange-brown and finally to gray. Bark smooth, grayish, becoming

roughened in horizontal lines on old trunks. Leaves 6-16 inches long, composed of 7-13 elliptical to obovate leaflets, toothless (rarely few-toothed or lobed), 1-6 inches long. Fruit loose clusters of pale, yellow-white, shining nutlets. Found in swamps from western Maine to Minnesota and southward. Both Nos. 1 and 2 are poisonous to most people if even touched, causing burning inflammations. A paste of baking soda applied to the affected parts is a first aid remedy.

3. SHINING SUMAC (*R. copallina* L.). Usually a shrub with stout, velvety, greenish red twigs becoming red-

brown. Bark smooth, brownish, becoming roughened in horizontal lines and sometimes cracking into papery scales. Leaf 6-12 inches long, composed of 9-21 somewhat leathery, shining leaflets, usually toothless, and with green, leafy outgrowths between each pair of leaflets. Fruit in dense, hairy, red clusters. Found on dry hills from southern Maine to Minneapolis and southward.

4. STAGHORN SUMAC (*R. typhina* L.). A shrub or small tree often with crooked stem and a few coarse branches. Twigs pinkish, velvety, becoming green and finally smooth

and brownish. Bark dark brown, smooth, but rough-dotted becoming on old stems roughened in horizontal lines and often cracking into papery scales. Leaves 1-2 feet long, composed of 11-31 sharp-toothed leaflets. Fruit in dense, reddish, conical clusters. Found in poor soils from Nova Scotia to Ontario and South Dakota and southward. (See illustration, bottom p. 148.)

5. SMOOTH SUMAC (*R. glabra* L.). Resembles No. 4, but the twigs are smooth and covered with a bluish white coating; the bark lighter-colored and grayish. The leaves are very whitish beneath. Forms with deep cut or with smooth-margined leaflets also occur. Numbers 4 and 5, or varieties of them, are sometimes cultivated. Found in dry soils from eastern Canada to Ontario and Minnesota and southward.

Holly (*Ilex* L.)

Shrubs or small trees with slender ascending or spreading branches; found in swamps or moist ground. Bark smoothish, gray or brown. Leaf margin with or without teeth. Flowers minute, green or white, solitary or in clusters on the branchlets. Fruit small, berry-like, shining bright red, yellow, or black, containing 4-8 nutlets.

Key to the Hollies.

Leaves evergreen. 1. American Holly.
Leaves not evergreen.
    Nutlets of fruit roughish.
        Leaves mostly obovate. 2. Possumhaw.
        Leaves mostly elliptical 3. Mt. Winterberry.
    Nutlets of fruit smooth. 4. Winterberry.

1. AMERICAN HOLLY (*I. opaca* Ait.). A handsome tree with horizontal, sometimes drooping, branches forming a conical top. In the North sometimes a shrub. Twigs finely

rusty-hairy, soon becoming smooth, and pale brown. Bark light gray or yellowish brown, smooth and firm, sometimes becoming warty or wrinkled. Leaves stiff, usually with spine-tipped teeth, somewhat shining, deep green, 2-4 inches long. Fruit a shining red berry, ⅓ inch broad, remaining on branches through the winter. Found on moist soil near water, from Maine along the coast southward, and up the Mississippi River basin to Illinois and Indiana.

The thoughtless and wasteful use of this plant for Christmas decoration is rapidly exterminating it. Every one should refuse to buy or to cut a piece of this tree.

2. POSSUMHAW. SWAMP HOLLY (*I. decidua* Walt.). This is usually a shrub, rarely a straggling tree. Twigs smooth, silvery gray or tinged with yellow. Bark grayish, smooth, often mottled, sometimes warty. Leaves obovate, teeth rounded or lacking, hair beneath on middle vein, 1-3 inches long. Fruit clustered on short stems, scarlet or orange-red. Grows on borders of streams and swamps from Virginia, Illinois, and Kansas southward.

3. MOUNTAIN WINTERBERRY (*I. monticolor* Gray). A shrub or small tree with short trunk and slender, spreading branches. Twigs smooth, light brown, becoming dark gray. Bark light brown, smooth, becoming roughened with numerous warty outgrowths. Leaves thin, elliptical to lan-

ceolate, smooth, teeth sharp and short, 2-6 inches long. Fruit scarlet, nearly ½ inch broad. Found in mountains from New York southward along the Alleghenies.

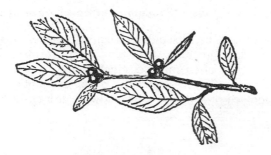

4. WINTERBERRY. BLACK ALDER (*I. verticillata* Gray). One of our most attractive swamp shrubs, rarely a small tree. Twigs smooth or slightly hairy, pale gray or brownish. Bark smooth, gray-brown. Leaves elliptical to obo-

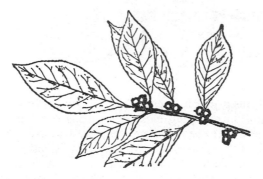

vate, sharp or indistinctly toothed, hairy beneath, 1-4 inches long. Fruit clustered on twigs, bright red, rarely yellowish. Common from eastern Canada to Ontario and Wisconsin and southward.

5. THE SMOOTH WINTERBERRY (*I. laevigata* Gray). A shrub similar to the Winterberry, with leaves smooth, teeth lacking or very short. Fruit orange-red, not clus-

tered. Grows from Maine south, through the mountains to North Carolina and Kentucky.

Wahoo. Burningbush (*Euonymus atropurpureus* Jacq.)

A small tree or shrub with slender, often four-sided twigs, at first greenish, becoming purple-brown. Bark smoothish, gray often mottled, cracking on old stems into shallow ridges. Leaves opposite, ovate to elliptical, minutely toothed, 2-5 inches long. Flowers in long-stemmed

clusters, deep purple, nearly ½ inch broad. Fruit a four-lobed pod in drooping clusters, splitting open in the fall, showing scarlet seed. Found from western New York to South Dakota and southward. Often cultivated.

The Spindletree (*E. europæus* L.) is a similar cultivated species that sometimes escapes. Leaves smaller, 1-2 inches long.

American Bladdernut (*Staphylea trifoliata* L.)

A slender shrub, rarely 20 feet high. Twigs smooth, greenish, somewhat shining, becoming brown and striped with whitish lines. Bark smooth, gray, striped with green or white. Leaves opposite, composed of three mostly ovate, narrow-pointed leaflets, smooth, toothed, 1-3 inches long. Flowers white, in drooping clusters about 4 inches long. Fruit a papery, bladder-like, three-lobed

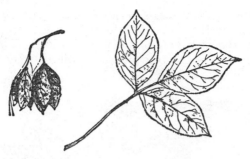

pod, nearly 2 inches long. Found in thickets from Quebec to Minnesota and southward.

Maple *(Acer L.)*

A group of large trees valuable for timber and for use as shade trees; familiar to every one and greatly admired for the beuaty of their foliage. The leaves are large and broad, opposite on the twigs, conspicuously lobed, generally toothed, with large veins branching from the petiole. The bark is gray to brown, smooth, scaly or ridged. In one form the leaves are composed of 3-5 leaflets. The flowers are small, reddish or yellow-green, in loose or close clusters. The fruit has a blade-like outgrowth or wing.

Key to the Maples.

Leaf compound. 1. Box Elder.
Leaf not compound.
    Sinus (space between lobes) rounded.
        Sinus broad, lobes short. 2. Sugar Maple.
        Sinus narrow, lobes long. 3. Silver Maple.
    Sinus (space between lobes) sharp angled.
        Bark grayish, becoming scaly.
            Twigs reddish. 4. Red Maple.
            Twigs brownish. 3. Silver Maple.

Bark brownish or red-gray, smooth.
    Bark not striped.   5. Mt. Maple.
    Bark striped with white or black.
                         6. Striped Maple.

1. Box Elder. Ash-leaved Maple (*A. negundo* L.). A small tree rarely 50 feet high, with short trunk and stout, spreading, often drooping branches. Twigs greenish to purple and often covered with a whitish coating.

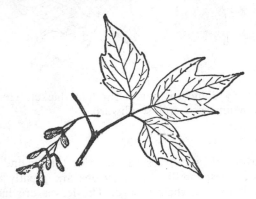

Bark smooth, grayish brown, becoming cracked into deep, firm ridges, rarely scaly. Leaves composed of 3-7 (usually 3) ovate to obovate leaflets, usually coarsely toothed and sometimes lobed, 2-5 inches long. Flowers and fruit in long, drooping clusters. Found from Vermont to southern Ontario and southward throughout our range. A handsome tree, extensively cultivated in many forms and colors.

2. Sugar Maple (*A. saccharum* Marsh.). A tree of 40-100 feet with ascending, regularly dividing branches forming a symmetrical ovoid top. Twigs smooth, green, soon reddish brown or orange-brown. Bark smooth, light brown, becoming brown-gray on old trunks and cracked into coarse scales or vertical broken plates. Leaves heart-shaped at base, 3-5 lobed (mostly 5), the lobes with 3-5 roundish teeth, light to dark green above, paler and often hairy on veins beneath; in the fall passing through shades of red, purple, and yellow, 3-6 inches long. Flowers cover the tree in spring in yellow, lacy clusters. Wings of fruit ½-1 inch long, parallel or slightly spreading. Prefers hilly country. Found from eastern Canada to Manitoba and southward. Perhaps the most extensively cultivated native tree in the East and the principal source of maple sugar. Several forms are recognized, notably the Black

Maple (*A. nigrum* Michx.), which has in its extreme form yellowish twigs, scaly, dark brown or almost black bark, and leaves commonly three-lobed, hairy beneath and toothless.

The Norway Maple (*A. plantanoides* L.), introduced from Europe, is much cultivated and occasionally escapes. Bark brown, cracking into a network of shallow ridges. Leaves larger than Sugar Maple, juice milky (break petiole). Flowers in conspicuous, flat, yellow clusters. Fruit with wings at right angles, 2 inches long.

3. SILVER MAPLE (*A. saccharinum* L.). A graceful tree, usually with short trunk and stout, ascending and dividing branches; the branchlets often drooping and curving upwards at their tips. Twigs smooth, green, soon becoming brown, often tinged with red, unpleasant odor when bruised. Bark smooth, gray, cracking on old trunks into

thin, somewhat curved scales of gray-brown color. Leaves usually with five deep lobes, silvery white beneath (hairy when young), teeth irregular, 3-6 inches long. Flowers appear before leaves in close bunches on the twigs, greenish yellow or reddish. Fruit with large, spreading wings, 1-2 inches long. Found on river banks and bottom lands from New Brunswick to southern Ontario and eastern Dakota southward. Much cultivated, though the branches are easily broken by snows and winds.

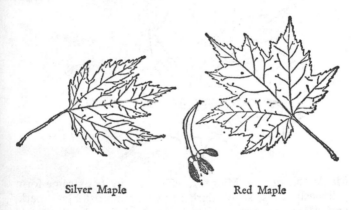

Silver Maple   Red Maple

4. RED MAPLE (*A. rubrum* L.). A tree 40-80 feet high with strong, ascending branches forming an ovoid top. Twigs smooth, green, soon shining, light or dark red. Bark grayish, smooth, becoming, on old trunks, ridged and covered with long, plate-like scales of a dark, gray-brown color. Leaves with three broad lobes, and usually with two small lobes at base, irregularly double-toothed, light or dark green above, paler or whitish beneath, sometimes hairy, 2-6 inches long. Flowers deep red or slightly yellow, covering the twigs in the spring before the leaves appear. This tree leads the red procession in the spring and in the fall. Fruit small, about 1 inch long. Found in wet soils from Nova Scotia to western Ontario and southward.

The Carolina Maple (*A. carolinianum* Britt.) is a similar tree, ranging from Massachusetts to southern Illinois southward. Leaves usually three-lobed, few toothed, whitish and usually hairy beneath.

5. MOUNTAIN MAPLE (*A. spicatum* Lam.). A bushy little tree generally found in clumps on the margin or in

the openings of rather moist woods, especially along streams. Twigs slightly hairy, yellow-green to reddish, becoming smooth and red-brown. Bark smoothish, dark gray or reddish brown, often mottled, and on old trunks sometimes slightly ridged. Leaves thin, with 3-5 short lobes and coarse teeth, downy on veins beneath, 3-6 inches long. Flowers appear after leaves in long, erect, hairy clusters. Fruit in bright red or yellow drooping clusters, becoming brown. Found from eastern Canada to Manitoba and south to Minnesota, Michigan, Ohio, and along the mountains to Tennessee.

6. STRIPED MAPLE (*A. pennsylvanicum* L.). A shrub or small forest tree, rarely exceeding 30 feet, with short trunk and straight, slender branches. Twigs smooth, yellow-green, sometimes mottled with black, becoming red-brown and often white-streaked. Bark smooth, reddish brown or dark green, white- or black-striped, becoming dark brownish gray and somewhat cracked on old trunks. Leaves very thin, roundish, with three short lobes

above the middle (hence the name "goose-foot"), nearly smooth (hairy when young), fine-toothed, 4-8 inches long. Flowers and fruit in long drooping clusters. Found

in rich woods from Nova Scotia through Quebec and Ontario to Minnesota and southward along the mountains to Tennessee.

7. THE SYCAMORE MAPLE (*A. pseudoplatanus* L.) is a much cultivated tree that occasionally escapes. Twigs

smooth, shining, yellow-green or light brown. Bark smooth, brown or gray, cracking into short, flat scales on old trunks. Leaves usually firm, with three rounded lobes and coarse, blunt teeth, deep green above, paler and hairy on veins beneath, 4-8 inches broad. Fruit in large, drooping clusters.

Horsechestnut. Buckeye (*Aesculus* L.)

Trees with stout twigs, large scaly buds, and rough bark. Leaves large, opposite, composed of 3-9 leaflets radiating from the petiole, veins running straight to leaf margin. Flowers pale yellow, white or red, in large, erect, showy clusters. Fruit roundish, leathery, smooth or prickly; contains one or more smooth, shining, brownish nuts with whitish spot ("buck's eye") on one side.

Key to the Buckeyes.

Fruit prickly.
    Leaf coarsely toothed. 1. Horsechestnut.
    Leaf fine-toothed. 2. Ohio Buckeye.
Fruit smooth.
    Bark scaly. 3. Yellow Buckeye.
    Bark smooth. 4. Red Buckeye.

1. HORSECHESTNUT (*A. Hippocastanum* L.). An introduced tree extensively cultivated in many varieties. Twigs

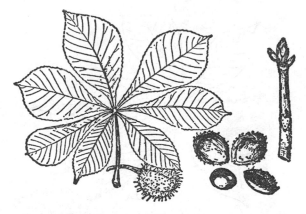

smooth, reddish brown with sticky winter buds; bark smooth, dark brown, cracking on old trunks into flat, irregular, scaly plates. Leaves composed of 5-7 (usually 7) wedge-shaped leaflets, abruptly narrowed at tip, coarsely toothed, 4-8 inches long. Flowers white with red or yellow spots, in large pyramidal clusters. Fruit prickly, about 1½ inches broad, containing one or more shining, brown-red nuts.

2. OHIO BUCKEYE (*A. glabra* Willd.). A medium-sized tree with fine hairy, orange-brown twigs, becoming smooth, reddish brown or gray; ill-smelling when crushed; buds not sticky. Bark gray, cracking into coarse plates. Leaves composed of 5 (rarely 7) elliptical leaflets, irregularly fine-toothed, hairy on middle vein beneath, 4-8 inches long. Flowers pale greenish yellow. Fruit as in No. 1. Found in moist soil from western Pennsylvania to Illinois and Nebraska southward. A related form (*A. arguta* Buckl.) has 6-9 lanceolate leaflets with very sharp teeth.

3. YELLOW BUCKEYE (*A. octandra* Marsh.). A large forest tree (sometimes shrubby). Twigs as in No. 2. Bark

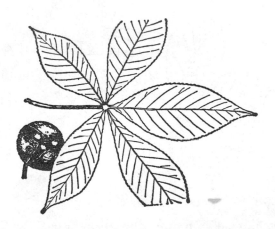

light or dark brown, cracking into irregular, thin scales. Leaves as in No. 2, but sometimes obovate with fine regular teeth, 4-10 inches long. Flowers yellowish, rarely pinkish. Fruit smooth. Range from western Pennsylvania to southern Iowa and southward.

4. RED BUCKEYE (*A. pavia* L.). Usually a shrub with smooth, gray or brown bark. Leaflets commonly 5, elliptical to obovate, fine-toothed, shining, 2-6 inches long. Flowers red. Fruit smooth. Found in woods and along streams from Virginia, Kentucky, and Missouri southward.

Carolina Buckthorn (*Rhamnus caroliniana* Walt.)

A tall shrub or small tree with slender branchlets, at first fine-hairy, light brown, with reddish tinge, becoming

smooth and gray. Bark smooth, ash-gray, often black-blotched. Leaves elliptical, faintly toothed or smooth margined, 2-5 inches long. Flowers minute, in small, hairy clusters. Fruit roundish, changing from red to black, sweet, ⅖ inch broad. Found in swamps, on river banks and hillsides from New Jersey to Kansas southward.

THE COMMON BUCKTHORN (*R. cathartica* L.) has been used for hedges and is now established in many places, especially in the East. It is a shrubby plant, sometimes 30 feet high with crooked branches often spiny. Bark smooth, dark brown, cracking into thin strips and finally becoming ridged. Fruit black and bitter.

Jersey-Tea *(Ceanothus americanus* L.)

One of our most attractive shrubs, rarely exceeding 5 feet in height. Twigs yellow-green. Bark smooth and brown. Leaves ovate to broad-lanceolate, thin, three-veined from petiole, toothed, 1-4 inches long. Flowers

showy, white, in lacy clusters. Fruit roundish, three-lobed. The leaves remain green until late in the fall. This plant was used in Revolutionary times as a substitute for tea. It is found in dry, open woods from Maine to western Ontario and southward.

Linden. Basswood *(Tilia* L.)

These are mostly large trees with grayish, ridged bark, inner bark tough and fibrous, juice mucilaginous. The foliage is attractive; leaves large and broad with base mostly heart-shaped and unequal, teeth coarse. The flowers are fragrant, creamy or white in flattish, showy clusters, drooping on a long stem from an oblong leaflet. Fruit a roundish, hairy nutlet. Valuable timber trees, much cultivated in many varieties.

1. AMERICAN LINDEN. BASSWOOD (*T. americana* L.). A large forest tree with numerous slender branches forming a rounded or ovoid top. Twigs greenish, nearly smooth, becoming reddish gray or brown. Bark smooth, brownish gray, cracking on old trunks into deep, firm, flat ridges. Leaves thick and firm, broadly ovate or roundish, gen-

erally unevenly heart-shaped at the base, hairy in angles of veins beneath, teeth coarse and sharp, 3-6 inches long. The leaflet of the flower cluster is oblong and very short-

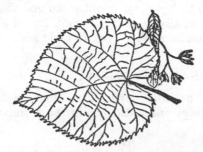

stemmed. Found in rich woods from eastern Canada through southern Quebec and Ontario to Manitoba and southward.

2. BEETREE LINDEN. WHITE BASSWOOD (*T. heterophylla* Vent.). Resembles the American Linden but is somewhat smaller. Recognized by its longer leaves (5-8

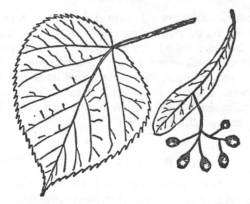

inches) which are white- or gray-hairy beneath. The leaflet of the flower cluster has a decided stem. Found mostly in mountain woods on limestone soils, from southern New York to Indiana and Illinois southward.

3. GRAY LINDEN (*T. Michauxii* Nutt.). A beautiful tree with broadly ridged dark bark and silvery gray branches. The leaves are usually smaller than those of the other Lindens, 2-6 inches long, bright green and shining above, densely gray or silvery-hairy beneath. Found along waterways from southern New York to Ohio and southward.

Hercules Club (*Aralia spinosa* L.)

A shrub or small tree with stout, wide-spreading branches. Twigs stout and brown, bark smooth, becom-

ing a coarse network of firm ridges; the entire plant armed with hard, slightly curved prickles. The enormous leaves (2-4 feet long) are composed of numerous leaflets, toothed, dark green above, pale beneath, 1-4 inches long. Flowers minute, white, arranged in huge, branching clusters, 2-4 feet long. Fruit a small, blackish berry. Found in moist woodlands from southern New York to Indiana and southward.

Tupelo. Water Gum (*Nyssa* L.)

TUPELO. SOUR or BLACK GUM (*N. sylvatica* Marsh.). A large tree, 30-100 feet high, with straight trunk and small, usually strikingly horizontal branches. Twigs generally smooth, greenish yellow becoming grayish or red-brown. Bark smooth, grayish; becoming scaly reddish brown to dark gray-brown; and on old trunks broken into deep, coarse blocks or irregular, short ridges. Leaves ovate to obovate, narrow-pointed, margins smooth or rarely with a few teeth, usually shining and dark green, 2-5 inches long; strikingly colored in the fall. Flowers minute, greenish, in small clusters. The pollen- and seed-

producing flowers on separate trees. Fruit berry-like, 1-3 on a long stalk, dark-blue. Usually found on wet or moist soils, from southern Maine to Ontario westward to Michigan and Illinois and southward.

WATER GUM (*N. biflora* Walt.) grows in marshes from New Jersey southward. The trunk is greatly swollen at the base; the leaves narrower, blunter and more leathery than in the Tupelo.

Dogwood (*Cornus* L.)

FLOWERING DOGWOOD (*C. florida* L.). A small flat-topped tree familiar to all who love the spring woods. Twigs smooth purplish green, becoming grayish and bent upward at tip. Bark smooth, light brown or red-gray becoming darker or nearly black and broken into irregular, squarish blocks. Leaves opposite, elliptical to ovate, slightly hairy, margin sometimes wavy or roughened, pale or sometimes whitish below, 2-7 inches long. Flowers minute, greenish, in showy clusters, 3-4 inches broad; the outer part of the cluster consists of four white or pink obovate leaflets, notched at the end and about 2 inches long. Fruit a scarlet berry (rarely yellowish).

Found in open forests from southern Maine to Ontario and Minnesota and southward. This tree needs your

earnest effort to save it from destruction. The automobile has made it the prey of every town and city.

1. ROUGHLEAF DOGWOOD (*C. asperifolia* Michx.). A small, narrow-topped tree, or more often a shrub. Twigs slender, hairy, light yellow-green, becoming gray- or red-brown. Bark smooth, dark brown with tinge of red, cracking on old stems into irregular, shallow, scaly ridges. Leaves elliptical to oblong, usually tapering to a sharp point, rough above, somewhat hairy beneath (very hairy when young), 2-6 inches long. Flowers small, in cream-white, flattish clusters. Fruit white. Found in moist soil, from southern Ontario to Minnesota and southward.

2. THE SILKY DOGWOOD (*C. Amomum* Mill.) is common throughout our area. Twigs purplish; bark on old stems yellow-brown; the under surface of leaves silky-downy, often rusty. Fruit pale blue.

3. THE PAGODA DOGWOOD (*C. alternifolia* Michx.). An odd but attractive shrub or small tree; its whorled branches widely separated, producing a pagoda-like appearance. Twigs smooth, yellow or purplish green, becoming dark green, often white- or gray-striped. Bark smooth, reddish brown, breaking on old stems into firm, rather oblong scales or plates. Leaves alternate (rarely

opposite), ovate, sometimes slightly toothed, whitish beneath, 2-4 inches long. Flowers in flat, white clusters.

Fruit bluish black. Found on borders of forests and in open fields, from Nova Scotia to Quebec, Ontario and Minnesota southward.

Clethra (*Clethra* L.)

1. SUMMERSWEET CLETHRA (*C. alnifolia* L.). An attractive shrub or small tree with slender, mostly erect

stems. Twigs slightly hairy, light brown, becoming on old stems smooth, dull brown. Leaves thin, obovate, strongly narrowed at base, sharply fine-toothed towards tip, 1-3 inches long. Flowers appear in midsummer, small, white or pinkish, in erect and usually branching clusters, spicy odor. Fruit a small, smooth pod. Found in wet soils from Maine southward along the Atlantic States.

2. CINNAMON CLETHRA (*C. acuminata* Michx.) is a similar plant found in the Alleghenies from Virginia southward. Bark smooth, light reddish brown, cracking into thin scales. Leaves ovate to oblong, rounded or slightly narrowed at base, 3-8 inches long. Flower-clusters somewhat drooping. Fruit-pods roughish.

Rosebay. Rhododendron *(Rhododendron maximum L.)*

A small shrubby tree (rarely 40 feet high and often only 10-15 feet) with very crooked stems and branches.

The dense thickets of these plants, with their shining deep green foliage and showy flowers, present an attraction rarely equalled. Twigs green with tinge of red, becoming smooth, green and finally red-brown or gray. Bark smooth, cracking on old stems into small, thin, red-brown scales. Leaves remain on trees for 2-3 years; they are elliptical to obovate, leathery, 4-10 inches long, pale or whitish beneath (hairy when young). Flowers in large, close clusters, pink to white. Fruit a brown ovate pod about ½ inch long. Found in rocky woods, along streams and swamps, from Nova Scotia to southern Quebec and Ontario and southward along the mountains. Cultivated in many forms.

Mountain Laurel (*Kalmia latifolia* L.)

A shrub or small tree with crooked stems and branches. Few plants add more beauty to the open woods

at all seasons of the year. Twigs at first sticky-hairy becoming smooth, shining green, and finally red-brown. Bark on old stems cracks into long, narrow, red-brown scales. Leaves clustered at ends of twigs, sometimes 2-3 at the same level on the twig, falling off after one or two years; leathery, smooth, dull green when mature, elliptical to obovate, 2-5 inches long. Flowers white to pink, about 1 inch broad, in large, flat clusters. Fruit a small, roundish pod about ⅕ inch broad. Prefers rocky woods. Found from New Brunswick to Ontario and Indiana and southward. This plant is being exterminated in many places by the thoughtless use of it for decoration.

Sourwood (*Oxydendrum arboreum* DC.)

A tree 20-50 feet high with straight, slender stem and spreading branches, forming a rather narrow top. Twigs smooth, yellow-green, changing to orange or red-brown.

Bark smooth, gray-brown, cracking on old trunks into short, broken, rounded ridges. Leaves elliptical to oblong, narrow-tipped, with fine incurved teeth. Smooth and shining, acid to taste, scarlet in the fall, 4-8 inches long. Flowers small, white, in long, drooping and branching, one-sided clusters. Fruit a small, ovoid woody pod. Found from Pennsylvania and Indiana southward, especially along the mountains.

Farkleberry (*Vaccinium arboreum* Marsh.)

A shrub or small tree with short, crooked stem and branches. Twigs slender, hairy, light red-brown becoming

smooth and dark red. Bark smooth, red-brown; cracking into long, thin scales. Leaves leathery, obovate to elliptical, teeth minute or lacking, nearly smooth, shining dark green, ½-2 inches long. Flowers small, white, clustered on leafy twigs. Fruit a small berry, shining black, sweet. Found in moist soils from southern Illinois and Indiana to North Carolina and southward. This tree belongs to that large group of shrubs called Blueberries and also Huckleberries.

Bumelia (*Bumelia* Pers.)

1. WOOLLY BUMELIA (*B. languinosa* Pers.). A small tree or shrub (rarely exceeding 50 feet), sometimes with spiny branchlets. Twigs very rusty or pale-hairy becom-

ing smooth, reddish brown or gray; cut twigs exude a gummy juice. Bark dark gray-brown, cracking on old stems into a network of firm ridges. Leaves clustered on short stems, leathery, obovate, rounded at tip, rusty or white-hairy beneath, 1-3 inches long. Flowers small, white, in dense clusters. Fruit cherry-like, black, about ½ inch broad. Found in woods from southern Illinois and Kansas southward.

2. BUCKTHORN BUMELIA (*B. lycioides* Pers.). A similar tree but smaller, with slightly hairy twigs and smooth grayish bark that cracks into thin scales; on old trunks may become slightly ridged. Leaves firm, elliptical to oblanceolate, with sharp tips, nearly smooth, 2-6 inches long. Found in borders of swamps and streams from southern Illinois and Indiana southward.

Persimmon (*Diospyros virginiana* L.)

A slender tree with spreading branches forming a narrow or broad rounded top. Twigs hairy-greenish, becoming gray or red-brown. Bark smooth, dark reddish brown, cracking into thick, squarish blocks. Leaves ovate to ellip-

tical, firm, nearly smooth, shining dark green, 2-6 inches long. Flowers small, greenish yellow, solitary or few-clustered; the pollen and seed-bearing flowers usually on separate trees. Fruit yellowish when ripe, sweet, usually not edible until after frost, ½-2 inches broad. Our cultivated Japanese varieties have larger fruits. Found in woods and old sandy fields from Connecticut and southern Iowa and southward.

Great Silver Bell (*Halesia caroliniana* L.)

A beautiful shrub or small tree with stout ascending and spreading branches. Twigs hairy, usually soon smooth and yellow-brown. Bark smooth, reddish brown, cracking into shallow ridges separated by yellowish furrows; on old trunks broken into broad, flat, scaly ridges. Leaves elliptical to obovate, teeth minute, deep green above, paler and often hairy beneath, 2-7 inches long. Flowers white, about ½ inch long, in drooping clusters. Fruit oblong, four-winged, usually over 1 inch long.

Found on banks of streams from Virginia to Illinois and southward. Much cultivated.

Common Sweetleaf (*Symplocos tinctoria* L'Her.)

A shrub or small tree with slender upright branches forming an open top. Twigs green, usually hairy, becoming smooth, brownish or grayish. Bark gray, smooth,

finally developing short, roughened cracks, separated by broad, flat spaces. Leaves elliptical to obovate, teeth indistinct, shining dark green above, slightly hairy beneath, with sweetish taste, 3-6 inches long. Found in rich woods from Delaware southward and in the Blue Ridge from North Carolina southward.

Ash (*Fraxinus* L.)

These valuable timber trees grow for the most part in moist or swampy ground. The branchlets are stout, with oppositely placed coarse and blunt twigs. Bark grayish, ridged or scaly. Leaves large, opposite, and composed of 5-11 leaflets. Flowers, appearing in early spring, very small, in branching clusters, and of two kinds; each kind usually on different trees. The pollen-bearing flowers are in very dense clusters and red-purple, becoming yellowish when the pollen is shedding. The seed-forming clusters are more branching, and the minute flowers develop into hard, cylindrical or flattened, one-seeded pods that spread out into a paddle-shaped wing. The leaves of the Ashes are exceedingly variable, but the winged fruits are more reliable guides to the various forms.

Key to the Ashes.

Leaflets without petioles. 1. Black Ash.
Leaflets with petioles.
  Twigs square. 2. Blue Ash.
  Twigs rounded.
    Twigs smooth or nearly so. 3. White Ash.
    Twigs hairy or velvety.
      Trees of very wet swamps. 4. Pumpkin Ash.
      Trees of drier soils.
        Wing at tip of seed pod. 5. Biltmore Ash.
        Wing extending down side of seed pod.
                      6. Red Ash.

1. BLACK or HOOP ASH (*F. nigra* Marsh.). A tall slender tree of swamps. Twigs soon smooth, greenish, becoming gray or with tinge of yellow. Bark gray, rough-warted, cracking on old trunks into large irregular plates covered with thin, soft scales. Leaves 12-16 inches long, composed of 7-11 oblong, narrow-pointed leaflets, toothed, very nearly smooth (rusty-hairy beneath when young), 3-5 inches long, without petioles. Fruit with ob-

long wing extending around the flat seed portion. Found from eastern Canada to Manitoba, southward to Delaware and Arkansas.

2. BLUE ASH (*F. quadrangulata* Michx.). A valuable western timber tree. Twigs squarish, rusty-hairy, reddish or orange-colored, becoming brownish or grayish. Bark smooth, gray tinged with red, cracking on old stems into

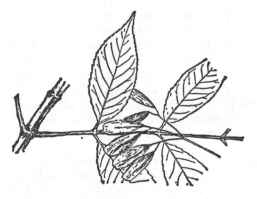

irregular, thick plates covered by thin, small scales, often shaggy. Leaflets usually 7 (7-11) sharp-toothed, nearly or quite smooth, 3-5 inches long. Fruit with oblong wing, rounded or notched at tip, and forming a narrow margin around the flattened seed portion. Found in dry or moist woods from southern Ontario and Minnesota southward to eastern Tennessee and Arkansas.

3. WHITE ASH (*F. americana* L.). A large and valuable forest tree with massive, straight trunk and large ascending branches. Twigs greenish, often with tinge of orange or red, becoming light brown or gray, and polished. Bark dark gray or brown (inner bark of branches green or tan), cracking into a regular network of deep, firm

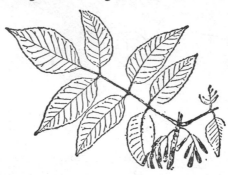

ridges. Leaves 6-12 inches long, composed of 5-9 ovate or lanceolate-oblong leaflets with smooth or fine-toothed margins, light or dark green above, paler or silvery and often lightly hairy on veins beneath, 2-6 inches long; petiole smooth. Fruit in long branched clusters; the wing lanceolate or oblong-lanceolate, blunt-tipped and attached to the end of the cylindrical seed portion. Common in rich, moist soils from Minnesota to Lake Superior southward and eastward.

4. PUMPKIN ASH (*F. profunda* Bush.). A tall slender tree with greatly enlarged base (pumpkin) growing in deep swamps that are often covered with water for months at a time. Twigs light gray and usually hairy. Bark gray, cracking into broad, shallow, scaly ridges. Leaves 9-18 inches long, with 7 or 9 leaflets, resembling the White Ash though more hairy. Fruit with narrow, oblong wing, rounded (often notched at tip), and extend-

ing nearly to the base of the slightly flattened seed portion. Found from western New York to southern Illinois and southward.

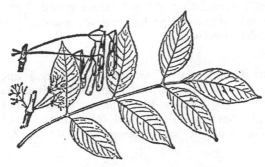

5. BILTMORE ASH (*F. biltmoreana* Beadl.). A tree resembling the White Ash but with very hairy twigs and petioles. Bark dark gray and cracked into a less pronounced network of narrow ridges. Fruit with narrow, oblong wing. Found on banks of streams from western New Jersey along the Appalachians to Alabama.

6. RED ASH (*F. pennsylvanica* Marsh.). A tree usually smaller than the White Ash but resembling it in many respects. It is found in moister soils, as low river banks

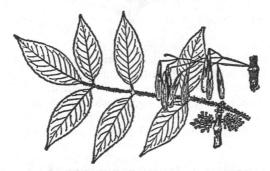

and borders of swamps. Twigs greenish gray and usually velvety, becoming light gray or brown. Bark smooth, gray or brown (the inner bark of branches reddish) becoming cracked into shallower and flatter ridges. Leaflets hairy or downy beneath. Fruit with wing extending to at least the middle of the cylindrical seed portion, and gradually broadening above it into a rounded or notched or slightly pointed tip. Range from eastern Canada to Manitoba southward.

7. THE GREEN ASH (var. *lanceolata* Sarg.) appears in some sections as a distinct form of the Red Ash, with smooth twigs, leaflets long, narrow-pointed and sharp-toothed above middle. Found from Maine and the St. Lawrence valley to Saskatchewan and southward.

Texas Adelia. Swamp Privet (*Forestiera acuminata* Poir.)

A shrub or small tree with spreading and sometimes thorny branches. Bark dull brown, smooth, becoming

slightly roughened or ridged. Leaves opposite, elliptical, tapering at both ends, faintly toothed, smooth, 1-4 inches long. Flowers yellow-green, in small clusters before the leaves appear. Fruit oblong, bluish, cherry-like, about 1 inch long. Found on borders of streams and swamps from southern Indiana and Illinois southward.

White Fringetree (*Chionanthus virginiana* L.)

A beautiful shrub or small tree of rocky soils and river banks. Twigs green, usually hairy, becoming smooth, light brown or orange-colored. Bark smooth, reddish brown, cracking into irregular scales or sometimes ridged. Leaves opposite, elliptical to obovate,

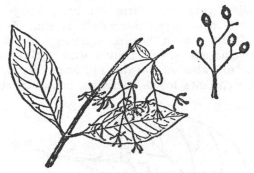

margins wavy, shining above, hairy beneath on veins, 2-8 inches long. Flowers fragrant in graceful, drooping, snow-white clusters 4-8 inches long. Fruit cherry-like, 1 inch long, dark blue or black. Found from southern New Jersey and Pennsylvania southward. Often cultivated.

European Privet (*Ligustrum vulgare* L.)

A shrub or small tree much used for hedges. Escaping from Maine to Ontario and southward. Cultivated in

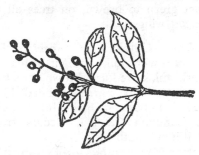

many varieties. Leaves opposite, elliptical, leathery, smooth, deep green, ½-2 inches long. Flowers small, white, in compact, erect clusters. Fruit berry-like, black.

Catalpa (*Catalpa* Scop.)

1. COMMON CATALPA (*C. bignonioides* Walt.). A widely cultivated tree with short, often crooked trunk and widely spreading coarse branches. Twigs reddish purple becoming gray to reddish brown. Bark thin, smooth, light reddish brown, cracking on old trunks into irregular thin scales. Leaves with unpleasant odor, opposite or whorled, ovate or heart-shaped, short-pointed, sometimes lobed, somewhat hairy beneath, 4-10

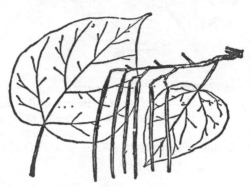

inches long. Flowers white, thickly blotched with yellow or brown, about 2 inches long; in spreading, erect, many-flowered clusters, 6-10 inches long. Fruit long slim pods, changing from green to brown, on trees all winter; seed with two fringed wings.

2. THE WESTERN CATALPA (*C. speciosa* Engle.) is a large forest tree with tall, straight trunk and slender branches. Bark thick, reddish brown, cracking into flat scaly ridges. Leaves long, narrow-pointed. Flowers white, slightly blotched at base; in erect, few-flowered clusters. Fruit as in Common Catalpa. Occurs from southern Indiana and Illinois southward.

3. ROYAL PAULOWNIA (*Paulownia tomentosa* Bail.). A much cultivated tree from Japan, strongly resembling the Common Catalpa. Twigs hairy, becoming smooth, brown.

Bark smooth, light to dark brown, cracking into shallow, irregular, smooth, flat ridges. Leaves more hairy beneath. Flowers violet, in erect clusters often a foot long. Fruit a leathery pod about 2 inches long. Found from New York and New Jersey southward.

Common Buttonbush (*Cephalanthus occidentalis* L.)

A shrub or small tree with spreading crooked branches forming a round, bushy top. Twigs often whorled, light

green, changing to reddish brown. Bark smooth, brownish, becoming darker on old stems and cracked into narrow, loose scales. Leaves opposite or whorled, ovate to lanceolate, deep green, smooth, 2-8 inches long. Flowers small, fragrant, creamy white, in rounded clusters. Fruit in greenish or brownish balls about ⅔ inch broad. Found in swamps and along streams from New Brunswick to Nebraska southward.

Elder (*Sambucus* L.)

1. AMERICAN ELDER (*Sambucus canadensis* L.). A shrubby plant of common occurrence in open fields throughout our range. Twigs thick but soft, greenish, becoming light brown with purplish tinge. Bark smooth, dark brown with small warts, becoming scaly on old

stems. Leaves have unpleasant odor when crushed; they are opposite, composed of 5-11 leaflets, ovate to oblong and fine-toothed. Flowers small, white, in large flat clus-

ters 3-10 inches broad. Fruit a small, purplish black, sweetish berry.

2. RED ELDER (*S. racemosa* L.) has hairy twigs and leaves; flowers in ovoid clusters; fruit bright red. Found in open, rocky woods. There are also several cultivated forms.

Viburnum (*Viburnum* L.)

A large and widely distributed group of shrubby plants, only four of which may be called tree-like. They are

found under widely different conditions; such as open woods or dense thickets, dry hills or wet swamps. Attractive in foliage, flower and fruit; cultivated in many varieties. The Snowball tree or Guelder Rose is an example. Leaves opposite, usually toothed, and without lobes in the tree forms. Flowers small, white, in broad, flat clusters. Fruit cherry-like, often bluish.

Key to the Viburnums.

Leaf sharp-toothed.
  Leaf long, narrow-pointed. 1. Nannyberry.
  Leaf blunt or short-pointed.
    Leaf smooth or nearly so. 2. Blackhaw.
    Leaf red-hairy beneath. 3. Southern Blackhaw.
Leaf toothless or nearly so. 4. Smooth Withe-rod.

1. NANNYBERRY (*V. Lentago* L.). A shrub or small tree with short trunk and slender, drooping branches forming a rounded, bushy top. Twigs foul-smelling when bruised, greenish, slightly rusty-hairy, becoming scurfy, light red, and finally smooth red-brown. Bark dark reddish brown, broken on old stems into small, thick plates. Leaves ovate to obovate, taper-pointed, fine-toothed, at first rusty-hairy, becoming smooth, shining, 2-4 inches long. The leaves at the tips of the twigs usually have petiole with minute wings. Fruit blue-black, sweet. Found in borders of forests, in moist ground, from Quebec to Manitoba and southward.

2. BLACKHAW (*V. prunifolium* L.). A shrub or small tree usually with crooked stem and stiff spreading

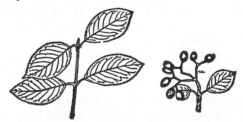

branches often bearing spine-like twigs. Twigs at first nearly smooth and reddish, soon turning green and finally reddish gray or brown. Bark smooth, red or gray-brown, breaking on old stems into irregular, thick, rounded or squarish plates. Leaves elliptical to obovate, usually blunt or short-pointed, fine-toothed, smooth, dark green, 1-3 inches long. Fruit blue-black, sweet. Found on dry hills and along fences from Connecticut to Michigan and Kansas and southward.

3, SOUTHERN BLACKHAW (*V. rufidulum* Raf.). Resembles the Blackhaw but the young twigs are rusty-hairy, as are the under surfaces of the leathery leaves and their winged petioles. Leaf 3-4 inches long.

4. SMOOTH WITHE-ROD (*V. nudum* L.). A shrub or small tree with nearly horizontal branches. Twigs at first scurfy, soon becoming smooth, shining, red-brown, and finally greenish brown. Bark reddish brown and broken on old stems into irregular, thick plates. Leaves elliptical to obovate, blunt or short-pointed, margins sometimes wavy or faintly toothed, thick, shining and smooth above, slightly scurfy on veins beneath (very scurfy when young), 3-8 inches long. Flowers white, in flat or curved clusters 2-4 inches broad. Fruit pink to deep blue. Found in swamps and moist, rich soil, from Connecticut to Kentucky and southward.

5. THE WITHE-ROD (*V. cassinoides* L.) is a shrub similar to the above species but with slender, ascending branches. Twigs scurfy, light brown or gray; leaves smaller (1-4 inches long), ovate to elliptical, duller above. Found in swamps and wet soils, from Newfoundland to Manitoba and southward.

There are several common shrubby Virburnums easily recognized by their leaves, as: 1. The Mapleleaf Virburnum (*V. acerifolium* L.) of rocky, open woods, with maple-like leaves, soft, downy beneath (see No. 4, page 156); 2. The Cranberry-bush (*V. opulus* L.), found along water ways, with deeply 3-5 lobed, smooth leaves, fruit red, sour, used as cranberries; 3. The Hobblebush (*V.*

alnifolium Marsh.) found in moist woods, with rounded leaves heart-shaped at base, rusty-hairy on veins beneath, 4-8 inches broad, the branches often nearly horizontal and touching the ground; 4. The Arrow-wood (*V. dentatum* L.), erect, tall shrubs of wet soil, leaves broadly ovate to rounded, smooth, strongly veined, regular sharp teeth, 2-3 inches long. The Indians used the straight branches for arrow shafts; 5. The Downy Viburnum (*V. pubescens* Pursh.), a low straggling shrub of rocky woods, with leaves resembling the Arrow-wood but downy beneath and with less prominent veins and teeth.

TREES OF THE SOUTHERN REGION

Pine (*Pinus* L.)

(See also p. 39.)

Key to the Species of Southern Pines.

Leaves in clusters of two.
    Cones ½-2 inches long. 1. Cedar Pine.
    Cones 2-3½ inches long. 2. Sand Pine.
Leaves in clusters of two and three.
    Leaves 8-12 inches long; cone 3-6 inches long.
                          3. Slash Pine.
    Leaves shorter, 3-5 inches long; cone small, 2 inches
                        long. 4. Yellow Pine.
Leaves in clusters of three.
    Leaves very long, 8-18 inches long. 5. Long-leaf Pine.
    Leaves shorter, 6-9 inches long.
        Mature cone oblong, 2-6 inches long.
                          6. Loblolly Pine.
        Mature cone roundish, 2-2½ inches long.
                          7. Pond Pine.

1. CEDAR PINE (*P. glabra* Walt.). A large tree, sometimes 120 feet high, attaining its greatest development

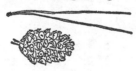

in northern Florida, its slender leaves in clusters of two, 1½-3 inches long; cones ½-2 inches long, with thin scales tipped with a small spine which eventually falls off. Found from South Carolina to Florida, westward to Louisiana.

2. SAND PINE (*P. clausa* Sarg.). A small tree, rarely exceeding 20 feet in height, its branches usually present right down to the soil level; leaves two in a cluster, 2-3½ inches long; cones are conical or ovoid-conical, 2-3½

inches long, the scales tipped with a short, thickish prickle. Usually found near the coast, Alabama and Florida.

3. SLASH PINE (*P. caribæa* Morel.). A large tree with orange-colored twigs. The leaves are 8-12 inches long, in clusters of both two and three; cones are ovoid, 3-6

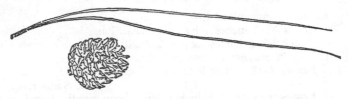

inches long with thin scales armed with a minute spine. Distributed along the coast from South Carolina to Florida to Louisiana. Second to the Long-leaf Pine in importance for the production of turpentine and rosin. Saplings are used for paper making.

4. YELLOW PINE (*P. echinata* Mill.). See p. 42. Predominantly southern in distribution with best development west of the Mississippi River.

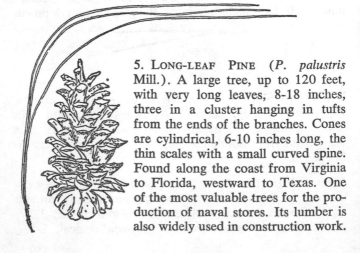

5. LONG-LEAF PINE (*P. palustris* Mill.). A large tree, up to 120 feet, with very long leaves, 8-18 inches, three in a cluster hanging in tufts from the ends of the branches. Cones are cylindrical, 6-10 inches long, the thin scales with a small curved spine. Found along the coast from Virginia to Florida, westward to Texas. One of the most valuable trees for the production of naval stores. Its lumber is also widely used in construction work.

6. LOBLOLLY PINE (*P. tœda* L.). See p. 41. Chiefly a southern species with its greatest development west of the Mississippi, extending westward to Texas.

7. POND PINE (*P. serotina* Michx.). A medium-size tree, with relatively broad leaves arranged in clusters of three,

6-8 inches long, triangular in section. The mature cones are globose, 2-2½ inches, with thin, flat scales having a slender spine which tends to fall off. Located in wet places near the coast, North Carolina to Florida. It is sometimes considered a variety of the Pitch Pine, *Pinus rigida,* p. 42.

Common Bald Cypress (*Taxodium distichum* Rich.)

See p. 53. Mostly southern in distribution, reaching its greatest development in the South Atlantic and Gulf States.

White Cedar (*Chamaecyparis thyoides* BSP.)

See p. 55. A swamp plant found in both northern and southern regions. In the latter it is distributed along the Atlantic and Gulf coasts.

Juniper (*Juniperus* L.)

Trees with small scale-like, overlapping leaves which are usually appressed to the stem; the cones are berry-like. In species 1-3 below the berry is blue and covered with a whitish bloom; in species 4 it is bright red.

1. RED CEDAR (*J. virginiana* L.). See p. 56. Northern and southern in distribution, extending westward to eastern Texas. "Berries" about ¼ inch in diameter.

2. SOUTHERN RED CEDAR (*J. lucayana* Britt.). This differs from the Red Cedar by the conspicuous oblong resingland on the back of the leaves, and the much smaller "berries." Found in swamps from Florida to Texas; often cultivated.

3. ROCK CEDAR (*J. mexicana* Spreng.). The appressed leaves of this juniper are fringed along the margin; the leafy branchlets are 4-angled. Its "berries" are about the size of those of the Red Cedar. Oklahoma and Texas.

4. PINCHOT'S CEDAR (*J. Pinchotii* Sudw.). Leaves similar to the Red Cedar. "Berries" are a bright red. A small tree rarely 20 feet high, more often a shrub with a few stems 1-12 feet high. Western Texas, extending into Arizona.

THE BROAD-LEAVED TREES

Poplar. Cottonwood (*Populus* L.)
(See p. 58.)

SOUTHERN COTTONWOOD (*P. deltoides* Marsh.). See p. 60. Found in the Atlantic and Gulf States to western Texas.

SWAMP COTTONWOOD (*P. heterophylla* L.). See p. 62. Inhabits borders of swamps in the Atlantic and Gulf States to western Louisiana, reaching its greatest development in Missouri, Arkansas and Mississippi.

Willow (*Salix* L.)
(See p. 64.)

HARBISON WILLOW (*S. Harbisonii* Schn.). A shrub or sometimes a tree 50 feet high; branchlets usually hairy the first season becoming smooth and purplish in the second, easily broken at the joints. The leaves are 4-5 inches long, linear-lanceolate, finely saw-toothed, green above, pale beneath. Found along the edge of streams and swamps from Virginia to Florida.

Several of the northern willows are also found in the southern region:

BLACK WILLOW, p. 69, extends southward to Georgia and Alabama and westward to Texas. It occurs as the variety *altissima* in Arkansas, Louisiana and Texas, where it may attain a height of 120 feet. It differs from the species in the greater hairiness of leaves and branchlets.

LONGLEAF or SANDBAR WILLOW, p. 67, may be found from Alabama westward.

PEACHLEAF WILLOW, p. 72, reaches into the southern region in Oklahoma and Texas.

Corkwood (*Leitneria floridana* Chapm.)

A small tree to 20 feet, the leaves are elliptical, tapering at both ends, 4-6 inches long, shiny above; petioles

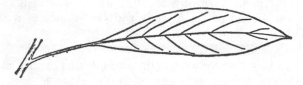

1-2 inches long. The young branches are covered with hairs. It inhabits the shores of saline swamps in Florida and the Gulf States and river swamps in Texas, Arkansas and Missouri. The wood is sometimes used in place of cork as floats for fishnets.

Wax-Myrtle (*Myrica cerifera* L.)

See p. 75. Found chiefly along the coast from Maryland to Florida, Texas and Arkansas.

Walnut (*Juglans* L.)

See p. 77. Both the Butternut and Walnut are found in the southern region, as well as in the northern. *J. major* and *J. rupestris* are present in Texas.

Hickory (*Hicoria* Rafn.)

(See p. 79.)

Key to the Hickories of the South.

Bud-scales few, not overlapping.
  Lateral leaflets not curved, nor tapering gradually to a point.
  Leaflets mostly 7, sometimes 9. 1. Nutmeg Hickory.

Lateral leaflets curved and tapering to a point.
Leaflets 7-9. 2. Bitternut.
Leaflets 9-17.
    Leaflets on a short, stout stalk. 3. Pecan.
    Leaflets without stalk, or essentially so.
        Bark close, in plate-like scales. 4. Bitter Pecan.
        Bark loose, in long strips. 5. Water Hickory.
Bud-scales numerous, overlapping one another.
    Bark loose, in long strips.
        Leaflets 7, sometimes 5 or 9. 6. King Nut.
        Leaflets mostly 5.
            Leaflets commonly 5, less often 7; broad (oval).
                                7. Shagbark Hickory.
            Leaflets commonly 5, less often 3; narrow
                (lanceolate). 8. Southern Shagbark Hickory.
    Bark close, not separating in long strips.
        Leaflets 5, less often 7.
            Finely serrate. 9. Pignut.
            Coarsely serrate, with tough teeth.
                                10. Florida Hickory.
        Leaflets 7, less often 5 or 9.
            Uppermost leaflets lanceolate, nuts white.
                                11. Pale Hickory.
            Uppermost leaflets broader (ovate or obovate);
                nuts reddish.
                Leaves fragrant; petiole, rachis and lower sur-
                    face leaflets hairy; winter buds not rusty-
                                hairy. 12. Mockernut.
                Leaves not fragrant, petiole and rachis becom-
                    ing smooth.
                    Winter buds rusty-hairy.
                                13. Buckley's Hickory.
                    Winter buds hairy but not rusty.
                                14. Louisiana Hickory.

Supplementary aid from conspicuous characteristics

A. Those in which the lower surface might be silvery.
    1. Nutmeg Hickory.
    13. Buckley's Hairy Hickory.
    11. Pale Hickory
B. Those often with more than 9 leaflets.
    3. Pecan

        4. Bitter Pecan
        5. Water Hickory
C. Those with loose bark.
        5. Water Hickory
        6. King Nut
        7. Shagbark Hickory
        8. Southern Shagbark Hickory
D. Those that usually have 5 leaflets.
        7. Shagbark Hickory
        8. Southern Shagbark Hickory
        9. Pignut

1. NUTMEG HICKORY (*H. myristicæformis* Nutt.). Leaves 7-14 inches long with slender, hairy petiole; 7, or occasionally 9, ovate to obovate, coarsely toothed

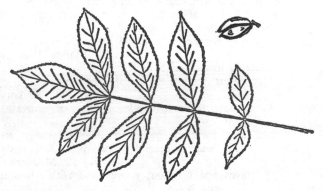

leaflets, 4-5 inches long, dark green above, silvery-white below; midribs hairy (late in season brown-hairy). The husk of the fruit is thin, splitting to base at maturity along the 4 thick ridges. The nut is ellipsoidal, about 1 inch long, reddish-brown. Distributed from South Carolina through central Alabama and Mississippi to southern Arkansas.

2. BITTERNUT (*H. cordiformis* Koch.). See p. 80. Ranges from northwestern Florida westward.

3. PECAN (*H. pecan* Engl. and Graebn.). See p. 79. Most abundant in Arkansas and eastern Texas.

4. BITTER PECAN (*H. texana* Schn.). Leaves 10-12 inches long with slender, grooved petiole; 7-11 leaflets which are lanceolate, tapering at the tip, finely saw-toothed, at first hoary-woolly, later dark green and smooth above and yellow-green, somewhat hairy below, 3-5 inches long. The lateral leaflets are often unequal at the base. The fruit is oblong, 1½-2 inches long, the thin husk slightly 4-angled at the base. The nut is thin-shelled and bitter. Along streams western Mississippi to Arkansas and Texas.

5. WATER HICKORY (*H. aquatica* Nutt.). Leaves 9-15 inches long with slender, red, hairy petioles; 7-13 lance-

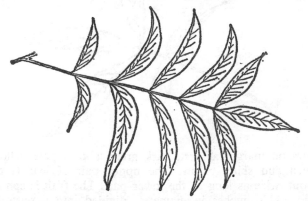

olate leaflets, tapering at the tip, unequal at the base, very finely serrate, 3-5 inches long, dotted with yellow glands, dark green above, brown and lustrous, or woolly below. The fruit is ellipsoidal, tapering to the tip, strongly 4-winged, dark brown covered with bright yellow scales, the thin husk splitting only to the middle. Nut 4-angled, obovoid, reddish-brown. Found in river swamps of southeastern Virginia southward to Florida and westward to Texas.

6. SHELLBARK HICKORY. KING NUT (*H. laciniosa* Loud.). See p. 85. In the South found chiefly in Missouri, Arkansas and Oklahoma.

7. SHAGBARK HICKORY (*H. ovata* Koch.). Ranges in the South to Florida and to eastern Texas and Oklahoma.

8. SOUTHERN SHAGBARK HICKORY (*H. carolinae-septentrionalis* Engl. and Graebn.). Leaves 4–8 inches long with slender glabrous petiole; usually having 5 lanceolate leaflets, tapering at apex and base, fine-toothed, with long

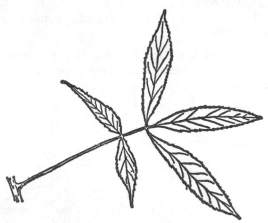

hairs on margin at first, dark green above, pale yellow-green and shiny below. The upper pair of leaflets are about twice as long as the lower pair. The fruit is spherical, ¾-1½ inches in diameter, divided into 4 parts by furrows along which the thick husk splits to the base. Distributed from North Carolina to Georgia, westward to Mississippi, and in Tennessee.

9. PIGNUT (*H. glabra* Sweet.). See p. 82. In the southern region it may be found from Virginia to Florida and westward to Louisiana.

10. FLORIDA HICKORY (*H. floridana* Sarg.). Leaves 6-8 inches long with slender petiole becoming smooth although rusty-hairy when young; usually 5 leaflets, the upper three 3-4 inches long and about twice as large as

the lower pair, coarsely saw-toothed with hard teeth; smooth at maturity. The fruit is obovoid, about 1 inch in diameter, the moderately thick husk splitting to the base

along 2 or 3 furrows. The nut is reddish. Found in Florida.

11. PALE HICKORY (*H. pallida* Engl. and Graebn.). See p. 83. In the southern region it is found in southeastern Virginia, the Piedmont of North and South Carolina, Georgia, western Florida and westward to Louisiana.

12. MOCKERNUT (*H. alba* Koch.). See p. 83. The most common Hickory in the Southern States.

13. BUCKLEY'S HICKORY (*H. Buckleyi* Durand.). Leaves 8-12 inches long, petioles rusty-hairy becoming smooth; usually having 7 leaflets, tapering at the apex, serrate, dark green and shiny above, pale below, smooth or with tufts of hairs in the angles of the veins. The terminal leaflet is obovate, sometimes on a winged stalk. The upper three leaflets are 4-6 inches long, twice the size of the lowest pair. Fruit is spherical, 1¼-1¾ inches

in diameter with a moderately thick husk splitting to base. The nut is dark red. Found in Texas and central Oklahoma.

Var. *arkansana* Sarg. differs from the species in the characteristics of the fruit which is obovoid in shape, the husk splitting to the middle or near the base. The nut is pale brown. Found from eastern Taxes and western Louisiana northward; the common Hickory of the mountains in Arkansas.

BUCKLEY'S HAIRY HICKORY (*H. Buckleyi* var. *villosa* Sarg.). The petiole and rachis are rusty-hairy, becoming smooth late in the season. The fruit is obovoid or spherical, rusty-hairy, tardily splitting to the base along 1 or 2 furrows, or not opening at all. The nut is tinged with red. Virginia to Missouri and southward.

14. LOUISIANA HICKORY (*H. leiodermis* Sarg.). Leaves are 12-14 inches long; petiole and rachis hairy, becoming smooth, usually with 7 leaflets, saw-toothed, short-stalked, tapering at apex, uneven at base, becoming shiny green above, pale and slightly hairy below, especially on the midrib. The three upper leaflets are obovate, 4-5 inches long, twice as large or larger than the lowest pair. The fruit is broadly obovoid or spherical, opening to base along 2 furrows. The nut is tinged with red. Western Mississippi to Texas and Arkansas.

Hornbeam. Blue Beech (*Carpinus caroliniana* Walt.)

See p. 85. Distributed along streams in the Southern States to central Florida and westward to eastern Texas, Oklahoma and Kansas.

Hop Hornbeam (*Ostrya virginiana* Koch.)

See p. 86. Similar in distribution to Hornbeam, its greatest development occurring in Arkansas and Texas.

Birch (*Betula* L.)

See p. 88. Two birches are found in the South, both of which also occur in the North: the Cherry Birch (*Betula lenta* L.) and the River Birch (*Betula nigra* L.). See pp. 89, 90. The River Birch attains its greatest size in Florida, Louisiana and Texas, and is the only birch of these warm regions.

Beech. (*Fagus grandifolia* Ehrh.)

See p. 93. It extends into the southern region to east Texas and Oklahoma.

In the south var. *caroliniana* Fern. and Rehd. obtains. It differs from the species in its ovate leaves which are rounded at the base, and in the margins being less sharply toothed.

Chestnut (*Castanea* Adans.)

The Chestnut and Chinquapins are trees or shrubs with oblong leaves, coarsely toothed on the margin, the veins extending into the glandular teeth. The fruits (nuts) are enclosed by a very spiny covering (involucre) which splits into 2 or 4 parts at maturity. The inner surface of the involucre and the apex of the nuts are hairy.

Key to the Southern Chestnuts.

Leaves hoary beneath, petioles about ½ inch long.
1. Chinquapin.
Leaves smooth beneath.
Petioles about ½ inch long, leaves 6-8 inches long.
2 Chestnut (See p. 94).
Petioles shorter, considerably less than ⅛ inch long, leaves 3-4 inches long. 3. Florida Chinquapin.

1. CHINQUAPIN (*C. pumila* Mill.). A medium-size tree, usually shrubby east of the Mississippi River. The leaves are 3-5 inches long, elliptical, coarsely toothed, with rigid teeth, hoary or silvery on the lower surface. The petioles are flattened on the upper side, hairy and about ½ inch long. The branchlets are woolly. It is found in the At-

lantic and Gulf States to eastern Texas and Oklahoma and attains its best development in Arkansas and east Texas.

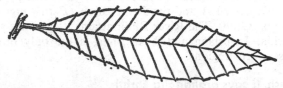

3. FLORIDA CHINQUAPIN (*C. alnifolia* var. *floridana* Sarg.). A shrub which attains tree-like dimensions only along the shores of St. Andrew's Bay, Florida. The leaves are 3-4 inches long, elliptical, irregularly serrate, the teeth ending in a short point. At maturity they are smooth below, although hoary when expanding. The petioles are smooth and considerably less than ⅛ inch long. The branchlets are almost smooth.

Oak (*Quercus* L.)

(See p. 95.)

Key to the Southern Oaks.

A. Leaves not deeply pinnately lobed, margin entire or toothed.
  B. Leaves relatively narrow.
    a. Margin usually entire, or only slightly wavy.
      b. Leaves conspicuously broadest at apex (1½ inches). 1. Water Oak.
      bb. Leaves conspicuously broadest at middle (1½-2 inches). 2. Southern Swamp Oak.
      bbb. Leaves not as above; lanceolate, elliptical or oblong.
        c. Woolly or hairy below.
          d. Margin curled back. 3. Live Oak.
          dd. Margin not curled back.
              4. Blue Jack Oak.
        cc. Smooth or essentially so.
          d. Elliptical with very short point at acute apex, sometimes 3-lobed at apex.
              5. Laurel Oak.
          dd. Lanceolate, without short point at acute apex. 6. Willow Oak.
    aa. Margin wavy above middle. 7. Chapman's Oak.

BB. Leaves relatively wide, abruptly widened at apex, margin with a few teeth and/or bristles, or slightly lobed at the broad apex.

    c. Leaves large, 6-7 inches long, lower surface orange or brown. 8. Black Jack Oak.

    cc. Leaves smaller, 2-3 inches long, lower surface pale green. 9. Arkansas Oak.

BBB. Leaves relatively wide, not abruptly widened at apex, margin coarsely wavy or toothed.

  a. Leaves sharply toothed; teeth curved toward tip of leaf, ending in very short projections.

                           10 Yellow Oak.

  aa. Leaves not sharply toothed, teeth usually rounded.

    b. Stem of acorn about twice as long as the acorn itself. 11. Swamp White Oak.

    bb. Stem of acorn lacking or shorter than the length of the acorn.

      c. Bark whitish, flaky. 12. Basket Oak.

      cc. Bark dark, firm. 13. Rock Chestnut Oak.

AA. Leaves deeply pinnately lobed, relatively large.

  B. Lobes sharply pointed, teeth mostly ending in a bristle.

    a. Leaves whitish on underside, covered with white or brownish hairs or wool. 14. Spanish Oak.

    aa. Leaves green on both surfaces; hairs, when present on the lower surface, are in angle of veins.

      b. Petiole yellow.

        c. Petiole 3-6 inches long, stout.

                      15. Black Oak.

        cc. Petiole ½-2 inches long, slender.

                      16. Pin Oak

      bb. Petiole green.

        c. Petiole grooved, stout, short (¼-¾ inch).

                      17. Turkey Oak.

        cc. Petiole not grooved, slender.

          d. Leaves small (2½ inches long), lowest lobe entire, its upper margin at right angles to midrib. 18. Georgia Oak.

        dd. Leaves larger, lowest lobe toothed or lobed.

          e. Tuft of hairs large on underside of leaf; leaves 6-8 inches long.

19. Texan Red Oak.

ee. Tufts of hairs absent or small.

f. Branchlets of current year red or brown; leaves about 3 inches long. 20. Texas Oak.

ff. Branchlets of current year green; leaves 3-6 inches long. 21. Scarlet Oak.

BB. Lobes rounded, bristles absent.

a. Leaves white below (woolly).

b. Terminal lobe (upper ½ of leaf) broad, oval, scalloped; rim of acorn fringed. 22. Burr Oak.

bb. Terminal lobe (upper ½ of leaf) 3-parted, not scalloped; nut almost covered by cup. 23. Overcup Oak.

aa. Leaves green below, *but* with fine hairs.

b. 5-lobed, the 2 middle ones largest, spreading and subequal, 2-parted; cup of acorn shallow. 24. Post Oak.

bb. 5-9 lobed; lobes not as above, nut almost covered by cup. 23. Overcup Oak.

aaa. Leaves green *and* smooth below.

b. Usually 5-lobed, upper lateral pair pointing forward and rather close together. 25. Southern White Oak.

bb. 7-9-lobed, lobes spreading and widely separated. 26. White Oak.

1. WATER OAK (*Q. nigra* L.). See p. 103. In the southern region it is found along the borders of swamps from Virginia to Florida, westward to Texas and eastern Oklahoma; planted as a shade tree in the South.

2. SOUTHERN SWAMP OAK (*Q. obtusa* Ashe.). A large

tree growing along swamps and in wet places in the coastal region. Its leaves, 3½-4 inches long, are widest in the middle (2 inches or less). They are dark green above with a yellow midrib, pale beneath, hairy in the angles of the veins; margin entire. The petioles are yellow. The acorn is ½ inch long or less, with a shallow cup at its base. It is found in the Dismal Swamp of Virginia, in west Florida and through the Gulf States to Texas. It is most abundant in Alabama and Louisiana.

3. LIVE OAK (*Q. virginiana* Mill.). A medium-size tree with a much enlarged base, above which it is divided into

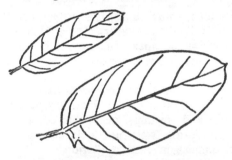

three or four large spreading branches. The leaves are oblong, 2-5 inches long, with usually entire, recurved margins, dark green and shiny above, pale and very hairy beneath. The ellipsoidal acorn is about 1 inch long, the cup enclosing about one-fourth of the nut. The wood is used in ship building. Found along the coast from Virginia to Florida, westward to Texas.

4. BLUE JACK OAK (*Q. cinerea* Michx.). Usually a small tree growing in dry soils. The leaves are oblong, 2-5 inches long, with entire margin, thick, blue-green and shiny above, pale and woolly beneath, with a short bristle

at the tip. The acorn is ½ inch long, ovoid, hairy at the apex. The cup is shallow or deep, covering up to one-half of the nut, usually much less. The scales of the cup are white and densely hairy, except at the brown margins. It is distributed mostly along the coastline from North Carolina to Florida, and westward to Texas.

5. LAUREL OAK (*Q. laurifolia* Michx.). A tree sometimes 100 feet high. The elliptical leaves are pointed at the tip, ending in a very short projection. They are thin,

3-4 inches long, shiny above, less so beneath. Petiole and midrib are yellow. The acorn is ½ inch long, ovoid, slightly hairy at the apex. The cup is shallow, coated on the outside with brownish scales which are hairy except on the margins.

There is a variety (var. *tridentata* Sarg.) in which the leaves are three-lobed at the apex. Found on the edges of streams and swamps near the coast from North Carolina to Florida, westward to Louisiana. It attains its best development in eastern Florida.

6. WILLOW OAK (*Q. phellos* L.). See p. 104. Found in wet places in the southern regions to Texas and Oklahoma.

7. CHAPMAN'S OAK (*Q. Chapmanii* Sarg.). A shrub or small tree with oblong leaves 2-3 inches long, with margin wavy above the middle. They are leathery, dark green

and shiny above, pale beneath, hairy along the midrib on the lower side. The petioles are very short, almost wanting. The acorn is ovoid, ½ inch long; the upper half of the nut is hairy. The cup encloses the nut for nearly half of its length. Found in the sand barrens along the coast from South Carolina to Florida. It is abundant only in western Florida.

8. BLACKJACK OAK (*Q. marilandica* Muench.). See p. 103. Distributed through the southern regions to western Texas and Oklahoma.

9. ARKANSAS OAK (*Q. arkansana* Sarg.). A medium-size tree with obovate leaves, very wide at the apex where they are slightly three-lobed, 2-3 inches long and about as wide at the apex; the apex and the two lateral lobes

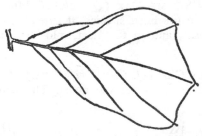

are tipped with a small bristle; light green and smooth (at maturity) above, paler beneath with hairs in the angles of the veins. The acorn is ovoid, ¼ inch long, with a shallow cup, the scales of which have a red margin. Found from Alabama to Arkansas in dry situations.

10. YELLOW OAK (*Q. Muehlenbergii* Engl.). See p. 105. Distributed along the Appalachian Mountains to Alabama and Mississippi.

11. SWAMP WHITE OAK (*Q. bicolor* Willd.). See p. 107. It reaches into the southern region only in northeastern Oklahoma.

12. BASKET or COW OAK (*Q. Michauxii* Nutt.). See p. 106. Distributed in both northern and southern regions.

13. ROCK CHESTNUT OAK (*Q. prinus* Engelm.). See p. 107. It extends along the Appalachian Mountains to northeastern Mississippi.

14. SPANISH OAK (*Q. digitata* Sudw.). See p. 101. Mostly a southern species growing in dry situations from Virginia to Texas and Oklahoma.

The Swamp Spanish Oak (*Q. pagodæfolia* Ashe.), sometimes considered a variety of the Spanish Oak, has less deeply cut leaves and wider lobes. Found mostly in the Southern States in low, rich soil. It is most abundant in central Mississippi.

15. BLACK OAK (*Q. velutina* Lam.). See p. 100. Distributed in both the northern and southern regions.

16. PIN or SWAMP OAK (*Q. palustris* Muench.). See p. 98. Mostly a northern species, it extends into Oklahoma and Arkansas, and in the East, into Virginia and North Carolina.

17. TURKEY OAK (*Q. Catesbæi* Michx.). A small tree of the sand barrens along the coast. The leaves, about 5

inches long, are deeply divided into 3 or 5 lobes, the terminal lobe elongate and three-toothed at the apex; thick, yellow-green and shiny above, paler and shiny below. Large clusters of rusty hairs are present in the angles of the veins on the lower side. The petiole is grooved. The acorn is ovoid, 1 inch long; the nut is woolly at the top, enclosed about one-third of its length by the cup, the scales of which are white-hairy with a red margin. Found from Virginia to Florida, westward to eastern Louisiana. It is most abundant in South Carolina and Georgia.

18. GEORGIA OAK (*Q. georgiana* Curtis.). The small leaves, about 2½ inches long, are usually 5-lobed, the lower pair of lobes are entire and their upper margins

are at right angles to the midrib; bright green and shiny above, paler beneath, tufts of hairs may be present or absent from the angles of the veins. The acorn is ellipsoidal or spherical, ⅓-½ inch long; the nut is enclosed one-third to one-half of its length by the thick cup, the scales of which are brownish. It is found only in central Georgia.

19. TEXAN RED OAK (*Q. Shumardii* Buckl.). See p. 98. The Spotted Oak (*Q. Shumardii* var. *Schneckii* Sarg.) differs from the species in the deeper cup of the acorn which covers one-third or more of the nut. In the species the cup is shallow and thick. The variety is more common than the species in Texas and the Mississippi Valley.

20. TEXAS OAK (*Q. texana* Buckl.). A small tree with leaves deeply divided into 5 or 7 lobes, 3-3½ inches long, dark green and shiny above, paler and shiny be-

neath. Occasionally small tufts of hair are present on the lower side, otherwise smooth. The acorn is ovoid,

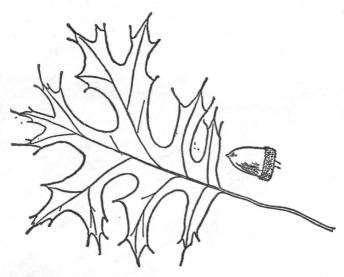

about 1 inch long, the cup covering one-third or less of the nut. Native to Texas.

21. SCARLET OAK (*Q. coccinea* Muench.). See p. 99. It is mostly a northern species but occurs in the southern region in the mountains of North Carolina to Georgia, Alabama, Mississippi and in Olkahoma.

22. MOSSYCUP or BURR OAK (*Q. macrocarpa* Michx.). See p. 108. Most abundant in the northern section, it is found sparingly in the southern region in Oklahoma, Texas and Louisiana.

23. OVERCUP or SWAMP POST OAK (*Q. lyrata* Walt.). See p. 109. Distributed mostly in the southern region along the Gulf and Atlantic States. Its greatest development is in Louisiana, Texas and Arkansas.

24. POST OAK (*Q. stellata* Wang.). See p. 109. Distributed in both northern and southern regions.

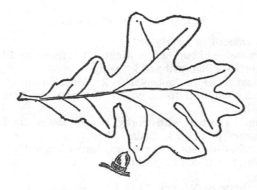

25. SOUTHERN WHITE OAK (*Q. austrina* Small.). A fairly large tree. The leaves are relatively narrow, cut

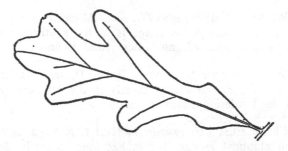

into 5 lobes which are entire, sinuses narrow. The second pair of lobes is much larger than the lower pair. They are glabrous, dark green and shiny above, paler beneath, 3-8 inches long. Acorns are ovoid, ½ inch long, the cup covering one-third or more of the nut. The scales are woolly. It is distributed from South Carolina to Florida westward to Mississippi.

26. WHITE OAK (*Q. alba* L.). See p. 110. Distributed in both the northern and southern regions.

Elm (*Ulmus* L.)

(See p. 110.)

Key to the Southern Elms.

Twigs smooth or nearly so.
  Branches without corky wings. 1. American Elm.
  Branches often with corky wings.
    Leaf ovate to lanceolate. 2. Winged Elm.
    Leaf elliptical to obovate. 3. September Elm.
Twigs hairy.
  Branches often with corky wings, leaves small (1-2 inches long). 4. Cedar Elm.
  Branches without corky wings, leaves larger (5-7 inches long). 5. Slippery Elm.

1. AMERICAN or WHITE ELM (*U. americana* L.). See p. 111. It is most abundant and best developed in the northern region, less common in the South.

2. WINGED ELM, WAHOO (*U. alata* Michx.). See p. 112. The greater part of its range is in the southern region, extending northward into Illinois and Indiana.

3. SEPTEMBER or SOUTHERN ELM (*U. serotina* Sarg.). See p. 112. Found locally mostly in the southern region and the bordering states to the north.

4. CEDAR ELM (*U. crassifolia* Nutt.). A large tree with small elliptical leaves, 1-2 inches long, coarsely doubly toothed, unequal or oblique at the base, leathery, dark green and shiny above, rough to the touch above, soft hairy beneath; petioles very short. Some of the branches have two corky wings, ¼ inch wide. The fruit is hairy, especially on the margin, ⅓ inch long, deeply notched at the tip. Distributed in Mississippi, Louisiana, Arkansas and Texas.

5. SLIPPERY ELM (*U. fulva* Michx.). See p. 113. Distributed in both the northern and southern regions.

Water Elm (*Planera aquatica* Gmel.)

See p. 114. Mostly confined to swamp lands in the South; extending into the northern region in Illinois, Kentucky and Indiana.

Hackberry. Sugarberry. Dwarf Hackberry (*Celtis* L.)

HACKBERRY (*C. occidentalis* L.) and Sugarberry (*C. laevigata* Willd.), p. 115, are also found in the South. The Hackberry is more common in the North, the Sugarberry in the South.

DWARF HACKBERRY (*C. georgiana* Small.) is a shrub or small tree ranging from North Carolina to Florida and Alabama. It is similar to *C. occidentalis* but has smaller leaves, 1½-2½ inches long. The leaves are ovate, pointed at the tip, with entire or saw-toothed margin, dark green and rough to the touch on the upper surface, pale beneath. The fruit is purplish and about ½ inch in diameter.

Mulberry (*Morus* L.)

See p. 116. The red and white Mulberries are found in both the northern and southern regions.

Paper Mulberry (*Broussonetia papyrifera* Vent.)

(See p. 117.)

Osage Orange (*Maclura pomifera* Schn.)

See p. 118. Native to Arkansas, Oklahoma and Texas, but cultivated and escaped in other parts of the southern and northern regions.

Pigeon Plum (*Coccolobis laurifolia* Jacq.)

A large tropical tree on the coast of southern Florida; the leaves are ovate, with entire or slightly wavy, re-

curved margins, leathery, 3-4 inches long, smooth; petiole ½ inch or less long, flattened. The large (⅓ inch) and transparent stipules at the base of the petiole entirely encircle the branchlet. The cherry-like fruits are ⅓ inch long and dark red.

Magnolia (*Magnolia* L.)

(See p. 118.)

Key to the Southern Magnolias.

Leaves without lobes at base.
    Leaves shiny above, leathery.
        Lower surface white. 1. Sweet Bay (see p. 119).
        Lower surface brownish. 2. Bull Bay (see below).
    Leaves not shiny, thin.
        6-8 inches long. 3. Cucumber Tree (see p. 119).
        8-24 inches long. 4. Umbrella Magnolia (see p. 120).
Leaves with ear-like lobes at base.
    Leaves light green beneath.
        10-12 inches long. 5. Fraser Magnolia (see p. 121).
    Leaves whitish beneath.
        5-8 inches long. 6. Pyramidal Magnolia (see below).
        20-30 inches long. 7. Bigleaf Magnolia (see p. 120).

2. BULL BAY, SOUTHERN MAGNOLIA (*M. grandiflora* L.). A tree attaining a height of 60 feet or more, oc-

casionally 135 feet; the branchlets thickly covered with rusty-colored hairs; leaves evergreen, leathery, glossy and smooth above, rusty-hairy on lower surface, 4-8

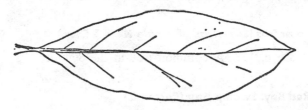

inches long, elliptical or oblong. Flowers 7-8 inches across, fragrant. Native to the southern region and widely cultivated.

6. PYRAMIDAL MAGNOLIA (*M. pyramidata* Pursh.). A small tree, rarely over 25 feet in height; leaves obovate, the apex abruptly narrowed to a short point, lobed at the

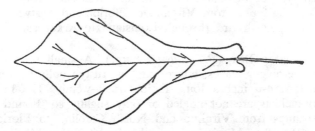

base, thin, smooth, covered with a whitish bloom on the lower surface, 5-8 inches long. Petioles 1-2½ inches long. Found locally in rich soils along streams in Georgia, Florida and Alabama.

Tulip Tree (*Liriodendron tulipifera* L.)

See p. 121. In the South this tree is found in the Atlantic States to northern Florida and westward to Mississippi and Arkansas.

American Pawpaw (*Asimina triloba* Dunal)

See p. 122. Distributed in northern and southern regions, especially in the Mississippi Valley.

Sassafras (*Sassafras officinale* Nees & Eber.)

See p. 123. A common tree in the South.

Red Bay. Swamp Bay (*Persea* L.)

RED BAY (*P. borbonia* Spreng.). A medium-size tree, inhabitant of swamps; with oblong leaves, pointed at apex and tapering at base, 3-4 inches long, thick and leathery, bright green and shiny above, pale and whitish beneath; margins entire. The petioles are reddish, flattened, and grooved on the upper side. The branchlets are angular the first year. Fruit is ovoid, about ½ inch long, shiny, blue or black, with thin dry flesh and ovoid seed. May be found from Virginia to Florida and westward to Texas, northward through Louisiana to Arkansas.

SWAMP BAY (*P. palustris* Sarg.). A small tree with lance-oblong leaves, entire margins, rusty-woolly on veins below, 4-6 inches long. Petiole rusty-woolly. The hairy branchlets are not angled or only slightly so. Found in swamps from Virginia and North Carolina to Florida, westward to Mississippi, mostly along the coast.

Witch-Hazel (*Hamamelis* L.)

Leaves smooth to the touch.
　　　　　　　　1. Northern Witch-Hazel (see p. 124)
Leaves rough to the touch.　2. Southern Witch-Hazel.

2. SOUTHERN WITCH-HAZEL (*H. macrophylla* Pursh.). This may be distinguished from the northern Witch-Hazel by the rough leaves covered abundantly on the

upper surface by stellate hairs (use hand lens). The leaves are obovate or elliptical, 3-5 inches long. Distrib-

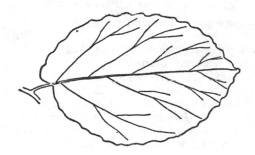

uted from Georgia to Florida, westward to Texas and Arkansas. It is best developed in Alabama and Louisiana.

Sweet Gum *(Liquidambar styraciflua* L.)

See p. 125. Distributed in the northern and southern regions.

Planetree Sycamore *(Platanus occidentalis* L.)

See p. 125. Northern and southern in distribution.

Shadbush *(Amelanchier canadensis* Md.)

See p. 131. Found in both North and South; best development in the northern region.

Hawthorn. Thorn. Haw (*Crataegus* L.)

(See p. 132.)

Plum. Cherry (*Prunus* L.)

(See p. 134.)

Key to the Southern Plums and Cherries.

Leaves evergreen, leathery, margin entire.
            1. Wild Orange.
Leaves not evergreen, margin toothed.
 Leaves relatively narrow.
  Leaves 1-2½ inches long.
   Leaves ½ inch wide. 2. Chickasaw Plum.
   Leaves 1 inch or more wide. 3. Sloe.
  Leaves 2-6 inches long (mostly more than 3 inches).
   Petiole hairy in groove. 4. Wild Goose Plum.
   Petiole not grooved nor hairy. 5. Black Cherry.
 Leaves relatively wide.
  Teeth on margin blunt, tipped with red gland.
            6. Wild Cherry.
  Teeth ending in a sharp point.
   Leaves relatively thick.
    Long white hairs on lower surface.
           7. Big Tree Plum.
    Without hairs, wrinkled. 8. Wild Plum.
   Leaves thin.
    Very hairy on lower surface.
          9. Woolly Wild Plum.

1. WILD ORANGE. MOCK ORANGE (*P. caroliniana* Ait.). A tree to 40 feet; evergreen leaves oblong, 2-4½ inches long, leathery, with entire margin somewhat recurved (occasionally a leaf with sharp teeth), lustrous and glabrous on upper surface, paler beneath. Petiole orange in color. Fruit black, shiny, ½ long, skin thick, flesh dry, stone cylindrical, ½ inch long. Found along the 'coast from North Carolina to Florida, westward to Texas.

2. CHICKASAW PLUM (*P. angustifolia* Marsh.). See p. 136. A small tree. Leaves lanceolate, pointed at both ends, toothed (the teeth glandular), not hairy or only when young, shiny above, dull beneath, 1-2 inches long. There are two red glands on the petiole near the blade. Native in Texas and Oklahoma, but established from

Delaware to Florida to eastern Texas along the borders of fields and dwellings.

3. SLOE, BLACK SLOE (*P. umbellata* Ell.). A small tree to 20 feet. Leaves lanceolate to oblong, abruptly pointed at both ends, fine-toothed (the glandular teeth curved toward the margin); two glands at base of the blade; dark green above (not shiny), paler beneath, about 2 inches long; midrib and veins orange in color. Fruit spherical, ½ inch in diameter, usually black, but sometimes yellow or red, covered with a white bloom, flesh thick, sour; stone flat. The fruit is used for preserves. Found from North Carolina to Florida, westward to eastern Texas and southern Arkansas.

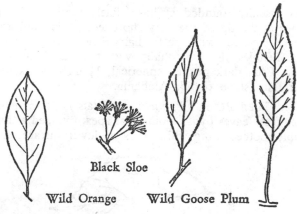

Black Sloe

Wild Orange   Wild Goose Plum

4. WILD GOOSE PLUM (*P. Munsoniana* Wight & Hedrick.) A small tree to 20 feet, spreading from the roots and forming thickets; leaves lanceolate, pointed at both ends, finely glandular-toothed, thin, shiny on upper surface, hairy below especially on veins, often with tufts of white hairs in the angles, 2½-4 inches long. Petioles with 2 glands near the blade, grooved on upper side, with white hairs in groove. Fruit is oblong, ¾ inch long, red with slight bloom, skin thin, flesh juicy, stone oval, flattened. Native in the South from Missouri westward to

Oklahoma and Texas. May be found as an escape from cultivation eastward to Georgia.

5. BLACK CHERRY (*P. serotina* Ehrh.). See p. 139. Widely distributed in northern and southern regions.

6. WILD CHERRY (*P. australis* Beadl.). A large tree, sometimes 60 feet high. Its leaves are ovate, pointed at

apex, usually rounded at base, finely toothed with red glands at the tip of the very short teeth, thin, dull green above, covered with rusty hairs below, 2½-4 inches long. Petioles also rusty-hairy with two glands near the blade. Fruit dark purple, spherical, ¼ inch in diameter, flesh thin, stone ovoid. Alabama.

7. BIG TREE PLUM (*P. mexicana* Wats.). A small tree to 20 feet, leaves ovate, pointed at apex, rounded at base, doubly toothed, long white hairs on lower surface, espe-

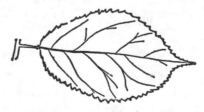

cially on veins, shiny on upper surface, paler beneath. Petioles hairy, usually with glands near blade. Fruit oblong, purple-red, with faint whitish bloom, 1⅓ inches long, thick juicy flesh, stone ovoid, flattened, about 1 inch long. Several varieties of this species have been described. Native from southern Kansas to Texas and Louisiana.

8. AMERICAN PLUM (*P. americana* Marsh.). See p. 134. Leaf thickish, wrinkled, fruit without bloom. Found along streams and marshes in northern and southern regions, extending into the Rockies in the West.

A variety *floridanum* Sarg. is found in Florida. It has thin, finely toothed leaves and purple fruit.

9. WOOLLY WILD PLUM (*P. lanata* Mack. & Bush.). Similar in many respects to the American Plum (8) from which it differs in the thin leaves which are glabrous above, pale and densely hairy on the lower side with longer hairs on the veins. Bark of the trunk is brownish-gray. Fruit crimson, covered with a whitish bloom, flesh thick, stone flattened. Found in the South from Oklahoma to Texas and Louisiana, extending into the northern region in Illinois, Indiana and Tennessee.

Redbud (*Cercis* L.)

Leaves ovate, apex pointed. 1. Redbud (see p. 140). Leaves circular, apex indented. 2. Texas Redbud.

2. TEXAS REDBUD (*C. reniformis* Engl.). A small tree with rounded leathery leaves, dark green and shiny

above, paler beneath, heart-shaped at base, 2-3 inches in diameter. The margin is wavy and the tip indented. Petiole is 1½-2 inches long. Texas.

Honeylocust. Waterlocust (*Gleditsia* L.)

HONEYLOCUST (*G. triacanthos* L.). See p. 140. It extends southward into the northern portions of the Gulf States from western Florida to Texas.

WATERLOCUST (*G. aquatica* Marsh.). See p. 141. Mostly southern in distribution, it reaches into Illinois and Indiana. Rare east of the Mississippi River.

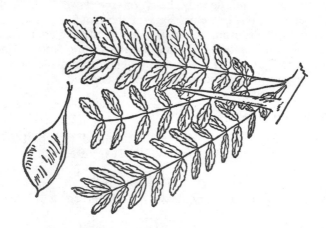

Kentucky Coffeetree (*Gymnocladus dioicus* Koch.)

See p. 141. Chiefly a northern species which is sparingly found in Arkansas and Oklahoma.

Cat's Claw. Huajillo. Ebony (*Pithecolobium* Mart.)

Trees or shrubs armed with a pair of spines, one on each side of the petiole. The leaves are bipinnate with glands on the leafstalks between the divisions of the compound leaf and between the leaflets. The small flowers are bunched in stalked round heads or more elongate spikes. The fruit is a flat pod.

CAT'S CLAW (*P. unguis-cati* Mart.). A small tree to 25 feet; branchlets armed with spines ¼ inch long. The compound leaves are composed of two stalks each with

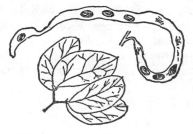

two leaflets, which are broadly oblong, rounded at the apex, oblique at the base, with one side of the leaflet rounded and the other narrowing sharply, ½-2 inches long, shiny and bright green above, paler beneath. Fruit 2-4 inches long and ½ inch wide, thickened on margin, twisted. Southern Florida.

HUAJILLO (*P. brevifolium* Benth.). A small tree or shrub found along the Rio Grande. The compound leaves are small, 2-3 inches long, and bear 8-10 secondary branches, each with 10-20 leaflets. The petiole is 1 inch long and bears an elongated gland in the middle. The leaflets are linear, oblique at the base, borne on short petiolules. They are light green above, paler beneath, without hairs, usually less than ¼ inch long. The pod is 4-6 inches long and about ⅔ inch wide, thin except for the thickened margins.

EBONY (*P. flexicaule* Coult.). A valuable tree 20-30 feet high, found along the lower Rio Grande. The leaves are smaller than the Huajillo, being 1½-2 inches long. The petiole is slightly hairy. The compound leaves have six branches (3 pairs) each with 8-12 leaflets. The leaflets are ovate, rounded at the apex, smooth, shiny green above, paler on the lower side, about ¼ inch long, borne on short stalks. The pod is 4-6 inches long and about 1 inch wide, thick and woody.

Mesquite (*Prosopis* L.)

Small spiny trees or shrubs with bipinnate leaves, which are usually composed of two secondary stalks bearing numerous leaflets. The petiole is tipped with a small spine between the two leaf-branches. The small greenish-white flowers are arranged in stalked spikes. Fruit is a pod.

MESQUITE (*P. juliflora* DC.). A small tree, more frequently shrubby. Each of the 2 leaf-stalks bears 12-22

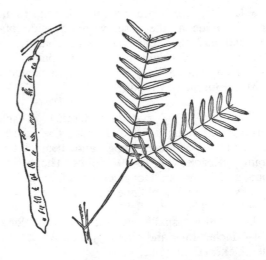

leaflets. The pod is straight. The branchlets are armed with spines ½-2 inches long, above the attachment of the leaves.

The more typical southern form is called the Glandular Mesquite (*P. juliflora* var. *glandulosa* Cock.). It has linear leaflets 2 inches long, dark green, not hairy. The tree, often 20 feet high, has a spreading crown with drooping branches. Found in the southern region from Louisiana to Texas and Oklahoma, extending into the western region to California.

"Acacia." "Mimosa" (*Albizzia julibrissin* Durazz.)

A small tree with glabrous bipinnate leaves about 14 inches long, composed of about 12 pairs of pinnae, each with about 25 pairs of leaflets. The tip of the leaf and of each pinna end in a short flexible spine. The leaflets

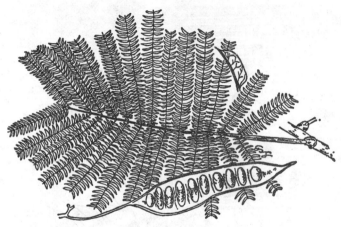

are about ¼ inch long, dark green but dull above, veins and midrib conspicuous on the light green lower surface, asymmetrical with the midrib along the upper edge and slightly prolonged beyond the tip. The base of the petiole is swollen and has a large gland on the upper side. The pod is about 5 inches long, thin and papery except at the thickened margins; constricted between the seeds and appearing corrugated. Native of Asia (Persia to China); much cultivated in the South, spreading northward to Virginia.

Black Locust (*Robinia pseudoacacia* L.)

See Common Locust, p. 143. In the southern region it is found in Arkansas, Oklahoma and Texas.

Jamaica Dogwood (*Ichthyomethia piscipula* Hitch.)

A common tropical tree in southern Florida, about 40 feet high, with compound leaves 4-9 inches long, with 5-11 stalked leaflets which are oval or oblong, leathery, smooth and shiny above, pale and more or less hairy beneath, margin entire and slightly wavy. The stalks of the leaflets are also hairy. The fruit is 3-4 inches long with four wings 1 inch or more wide; the pod proper is constricted between the seeds.

Prickly Ash (*Xanthoxylum* L.)

(See also p. 144.)

PRICKLY ASH. TOOTHACHE-TREE (*X. clava-Herculis* L.). A small tree or shrub, 25 feet high; branchlets armed

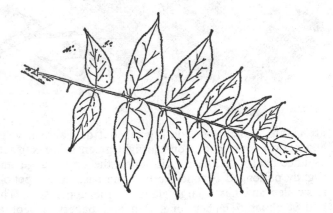

with spines ½ inch or more long; leaves compound, 5-8 inches long, with spiny petiole and rachis, 3-9 pairs of ovate-lanceolate leaflets, dark green and shiny above, slightly hairy below, 1-2 inches long, margin finely toothed with rounded glandular teeth. Distributed from southeastern Virginia to Florida, westward to Texas; best developed in Texas.

WILD LIME (*X. fagara* Sarg.). A small tree or shrub very common in southern Florida; it occurs also in south-

ern Texas; branchlets with hooked spines; leaves 3-4 inches long, with 7-9 abovate leaflets, ½ inch long or smaller, leathery, glandular, shiny above, rounded at apex, margin slightly scalloped.

Hoptree (*Ptelea trifoliata* L.)

See p. 144. Found in the northern and southern regions.

Sumac (*Rhus* L.)

The Shining Sumac and Staghorn Sumac, p. 148, may become trees 25-40 feet high in the South; the Poison Sumac, p. 147, is found in swamps in both North and South.

Holly (*Ilex* L.)

Key to the Southern Hollies.

Leaves with spiny margin. American Holly (see p. 149).
Leaves with entire margin.
    Broad (1 inch or more wide), midrib raised above upper surface. 1. Black-berried Holly.
    Narrower (less than 1 inch wide), midrib sunken on upper surface. 2. Dahoon.
Leaves with toothed margin.
    Slightly toothed above the middle, petiole not grooved.
                                   2. Dahoon.
    Toothed to base, petioles grooved.
        Leaves less than 2 inches long. 3. Cassena.
        Leaves 2 inches or more in length. Swamp Holly (see p. 150).

1. BLACK-BERRIED HOLLY (*I. Krugiana* Loesen.). A small tree growing in southern Florida. Its leaves are nar-

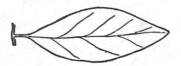

rowly ovate, tapering at both ends, margin entire and somewhat thickened, leathery, dark green and shiny above, pale beneath, 2½-4 inches long.

2. DAHOON (*I. Cassine* L.). Small tree or shrub; leaves oblanceolate, tapering at both ends, the margin is usually entire and curved back, but sometimes it is toothed above

the middle, shiny and dark green above, pale beneath, only slightly hairy on the midrib beneath, 1½-3 inches long; petioles short. Found along the coast from Virginia to Florida, westward to Louisiana.

3. CASSENA, YAUPON (*I. vomitoria* Ait.). Leaves are elliptical, leathery, dark green and shiny above, paler

beneath, 1-2 inches long, with short grooved petioles. The margin is toothed to the base. Found near the coast from Virginia to Florida, westward to Texas.

Maple (*Acer* L.)

Key to the Southern Maples.

Leaf compound. Box Elder (see p. 154).
Leaf not compound.
  Sinus (space between lobes) rounded.
    Sinus broad, lobes short.
      Leaf 4-5 inches across. Sugar Maple (see p. 154).
      Leaf 1½-3 inches across.
        Green on lower surface 1. White Bark Maple.
        White on lower surface.
                      2. Southern Sugar Maple.
    Sinus narrow, lobes long. Silver Maple (see p. 155).
  Sinus sharp angled.
    Twigs brown. Silver Maple (see p. 155).
    Twigs red. Red Maple (see p. 156).

1. WHITE BARK MAPLE (*A. leucoderme* Small.). A small tree, rarely over 25 feet high, with a close, light gray or gray-brown bark; leaves 3-5 lobed, yellow-green above and below, hairy on the lower surface, 2-3½ inches across. Found from North Carolina to Georgia, westward to Louisiana and Arkansas.

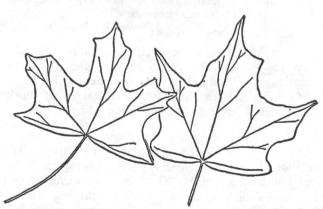

Southern Sugar Maple   White Bark Maple

2. SOUTHERN SUGAR MAPLE (*A. floridanum* Pax.). A large tree, occasionally to 60 feet; leaves 3-5 lobed, the

lobes themselves usually 3-lobed, dark green and shiny above, whitish and hairy below, woolly along the veins, 1½-3 inches across. The petiole is long and slender, enlarged at the base, almost encircling the twig. Its distribution is from Virginia to Florida, westward to Texas.

Buckeye. Horsechestnut (*Aesculus* L.)

(See also p. 159.)

Key to the Southern Buckeyes.

Fruits prickly. 1. Ohio Buckeye (see p. 160).
Fruits not prickly.
    Commonly shrubs.
        Petiole grooved; leaves pale (woolly) on lower surface. 2. Buckeye.
        Petiole not grooved; leaves green beneath, smooth or nearly so (not woolly).
            Midrib green.
                3. Red-flowered Buckeye (see p. 161).
            Midrib orange. 4. Georgia Buckeye.
    Commonly trees.
        Midrib of leaflets orange. 4. Georgia Buckeye.
        Midrib of leaflets greenish.
                5. Sweet Buckeye (see p. 159).

2. BUCKEYE (*A. discolor* Pursh.). A shrub or small tree occurring in several varieties in the South, from North Carolina to Florida, westward to Texas. The 5 leaflets are oblong, the margin saw-toothed except at the base, pale beneath due to a heavy coating of hairs.

4. GEORGIA BUCKEYE (*A. georgiana* Sarg.). A shrub or small tree 25-30 feet high, ranging from North Carolina to Florida, common in the Piedmont region of North and South Carolina and Georgia. The leaves consist of 5 oblong leaflets with finely toothed margins; leaflets 4-6 inches long, with a stout orange midvein; usually smooth beneath.

In the variety *pubescens* Sarg. the lower surface of the leaflets is hairy.

The variety *lanceolata* Sarg. has narrower, lanceolate leaflets. Found in Georgia.

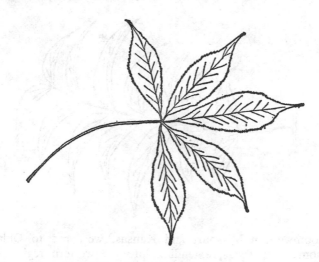

Soapberry (*Sapindus* L.)

Tree with alternate, pinnate leaves without terminal leaflets. The small white flowers are arranged in large clusters; the fruits are spherical berries.

Key to the Soapberries.

Rachis (main stalk of compound leaf) winged.
                                    1. Florida Soapberry.
Rachis not winged.   2. Wild China Tree.

1. FLORIDA SOAPBERRY (*S. saponaria* L.). A small tree, rarely 30 feet high, with evergreen, pinnately compound leaves made up mostly of 4 pairs of oblong leaflets which are 3-4 inches long, densely hairy on the lower surface. The rachis is winged. Southern Florida.

2. WILD CHINA TREE (*S. Drummondii* Hook. and Arn.). A tree sometimes 60 feet high with pinnately compound leaves which are made up mostly of 7 pairs of lanceolate,

curved leaflets, 2½ inches long or less, unequal on the two sides of the midvein. Distributed from Louisiana to

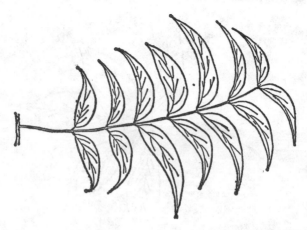

southwestern Missouri and Kansas, westward to Oklahoma and Texas, extending into the western region in Colorado, New Mexico and Arizona. The wood is largely used in basketry.

Red Ironwood (*Reynosia septentrionalis* Urb.)

A small tree, about 25 feet high, with opposite, shiny, leathery leaves, 1-1½ inches long, oval or obovate,

often indented at the apex, margins entire and curled backward; fruit spherical or obovoid, ½ inch long, dark purple or black. Southern Florida.

Black Ironwood (*Krugiodendron ferreum* Urb.)

A small tree, up to 30 feet; current year's branchlets velvety-hairy; evergreen leaves opposite, elliptical or ovate, 1-1½ inches long with entire margin, bright green and lustrous above, paler beneath, scattered hairs on upper surface and petiole. The cherry-like fruit, ⅓ inch long, is borne singly in the axils of the leaves. Florida.

Carolina Buckthorn (*Rhamnus caroliniana* Walt.)

See p. 161. Found in the South from Virginia to northern Florida, westward to eastern Texas.

Linden. Basswood (*Tilia* L.)

(See also p. 162.)

SOUTHERN LINDEN (*T. floridana* Small.). A tree sometimes 50 feet high; the ovate leaves are 3½-5 inches long,

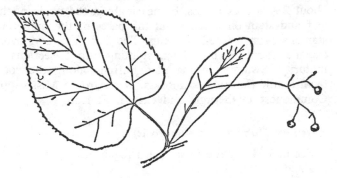

coarsely toothed, heart-shaped or unequal at the base, dark green above, paler beneath. Distributed from North Carolina to southern Florida and Texas.

CAROLINA BASSWOOD (*T. caroliniana* Mill.). The ovate leaves are 3-5 inches long, coarsely toothed, the lower surface densely hairy. Found from North Carolina to Georgia and Texas.

BEETREE LINDEN (*T. heterophylla* Vent.). See p. 163. Found in the South from Virginia to Florida, westward to Mississippi.

Loblolly Bay (*Gordonia lasianthus* Ell.)

A tree attaining a height of about 75 feet and a trunk diameter of 1½ feet; sometimes a shrub. The thick, dark green and shiny leaves are 4-5 inches long, lanceolate or

oblong, tapering gradually to the base, the margin saw-toothed above the middle. The fragrant white flowers are about 2½ inches across, borne singly in the angle of the leaf and stem on a red stalk; the bases of the numerous stamens form a five-lobed cup. The fruit is a dry, ovoid capsule about ¾ inch long, splitting into 5 sections at maturity. Swamps in the pine barrens along the coast from South Carolina to Florida, westward to Mississippi. Commonest in Georgia and eastern Florida.

Hercules' Club (*Aralia spinosa* L.)

See p. 164. Found in southern region to northern Florida and westward to Texas.

Mangrove (*Rhizophora Mangle* L.)

A tropical tree growing in tidal marshes. In the United States it is found along the coast of Florida. Commonly it attains a height of 20 feet, producing aerial roots from trunk and branches and forming dense thickets in the marshes. In drier localities it may reach a height of 70-

80 feet. The leaves are elliptical, narrowed to the base, dark green and shiny above, paler on lower surface, 3-5

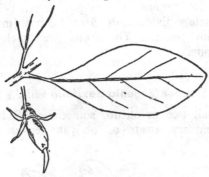

inches long. The margin is entire and slightly thickened. The bark is sometimes used for tanning.

Pawpaw. Papaya (*Carica papaya* L.)

A fast-growing tree attaining a height of about 15 feet,

native to southern Florida and frequently cultivated for their fruits which are considered to be a very enjoyable food in the tropics. The large leaves, 1-2 feet across, are palmately divided into 5 or 7 lobes (maple-like); on long stout petioles. The fruits are "melon-like," 4-12 inches long.

Spanish Stopper (*Eugenia buxifolia* Willd.)

A small tree or shrub, sometimes 20 feet high with small, leathery, ovate or obovate leaves, 1-1½ inches

long, margin entire or somewhat wavy; without petioles or on short stalks, in pairs on the branchlets. The fruits are ⅓ inch in diameter, spherical or oblong, black, the calyx remaining on top of the fruit; the skin is glandular, the flesh aromatic; containing one seed. Southern Florida.

Naked Wood (*E. dicrana* Berg.)

Similar in general characteristics to the Spanish Stopper, Naked Wood is a tree about 25 feet high, the leaves are thickly covered with black glandular dots. Southern Florida.

Tupelo. Water Gum. Cotton Gum (*Nyssa* L.)

Trees with alternate, simple leaves, and small greenish flowers aggregated at the end of a long axillary stalk; fruit olive-like, blue, red, or purple when ripe.

Key to the Tupelos of the South.

Leaves with entire margins.
Pale below, hairy especially on veins; petiole with longer hairs. 1. Tupelo, Sour Gum.
Pale below, whitish, smooth; petiole not hairy.
2. Water Gum.
Leaves (mostly) toothed. 3. Cotton Gum.

1. TUPELO. SOUR or BLACK GUM (*N. sylvatica* Marsh.). See p. 164. Distributed in northern and southern regions.

2. WATER GUM (*N. biflora* Walt.). See p. 165. Found in swamps near the coast from North Carolina to Louisiana.

3. COTTON GUM (*N. aquatica* Marsh.). Inhabits swamps from Virginia to Florida, westward to Texas. It is a

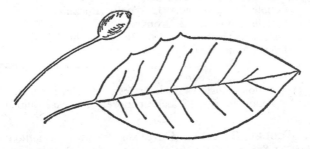

large tree with greatly swollen base, its leaves are 5-7 inches long, broadly ovate, some of them dentate, dark green and shiny above, downy on the lower surface.

Dogwood (*Cornus* L.)

See p. 165. The species of the northern region are also found in the South.

Sourwood (*Oxydendrum arboreum* DC.)

Extending southward to Florida and westward to Louisiana. See p. 170.

Farkleberry (Vaccinium arboreum Marsh.)

See p. 170. Mostly southern in its distribution. Its best development is along the coast from North Carolina to Florida, westward to Texas.

Bumelia (Bumelia Sw.)

Small trees or shrubs; branchlets armed with spines; leaves often crowded on very short spur branches; flowers very small, on long stalks, aggregated in the angles of the leaves; fruit black, like a small cherry or olive.

Key to the Bumelias of the South.

Lower surface of leaves hairy.
    Petiole not grooved. 1. Woolly Bumelia.
    Petiole grooved. 2. Ironwood.
Lower surface of leaves smooth or essentially so.
    Leaves thin, pointed at the apex.
                           3. Buckthorn Bumelia.
    Leaves thick, rounded at the apex.
        Petiole short, ⅛ inch or less. 4. Ant's Wood.
        Petiole longer, ¼ inch or more. 5. Texas Bumelia.

1. WOOLLY BUMELIA. CHITTAM WOOD (*B. lanuginosa* Pers.). See p. 171. Mostly southern in distribution, extending northward into Kansas and Illinois.

2. IRONWOOD. GOLDEN BUMELIA (*B. tenax* Willd.). A small tree or shrub with thin obovate leaves, 1-3 inches long, golden or white often becoming rusty-hairy beneath, dull green above, margins entire, thickened. Petioles slender, grooved, hairy. Found in dry sandy soil in South Carolina, Georgia and Florida, mostly coastal.

3. BUCKTHORN BUMELIA (*B. lycioides* Gaertn.). See p. 171.

4. ANT'S WOOD (*B. angustifolia* Nutt.). A small tree with pendulous branches; leaves obovate, rounded at the apex, tapering to base, 1-1½ inches long, smooth, thick, pale blue-green above, lighter beneath, petiole stout and grooved. Fruit oblong, ½-¾ inch long. Florida.

Golden Bumelia   Texas Bumelia

5. TEXAS BUMELIA (*B. monticola* Buckl.). A small tree or shrub, the lateral branchlets ending in spines; leaves rounded at apex, white-hairy beneath when young, becoming smooth, yellow-green and shiny above, lighter beneath. Petiole slender. Fruit oblong, ¼-⅓ inch. In dry locations, Texas.

Persimmon (*Diospyros virginiana* L.)

See p. 172. Widely distributed in North and South.

BLACK PERSIMMON or CHAPOTE (*D. texana* Scheele) occurs in southwestern Texas. It has small, thick, obovate leaves ¾-1½ inches long, dark green and shiny above, hairy beneath. Fruit spherical, ½-1 inch in diameter.

Silver Bell (*Halesia* L.)

Trees or shrubs; branchlets without terminal bud; leaves elliptical, toothed, pointed at the tip; flowers white, bell-shaped, pendulous on long stalks, in groups of 2 or 3 on a very short branch at the node of the leaves of the previous year; fruits are hard, dry, elongate, with 2 or 4 prominent wings.

Key to the Southern Silver Bells.

Fruit 4-winged.
    Leaves 8-11 inches long, flowers 2 inches long.
                                    1. Mountain Silver Bell.
    Leaves smaller (about 3 inches long); flowers smaller.
        Flowers about ½ inch long; fruit 1½ inches long, wings prominent. 2. Great Silver Bell.
        Flowers about ¼ inch long; fruit ¾ inch long, wings narrow. 3. Small-flowered Silver Bell.
Fruit 2-winged, leaves ovate, 3-4 inches long.
                                    4. Two-winged Silver Bell.

1. MOUNTAIN SILVER BELL (*H. monticola* Sarg.). A large tree to 90 feet; leaves large, 8-11 inches long, elliptical, long-pointed at tip, abruptly narrowed at base, smooth except for a few hairs on the veins beneath. Flowers are 2 inches long; fruits 1½-2 inches long with 4 prominent wings. Distributed in the mountains of western North Carolina, eastern Tennessee, Arkansas and western Georgia.

The variety *vestita* Sarg. is distributed in the southern region from North Carolina to eastern Oklahoma. The leaves are rounded at the base and hairy on the lower surface.

2. GREAT SILVER BELL (*H. caroliniana* L.). See p. 172.

3. SMALL-FLOWERED SILVER BELL (*H. parviflora* Michx.). A slender tree with elliptical leaves 2½-3 inches long, long pointed at the tip, minutely toothed with glandular teeth, veins hairy beneath; flowers ¼-⅓ inch long; fruit ¾-1½ inches long with 4 narrow wings. Northern Florida, Alabama, Mississippi and eastern Oklahoma.

4. TWO-WINGED SILVER BELL (*H. diptera* Ellis.). A small tree with ovate leaves 3-4 inches long, abruptly pointed at the tip sparingly and minutely toothed, lower

surface pale, soft-hairy, veins and veinlets conspicuous; flowers 1 inch long; fruits 1½-2 inches long with 2 wide

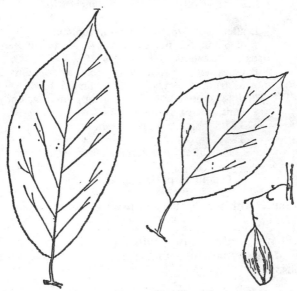

wings. Found from Georgia to Florida, westward to Texas and Arkansas.

Common Sweetleaf (*Symplocos tinctoria* L'Her.)

See p. 173. Distributed in the North and South.

Ash (*Fraxinus* L.)

(See also p. 174.)

Key to the Southern Ashes.

Leaflets with long petiolules.
  Leaflets 5 inches or more in length.
    Petiole woolly-hairy, midrib yellow.
                          1. Pumpkin Ash.
    Petiole pale, smooth, midrib greenish.
                          2. Carolina Ash.

Leaflets less than 5 inches long.
Usually 5 leaflets.
Leaflets woolly beneath, 3-4 inches long.
3. Water Ash.
Leaflets not woolly beneath, sometimes with tufts of hairs; 1-3 inches long. 4. Mountain Ash.
Usually 7 leaflets.
Petioles not grooved; wing broad surrounding body of fruit; swamps. 2. Carolina Ash.
Petiole grooved; wing not surrounding body of fruit; not of swamps.
Twigs hairy. 5. Red Ash.
Twigs smooth.
Petiolules of lateral leaflets ⅛-¼ inch long.
6. Green Ash.
Petiolules of lateral leaflets ¼-½ inch long.
7. White Ash.
Leaflets with short petiolules, twigs square in section.
8. Blue Ash.

1. PUMPKIN ASH (*F. profunda* Bush.). See p. 176. Found in swamps in both the northern and southern regions.

2. CAROLINA ASH, SWAMP ASH (*F. caroliniana* Mill.). A medium-size tree, leaves 7-12 inches long, petiole pale,

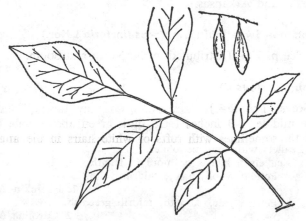

5-7 stalked leaflets, the mature leaflets ovate, toothed or

entire, 3-6 inches long, dark green above, paler beneath. The fruits are elliptical, 2 inches long, conspicuously veined. In swamps along the coast from Washington, D. C., to Florida, westward to Texas and Arkansas.

3. WATER ASH (*F. pauciflora* Nutt.). A tree 30-40 feet high; leaves 5-9 inches long with usually 5 petioled leaflets; the leaflets elliptical, pointed at both ends, toothed, 3-4 inches long, dark green above, densely hairy beneath. The fruits are oblong, 1-2 inches long, rounded at apex, the body of the fruit extending into the lower one-fourth of the wing. Occurs in swamps in southern Georgia and Florida.

4. MOUNTAIN ASH (*F. texensis* Sarg.). A tree rarely 50 feet high; leaves 5-8 inches long with 5, rarely 7, petioled

leaflets. The leaflets are ovate, coarsely toothed above the middle, 1-3 inches long, dark green above, pale beneath, sometimes with tufts of white hairs in the angles of the veins. Fruits with lanceolate wings on top of the body, rounded at the apex. Texas.

5. RED ASH (*F. pennsylvanica* Marsh.). See p. 177.

6. GREEN ASH (*F. pennsylvanica* var. *lanceolata* Sarg.). See p. 178.

7. WHITE ASH (*F. americana* L.). See p. 176.

8. BLUE ASH (*F. quadrangulata* Michx.). See p. 175. Extending into the southern region in Missouri, Arkansas and Oklahoma.

Texas Adelia (*Forestiera acuminata* Poir.)

See p. 178. Most abundant in Missouri, Arkansas and Texas; attains its largest size in Louisiana.

Fringetree (*Chionanthus virginica* L.)

See p. 178. Native to the northern and southern regions and often cultivated.

Devil Wood (*Osmanthus americanus* B.&H.)

An evergreen shrub or small tree, but occasionally attaining a height of 70 feet; leaves opposite, leathery, ob-

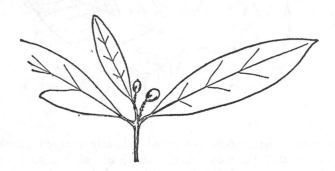

long lanceolate, tapering at both ends, 4-5 inches long, with entire, thickened margins. The olive-like fruits are about 1 inch long, dark blue in color when ripe. Mostly along the coast from North Carolina to Florida and Louisiana.

Desert Willow *(Chilopsis linearis* DC.)

See p. 313. Frequently cultivated in the South.

Fiddle Wood (*Citharexylon fruticosum* L.)

A tree or shrub with thick leaves oppositely arranged on angled branchlets which do not have terminal buds.

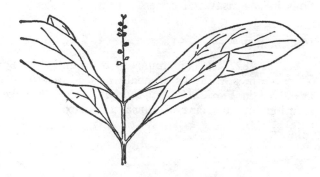

The leaves are oblong to obovate, hairless, 3-4 inches long, pointed at tip and gradually narrowed at base, margins entire and thickened; petioles grooved. Florida.

Catalpa *(Catalpa* Scop.)

(See also p. 180.)

CATALPA, INDIAN BEAN (*C. bignonioides* Walt.). See p. 180. Native to the Gulf States and often planted in the northern region.

WESTERN CATALPA (*C. speciosa* Engl.). In the southern region it is native to Missouri and Arkansas and naturalized through cultivation in Louisiana and Texas.

ROYAL PAULOWNIA (*Paulownia tomentosa* Bail.). See p. 180. Introduced from Japan, it has established itself in both northern and southern regions. It superficially resembles the Catalpa, from which it may be distinguished by its gray bark, pale violet flowers, persistent dry fruits (about 1 inch in diameter) and velvety leaves.

Buttonbush (*Cephalanthus occidentalis* L.)

See p. 181. Mostly a shrub, attaining tree-like proportions in Arkansas and eastern Texas.

Viburnum (*Viburnum* L.)

See p. 182. The Viburnums also occur in the South. They are mostly shrubs or small trees. *V. nudum* occurs as a tree in Florida; *V. rufidulum* reaches tree-like dimensions in Louisiana, Arkansas and Texas.

Cabbage Palmetto (*Sabal palmetto* R. and S.)

A tree attaining a height of 50 feet or more, with leaves 5-6 feet long and somewhat broader, divided into

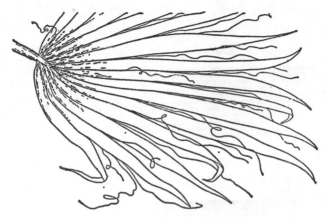

many narrow segments. Distributed in sandy regions near the coast from North Carolina to Florida. The leaves are locally used in basketry; the bark as scouring brushes.

Spanish Bayonet (*Yucca aloifolia* L.)

A small tree with erect, sword-shaped leaves, 1½-3 feet long and about 2 inches wide with a sharp brown

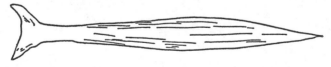

tip and hard, finely toothed margins. The base of the leaf is conspicuously and abruptly widened. Distributed on the dunes along the coast from North Carolina to Louisiana.

TREES OF THE WESTERN REGION

THE CONE-BEARING TREES

Pine (*Pinus* L.)

(See also p. 39.)

There are more different kinds of pines in the West than in the rest of the United States. At least twenty are recognized as distinct species.

Key to the Western Pines.

Leaves solitary, not in bunches. 1. Single-leaf Pine.
Leaves in clusters of two.
    Leaves short, 1-2 inches long, cones 1-2 inches long.
      Leaves not twisted; cones globose before opening.
                        2. Nut Pine.
      Leaves twisted; cones conic ovoid or oblong before opening.
        Leaves dark green, usually 1-1½ inches long.
                        3. Beach Pine.
        Leaves yellow-green, usually 2 inches long.
                        4. Lodgepole Pine.
    Leaves longer, 4-6 inches long; cones 2-3½ inches long, scales with stout spines. 5. Bishop Pine.
Leaves in clusters of three.
    Cones equally developed on all sides.
      Cones 3-5 inches long. 6. Western Yellow Pine.
      Cones 5-15 inches long. 7. Jeffrey Pine.
    Cones lopsided, at least at the base.
      Cones 5-6 inches long, scales without stout spurs.
        Cones ovate. 8. Monterey Pine.
        Cones elongate. 9. Knob-cone Pine.
      Cones 6-12 inches long, scales with stout spurs.
        Branchlets of current season dark orange or brown.
                        10. Big-cone Pine.
        Branchlets of current season covered with a white bloom. 11. Digger Pine.
Leaves in clusters of four. 12. Parry Piñon Pine.

Leaves in clusters of five.
  Leaves 8-13 inches long. 13. Torrey Pine.
  Leaves shorter, ¾-6 inches long.
    Scales of cone thin, not thickened at apex.
      Cones 11-21 inches long. 14. Sugar Pine.
      Cones up to 8 inches long.
        Leaves 4-6 inches long.
                              15. Mexican White Pine.
        Leaves 1-3½ inches long.
                              16. Western White Pine.
    Scales of cones thickened at apex.
      Scales tipped with a long bristle.
                              17. Bristle-cone Pine.
      Scales not tipped with a long bristle.
        Leaves closely appressed to ends of branches.
                              18. Foxtail Pine.
        Leaves not as above.
          Cones oval or globose, ½-3 inches long,
            scales greatly thickened at apex.
                              19. White-bark Pine.
          Cones cylindrical, 3-8 inches long, scales
            slightly thickened at apex.
                              20. Limber Pine.

1. SINGLE-LEAF PINE. ONE-LEAF PIÑON (*P. monophylla* Torr.) A small tree, about 20 feet high, with short spiny-tipped leaves, 1-2 inches long, arising singly from the branchlets. The cones are somewhat globose or elongate, from 2-3½ inches long, with scales greatly thickened at their apices. Found in arid mountainous regions of California, Arizona, Utah and Nevada.

Single-leaf Pine   Nut Pine Parry Piñon Pine

2. NUT PINE (*P. edulis* Engelm.). A tree 40-50 feet

high, similar to the Single-leaf Pine, but with the short needles, 1-2 inches long, arranged in clusters of two. The globose cones are 1-2 inches long, composed of thick scales. The seeds of this pine, the Single-leaf Pine (1), and the Parry Pine (12), are very tasty and find their way into commerce as a minor item of food. Found in arid mountainous regions of Arizona, Colorado, Utah, Wyoming, western Oklahoma and western Texas.

3. BEACH PINE (*P. contorta* Loud.). A small tree about 20 feet high, with needles in clusters of two, dark green,

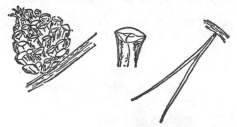

1-1½ inches long, stiff and occasionally twisted. Cones are slender, ovoid and sometimes oblique, 1-2 inches long, the scales having a slender prickle. Found mostly near the coast from Alaska to California.

4. LODGEPOLE PINE (*P. murrayana* Engelm.). A tree similar in general characteristics to the Beach Pine (3),

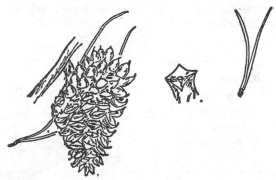

but it attains a much greater height, sometimes 80 feet;

leaves are yellow-green, mostly 2 inches long, in twos, stiff and twisted. Cones are ovoid (spheroid when mature), 1-1¾ inches long, the scales having a slender prickle. The most abundant conifer of the northern Rocky Mountains; its range extends from the Yukon River to Montana and Colorado, and the Pacific States.

5. BISHOP PINE (*P. muricata* Don.). A tree about 50 feet high, with stiff, twisted needles arranged in bundles of two, 4-6 inches long. The cones are ovoid and unequal at the base, 2-3½ inches long, with thick scales armed with large spines. California, along the coast.

6. WESTERN YELLOW PINE (*P. ponderosa* Laws.). A large tree, sometimes over 200 feet high, with needles

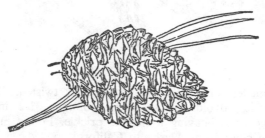

5-10 inches long, in clusters of three. The cones are ovoid, 3-5 inches long; the scales thickened at the apex and tipped with a fine prickle. The wood is hard and strong, valuable for construction purposes. Widely distributed throughout the West.

7. JEFFREY PINE (*P. ponderosa* var. *Jeffreyi* Vasey). Similar to *Pinus ponderosa* (6), from which it may be distinguished by its longer cones, 5-15 inches long, and the stouter prickle on the scale. California and Oregon.

8. MONTEREY PINE (*P. radiata* Don.). A tree often used for park plantings, 40-60 feet high; branchlets of the current season covered with a whitish bloom, later orange-colored; needles arranged in bunches of three, 4-6 inches long. The cones are unequal at the base, the lower scales

on the outer side are greatly swollen and tipped with a short point; they remain on the tree for many years. Native to California. Compare cone with illustration of that of Bishop Pine (5) which it closely resembles.

9. KNOB-CONE PINE (*P. attenuata* Lemm.). A small tree, about 20 feet tall, occasionally attaining a height of 100 feet; branchlets of the current season are dark orange in color; needles arranged in bundles of three, 4-5 inches long, three-sided. The cones are elongate and conical, unequal at the base where the outer scales are much thickened; they persist on the tree for many years. Most abundant in southwestern Oregon; also found in California. Cone similar to illustration of Bishop Pine (5).

10. BIG-CONE PINE (*P. Coulteri* Don.). A tree ranging from 40 to 90 feet in height; branchlets of the current season dark orange or brown; needles in bunches of three, three-sided, 6-12 inches long, in tufts at the ends of the branches. Cones oblong, 10-14 inches long; all the scales thickened and ending in a stout, flat spur, ½-1½ inches long. California.

11. DIGGER PINE (*P. sabiniana* Dougl.). Usually 40-50 feet tall, divided into three or four large branches about

15 feet from the ground; branchlets of the current season are covered with a white bloom; needles in bunches of three, 8-12 inches long, drooping from the ends of the branches; cones oblong or ovoid 6-10 inches long and almost as broad, all scales greatly enlarged and ending in large spurs, those at the base of the cone are curved downward. California and Nevada.

12. PARRY PIÑON PINE (*P. quadrifolia* Sudw.). A small tree about 30 feet high, with short, stiff, blue-green needles, ¾-1½ inches long, usually arranged in clusters of four, but varying from one to five. The cones are spheroidal, 1-2 inches in diameter, with scales thickened at the apex. (Similar to the *Nut Pine,* see illustration.) Arid situations in southern California.

13. TORREY PINE (*P. torreyana* Carr.). A tree usually 30-40 feet tall; branchlets of the current season bright

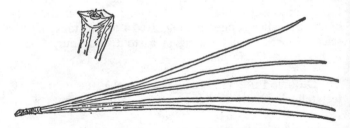

green; leaves in clusters of five 8-13 inches long, stiff and dark green; cones are broadly ovoid, 4-6 inches long, the thick scales with a triangular thickening at the apex. The seeds are edible. The most restricted of all the pines in the United States in its distribution, being found on the coast just north of San Diego, California, and on Santa Rosa Island, California. It is sometimes cultivated in the Pacific States.

14. SUGAR PINE (*P. lambertiana* Dougl.). A valuable tree, sometimes attaining a height of 230 feet, the wood is useful for interior finishes. The branchlets of the current season are coated with fine short hairs; needles in

groups of five, 2-4 inches long, bluish green; cones oblong-cylindrical, 11-21 inches long, their scales thin, not thickened at the apex. California and western Oregon.

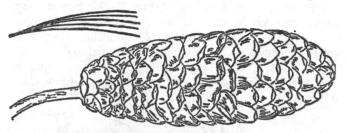

15. MEXICAN WHITE PINE (*P. strobiformis* Engelm.). The leaves are in bunches of five, 4-6 inches long, light green, slender and rigid. The cones are 5-8 inches long, with thin scales turned back at the tip; prickles absent. Distributed from Alberta to western Texas, southern New Mexico, Arizona, and California.

16. WESTERN WHITE PINE (*P. monticola* Don.). A tree occasionally 150 feet tall; branchlets of the current season coated with fine short hairs; the blue-green, slender

needles, 1-3½ inches long, are grouped in clusters of five. Cones are narrowly cylindrical, 6-8 inches long, with thin scales not thickened at the apex. Found in British Columbia and the Pacific States, and eastward to Idaho and Montana.

17. BRISTLE-CONE PINE. HICKORY PINE (*P. aristata* Engelm.). A small tree, sometimes 40 feet high; branchlets light orange-colored during the current season; the sharp-pointed needles in bunches of five, 1-1½ inches long, closely grouped in tufts at the ends of the branchlets. The cones are narrowly ovoid, 2-3½ inches long, with scales thickened at the tip and terminated by a brittle bristle about ¼ inch long. On high mountain slopes in Colorado, Utah, Nevada, Arizona and southern California.

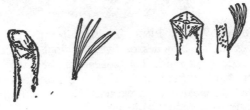

18. FOXTAIL PINE (*P. balfouriana* Balf.). A small tree about 30 feet, sometimes 90 feet high, with rigid needles ¾-1½ inches long arranged in clusters of five. The foliage is denser and appressed at the ends of the branches, suggesting a fox's tail. The cones are cylindrical, 2½-5 inches long, purple or brown, with scales thickened and four-sided at the apex, terminated by a very small prickle. California.

19. WHITE-BARK PINE (*P. albicaulis* Engelm.). A small tree 20-30 feet high; bark made up of white scales,

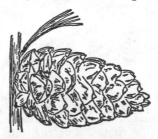

whence its name. The dark green, rigid needles, 1-2½ inches long, are grouped in fives. The cones are oval or globose, 1½-3 inches long, dark purple, and resinous, remaining closed at maturity. The scales are greatly thickened toward the apex and tipped by a short, blunt projection. The seeds are large and edible. At high altitudes in the Rockies: Idaho, Montana and Wyoming; and in the mountains of the Pacific States.

20. LIMBER PINE (*P. flexilis* James). A tree usually attaining a height of about 50 feet; needles in groups of five, 1-3 inches long, stiff and dark green. The cones are

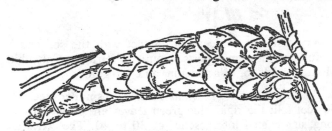

cylindrical, 3-8 inches long, the large scales not thickened at the apex, or only slightly so, spreading at maturity. Widely distributed in the western region and especially abundant in the Rockies.

Larch (*Larix*)

Two species of Larch are to be found in the West. They have the general characteristics of the eastern Larch, from which they differ in minor details (see p. 47).

Key to the Western Larches.

Leaves three-sided.
　Scales of cone not fringed.　1. Western Larch.
Leaves four-sided.
　Scales of cone fringed.　2. Alpine Larch.

1. WESTERN LARCH (*L. occidentalis* Nutt.). The sharp-pointed leaves are about an inch long, aggregated into rosettes of 15 to 30 on short spur-shoots. The cones are 1-2 inches long, margins of the scales entire, bracts conspicuous, long-tipped, longer than the scales. The young

branches are hairy, but not woolly. An important timber tree, sometimes it reaches a height of 188 feet. The wood

is very resistant to decay in contact with the soil and is useful for ties and posts. Southern British Columbia, Montana, Idaho, Washington and Oregon.

2. ALPINE LARCH (*L. lyalli* Parl.). A smaller tree, 25-50 feet tall; the rigid blue-green leaves are about an inch long, aggregated into rosettes of 30 to 40. The cones are 1-2 inches long, the margin of the scales fringed. As in the *Western Larch,* the bracts are longer than the scales. Young twigs are woolly. It may be found at the timber line: Southern Alberta and British Columbia, Washington, Oregon, Idaho and Montana.

Spruce (*Picea* Link.)

The short, sharp-pointed angular needles scattered on all sides of the branchlets, and the drooping cones are characteristic of the *Spruces.* In addition the branchlets are rough, retaining the short petioles after leaf-fall. (See p. 48.)

Key to the Western Spruces.

Twigs not hairy.
  Leaves square in section.   1. Colorado Spruce.
  Leaves flat.   2. Sitka Spruce.
Twigs hairy.
  Leaves square in section, scales of cone thin.
                                3. Engelmann Spruce.
  Leaves flat, scales of cone thick.   4. Weeping Spruce.

1. COLORADO SPRUCE. BLUE SPRUCE (*P. pungens* Engelm.). A tree usually 80-100 feet tall with bluish-green or whitish foliage. The leaves are about 1 inch

long, stiff and curved. The cones are 2-4 inches long, the thin scales having small teeth at the apex. It is distributed in southern Montana, Wyoming, Colorado, Utah and northern New Mexico.

2. SITKA SPRUCE (*P. sitchensis* Carr.). A large tree, valuable for its lumber; about 100 feet high, or occasionally 200 feet. The leaves of this Spruce are flat but sharp-pointed, about 1 inch long, green on the lower surface, white above. The cones are oblong-cylindrical, 2½-4 inches long; the scales thin, irregularly short-toothed above the middle. Found growing along the coast under moist or swamp conditions in Washington, Oregon and northern California.

3. ENGELMANN SPRUCE (*P. Engelmanni* Engelm.). A tree growing to about 120 feet in height; leaves very flexible (not rigid, as is characteristic of most Spruces), four-sided, blue-green, about 1 inch long, and strongly aromatic; cones are 2 inches long, oblong-cylindrical, the scales being thin and finely toothed. The wood is used for construction purposes. Widely distributed throughout the western region on high mountain slopes.

4. WEEPING SPRUCE (*P. Breweriana* Wats.). Usually 80-100 feet high, the horizontal or pendulous branches have hanging branchlets 7-8 feet long and only ¼ inch in diameter; the leaves are ¾-1 inch long, flattish, green below, whitish above, cones are ellipsoidal, 2-4 inches long, the thick, broadly obovate scales with entire margins slightly curled backward. Near the timber line, mountains of southern Oregon and northern California.

Hemlock (*Tsuga* Carr.)

Trees with slender, horizontal, usually pendulous branches, the leaves of which usually become arranged in one plane along the twigs to which they are attached by short stalks. These persist after leaf-fall, leaving the branchlets rough, as in the Spruces. The cones are pendulous at maturity; their scales circular or ovate and thin. For description of the eastern species, see p. 51.

Key to the Western Hemlocks.

Leaves flat; cones oblong to ovoid, about 1 inch long.
                               1. Western Hemlock.
Leaves not flat, rounded above; cones cylindrical, 1-3 inches long.   2. Mountain Hemlock.

1. WESTERN HEMLOCK (*T. heterophylla* Sarg.). A large tree, sometimes 200 feet high; the needles are ¼-¾ inch long, grooved and dark green above, with two white bands on the lower surface. The scales of the cone are oval. The bark is extensively used in tanning hides and the lumber for construction purposes. Found from Alaska to Washington, Oregon, northern California, Idaho and Montana. See illustration of *T. canadensis,* p. 51, which it closely resembles.

2. MOUNTAIN HEMLOCK (*T. hertensiana* Sarg.). In this Hemlock the leaves are not arranged in one plane along

the twigs, but usually stand out in all directions. The leaves are rounded on the upper surface, usually curved,

Mountain Hemlock

Western Hemlock

blue-green. The cones are large for the genus, reaching up to 3 inches long, cylindrical. The scales are obovate, purplish, or sometimes yellowish. It attains a height of 70-100 feet, exceptionally 150 feet, in mountains from Alaska, southward to Washington, Oregon, California, Idaho and Montana.

Douglas Fir (*Pseudotsuga taxifolia* Britt.)

A large tree, up to 250 feet, with yellow-green or blue-green (glaucous) needles, about 1 inch long, petioled.

The tips of the leaves are rounded, or occasionally pointed on leading shoots. The cones are pendulous, 2-4 inches long, cylindrical or oblong. The scales are thin and rounded at the apex, subtended by long bracts which are two-lobed, with a long arm projecting from between them. It has a wide distribution in the western region, attaining its greatest size in the coastal regions of Washington and Oregon. The lumber is widely used for construction purposes. It is very commonly seen as plywood under the name of Red Fir.

THE BIG-CONE SPRUCE (*P. macrocarpa* Mayr.) is a smaller tree, about 50 feet high, with blue-green leaves about 1 inch long, pointed at the tip. The cones are 4-6½ inches long. Found on mountain slopes in southern California.

FIR (*Abies* Link.)

The leaves of the Firs are not stalked and in falling leave a small circular scar on the branchlets. In all but one species the leaves are flat and grooved on the upper surface. In the one exception, they are four-sided. The cones are erect on the branches. The wood is used for crates and packing cases, or for cheap construction.

Key to the Western Firs.

Bracts of the cones exserted (visible without removing scales.)
    Bracts narrow, terminated by flat awn 1-1¾ inches long. Leaves shiny, yellow-green. 1. Bristle-cone Fir.
    Bracts terminated by shorter awns, leaves blue-green.
        Cones 4-5 inches long, scales nearly covered by the bracts; bracts with broad midrib extended into a short awn. 2. Noble Fir.
        Cones 6-9 inches long, bracts smaller, not nearly covering scales. 3. Shasta Fir.
Bracts of the cones not exserted.
    Leaves blue-green.
        Cones 6-9 inches long, leaves four-sided.

                                    3. Red Fir.
    Cones smaller (up to 5 inches long), leaves on sterile branches, flat.
        Leaves 2-3 inches long, ⅛ inch or less wide.

                                  4. White Fir.
        Leaves 1-1¾ inches long, less than half ⅛ inch wide. 5. Rocky Mountain Fir.

Leaves dark green (above).
  Leaves on non-cone-bearing branches not crowded,
    1½-2¼ inches long; ⅛ inch wide, two-ranked.
                                    6. Giant Fir.
  Leaves on non-cone-bearing branches crowded, ¾-
    1¼ inches long; less than half ⅛ inch wide; not
    two-ranked.   7. Cascade Fir.

1. BRISTLE-CONE FIR (*A. venusta* Koch.). A large tree,
to 150 feet, found only in the Santa Lucia Mountains of
California. The leaves are 1¼-2¼ inches long on non-

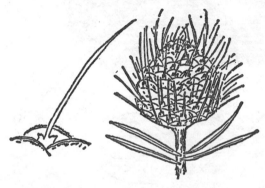

cone-bearing branches, dark green above, not grooved;
the midrib is prominent below with a silvery stripe on
each side of it. They become arranged in one plane by
the twisting of the lower part of the needles. The cone is
easily distinguished by virtue of the very long bristle, 1-
1¾ inches long, that tops the two-parted bracts.

2. NOBLE FIR (*A. nobilis* Lindl.). A large tree, sometimes reaching 250 feet. The leaves are 1-1½ inches long,
on non-cone-bearing branches, blue-green (thickly coated
with a white bloom the first season), grooved above,
ribbed below; closely crowded on the branches, those on
the lower side spreading out in two ranks, those on the
upper side of the branch curved upward with the base
of the leaf pressed against the branch. On the cone-bearing branches the leaves are four-sided. The bracts of the
cone are very conspicuous, curving back and nearly ob-

scuring the scales. They are finely saw-toothed along the margin, their broad midribs extended as a broad bristle beyond the rest of the bract. Most abundant in Washington, reaching into Oregon and California.

3. RED FIR (*A. magnifica* Murt.). A large tree, often 200 feet tall; with characteristic four-sided leaves which are blue-green with white lines on all faces; ¾-1½ inches

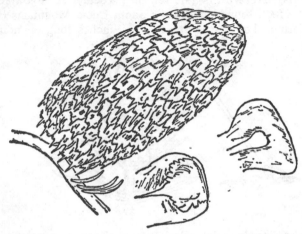

long; those on the lower side of the branch spreading in two ranks, while those on the upper side curve upward. The cones are 6-9 inches long, the bracts entirely obscured by the scales. Southern Oregon and northern California.

The Shasta Fir (*A. magnifica* var. *shastensis* Lemm.) differs from the species in the conspicuous bracts of the cone, which cover about one-half of the scale. Note bract on left scale above, as compared with the Red Fir bract and scale at right above. It is found within the same range as the species.

4. WHITE FIR (*A. concolor* Lindl. and Gord.). A tree attaining a height of 250 feet in the mountains of California, but usually about 120 feet tall; leaves are ¾-3 inches long and usually ⅛ inch broad, flat, blue-green

on both surfaces, with two white bands below. Cones are 3-5 inches long; bracts entirely hidden by the scales. Found in Oregon, California, Arizona, New Mexico, Colorado and Utah.

5. ROCKY MOUNTAIN FIR (*A. lasiocarpa* Nutt.). A tree usually 50-100 feet high, the leaves ¾-1½ inches long, flat, blue-green, grooved above, crowded on the branches and usually curved upward. The cones are 2-4 inches long, the bracts hidden by the scales. Found in the high mountain ranges from Alaska to Washington, Oregon, Idaho, Montana, Wyoming, Colorado, New Mexico, Arizona and Utah.

6. GIANT FIR (*A. grandis* Lindl.). Along the coast this tree reaches a height of 300 feet, but elsewhere it is about

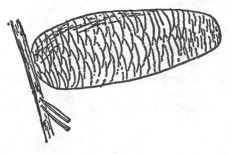

100 feet tall. The leaves on non-cone-bearing branches are 1½-2¼ inches long and ⅛ inch wide, dark green above, grooved, with two white stripes on the lower surface, flat, and notched at the apex, spreading in two ranks. Cones are 2-4 inches long, the bracts hidden by the scales. Found in California, Oregon, Washington, Idaho and Montana.

7. CASCADE FIR (*A. amabilis* Forbes). A tall tree, often 250 feet high; leaves flat, ¾-1½ inches long, dark green above, with two broad silver stripes on lower surface; crowded on the branches, those on the underside spreading horizontally, those above curved upward. The cones

are 3½-6 inches long; bracts entirely obscured by the scales. Southeastern Alaska to Washington and Oregon.

Giant Arbor Vitae (*Thuja plicata* Don.)

A large tree, to 200 feet, with buttressed base; the horizontal branches pendulous at the ends, lateral branchlets flattened. The scale leaves are appressed to

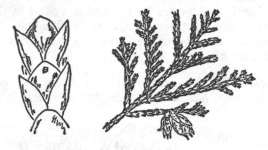

the stem, opposite, each succeeding pair at right angles to those above and below. Those on the leading shoot are about ¼ inch long; those on the lateral branches ⅛ inch or less long. Cones are ½ inch long with 8-10 thin and tough scales. Alaska to California, Oregon, Washington, Idaho and Montana.

"Cypress" (*Chamaecyparis* Spach.)

Trees with branchlets arranged in one plane, clothed with scale-like leaves closely pressed against the branchlet, or with their tips spreading. The scale-leaves are in pairs, at right angles to the pairs above and below them. The cones are small, erect, spheroidal, and composed of 4-6 scales.

LAWSON CYPRESS. PORT ORFORD CEDAR (*C. Lawsoniana* Parl.). A tree often attaining a height of 200 feet; scale-leaves bright green and conspicuously glandular. Cones ¼-⅓ inch in diameter; the center of the scale may bear a prickle. The lumber is very valuable. It is used extensively for matches. Southwestern Oregon and northwestern California.

YELLOW CYPRESS (*C. nootkatensis* Sudw.). A smaller tree usually not over 125 feet tall; scale-leaves blue-

green, usually without conspicuous glands. Cones ½ inch in diameter, scales usually tipped with a stout prickle. The lumber is often used in shipbuilding. Alaska to Washington and Oregon.

Incense Cedar (*Libocedrus decurrens* Torr.)

A tree 100 feet high, occasionally 150 feet, with irregularly fluted trunk 3-6 feet in diameter. The branch-

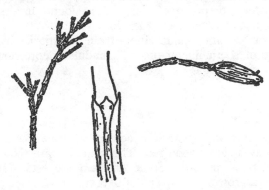

lets are flattened and arranged in one plane. The leaves are small (⅛ inch long), scale-like, arranged in four ranks, closely appressed to the branchlets, the lateral pair keeled and glandular, nearly covering the inner pair;

both pairs of equal length. The ¾-1 inch long cones are composed of three pairs of scales, the lowest pair being small and reflexed, the second pair much larger and thicker, the third pair united, splitting at maturity.

Cypress (*Cupressus* L.)

Trees with four-angled branchlets: the scale-like leaves in pairs at right angles to those above and below them; cones small, spherical, composed of 3-6 pairs of scales which are abruptly flattened at the apex.

MONTEREY CYPRESS (*C. macrocarpa* Gord.). A tree growing to 70 feet in height, the scale-like leaves are dark green, without glands. The cones are 1-1½ inches in diameter, made up of 4-6 pairs of scales. Native on only a small strip of land along the coast of California, but widely cultivated in the Pacific States.

ARIZONA CYPRESS (*C. arizonica* Greene.). A tree sometimes 70 feet high; the scale-like leaves pale green, coated with a white bloom when young; cones ¾-1 inch in diameter, composed of 6-8 scales. Found in eastern Arizona and western New Mexico.

The var. *bonita* Lemm. differs from the species by the presence of a circular or oblong glandular depression on the leaves. Arizona.

Redwood. Big Tree (*Sequoia* Endl.)

Large trees with pendulous cones and scale-like or flat linear leaves; heartwood red. The sequoias are the longest-lived trees on earth. Some of them are estimated to have been growing for over 4000 years.

REDWOOD (*S. sempervirens* Endl.). Among the tallest trees known, often reaching upward to 340 feet, it has two kinds of leaves; those on the lower branches are linear, ½-¾ inch long, with decurrent petioles, spreading in two ranks; dark green above, prominent midrib below with a whitish band on each side of it; those on some of

the leading shoots are short, linear scale-leaves about ¼ inch long, appressed against the branchlets or spreading somewhat. Cones are oblong, ¾-1 inch long. Found near the coast in northern California and southern Oregon. The wood is brittle, but very resistant to decay, and fire-resistant. It is used for construction, shingles, posts, etc.

BIG TREE (*S. gigantia* Decne.). A more massive tree, but not as tall as the tallest Redwoods, 275-320 feet high,

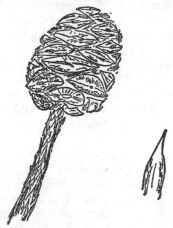

the diameter of the buttressed trunk is sometimes 35 feet. The leaves are short, lanceolate to scale-like, ⅛-½ inch long, resembling the scale-leaves of the Redwood. The cones are ovoid, 2-3½ inches long. Found in California in the Sierra Nevada Mountains.

Juniper (*Juniperus*)

Trees with small overlapping, scale-like leaves, usually appressed to the branchlets; the cones mature as a fleshy, spheroidal, "berry-like" structure. (See also p. 55.)

Key to the Western Junipers.

Fruits brown or reddish.
    Bark of trunk deeply divided into squares.
                        1. Checkered-bark Juniper.
    Bark of trunk not as above.
        Leaves opposite (in pairs). 2. Utah Juniper.
        Leaves in threes. 3. California Juniper.
Fruits blue or blue-black.
    Young branchlets four-sided.
                        4. Rocky Mountain Juniper.
    Young branchlets not four-sided.
        Bark grayish. 5. One-seeded Juniper.
        Bark brownish-red. 6. Western Juniper.

1. CHECKERED-BARK JUNIPER (*J. pachyphlaea* Torr.). A tree often 50 feet high with bark divided into square plates 1-2 inches across. Scale-leaves thick, glandular, blue-green, less than ⅛ inch long. The fruits are ⅓-½ inch in diameter, dark reddish-brown and coated with a white bloom; flesh thick, mealy and dry. Western Texas, New Mexico and Arizona, in dry situations.

2. UTAH JUNIPER (*J. utahensis* Lemm.). A small tree up to about 20 feet. The opposite scale-leaves are glandular, yellow-green, less than ⅛ inch long; the cone matures as a reddish-brown berry, coated with a white bloom, ¼-⅓ inch in diameter, the tips of the scales more or less prominent. Found in Idaho, Utah, Wyoming, Colorado, New Mexico, Arizona and southern California.

3. CALIFORNIA JUNIPER (*J. californica* Carr.). A shrub mostly, but it attains tree-like dimensions in the Mohave Desert (up to 40 feet high). The scale-leaves are arranged in threes, glandular, yellow-green, about ⅛ inch long. Cones similar to the Utah Juniper. They are sweet and edible.

4. ROCKY MOUNTAIN JUNIPER (*J. scopulorum* Sarg.). A tree 40 feet high, the young branchlets four-angled, scale-leaves opposite, obscurely glandular; cones ¼-⅓ inch in diameter, blue, coated with a white bloom; flesh resinous. Widely distributed in the eastern Rocky Mountains, Alberta, Montana, to Texas, westward to Oregon, Nevada and northern Arizona.

5. ONE-SEEDED JUNIPER (*J. monosperma* Sarg.). A tree to 50 feet, with large buttressed trunk; scale-leaves less than ⅛ inch long, blue-green, margin with very small teeth; cones ⅛-¼ inch in diameter, dark blue, thinly coated with a white bloom; flesh thin. Found in the eastern Rocky Mountains, Wyoming to Texas, westward in the south to Arizona and Nevada; abundant in Colorado and Utah, greatest size in Arizona. Used for fences and posts.

6. WESTERN JUNIPER (*J. occidentalis* Hook.). Usually a low tree about 20 feet high, with very thick trunk; scale-leaves blue-green, prominently glandular, about ⅛ inch long; cones ¼-⅓ inch in diameter, blue-black, covered with a whitish bloom; flesh thin and dry. Found in Idaho, Washington, Oregon and California.

California Nutmeg (*Torreya californica* Torr.)

A tree to 70 feet, with whorled branches and dark green, shiny foliage. The leaves are linear, 1-3 inches long, sharp-pointed at the apex, tapering at base to a decurrent petiole, dark green above, marked below by two narrow white bands; becoming two-ranked by twisting of the petioles. The cone matures into an ellipsoidal,

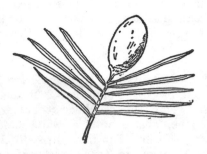

plum-like structure 1-1¾ inches long, green or streaked with purple, the flesh enclosing the single seed splitting at maturity into two parts. California.

Pacific Yew (*Taxus brevifolia* Nutt.)

A tree 50-70 feet high, with linear leaves ½-1 inch long, dark yellow-green and shiny above, paler beneath, narrowed at base to short yellow petioles which extend

down the branchlet and appear as part of the stem. The cone matures as a scarlet fleshy structure enclosing the seed, except at the apex. Never abundant: British Columbia, Washington, Oregon, California, Idaho and Montana.

THE BROAD-LEAVED TREES

Fan Palm (*Washingtonia filifera* Wendl.)

A tree with columnar trunk, occasionally 75 feet high, covered with dead leaves that hang downward. The

leaves are large, 5-6 feet long, and almost as broad, with 40-70 folds, cut ½-⅔ of the distance to the base, the margins of the segments have long thread-like fibers; petioles 4-6 feet long, armed with hooked spines. Native to southern California and widely cultivated there.

Joshua Tree (*Yucca brevifolia* Engelm.)

A tree 15-30 feet high, with leaves 5-10 inches long and ½ inch wide, crowded in clusters, the older ones pointed downward, the younger ones upward; blue-green

(coated with a whitish bloom) having a narrow, yellow margin which is very finely saw-toothed and lacking thread-like fibers. Distributed from southwestern Utah to the Mohave Desert, California.

Cottonwood. Poplars (*Populus* L.)

(See p. 58.)

Key to the Western Poplars.

Petiole laterally flattened, margin of leaf finely or coarsely toothed.
    Margin of leaf finely saw-toothed.
                1. Quaking Aspen (see p. 59).
    Margin of leaf coarsely toothed or scalloped.
      Branchlets hairy.
        Leaves thin, blue-green, teeth not glandular.
                2. MacDougal Poplar.
        Leaves thickish, shiny, teeth tipped with glands.
                3. Fremont Hairy Cottonwood.
      Branchlets not hairy.
        Leaves without glands.
          Branchlets green, later yellow; pedicels shorter than the fruit. 3. Fremont Cottonwood.
          Branchlets orange; pedicels longer then the fruit.
                4. Wislizen Cottonwood.
        Leaves (or some of them) with 1 or 2 small glands at the base of the blade. 5. Sargent Poplar.
Petiole not laterally flattened; margin of leaf finely saw-toothed.
      Leaves broadly ovate, white or rusty below.
                6. Black Cottonwood.
      Leaves not broadly ovate, pale green below.
        Leaves lanceolate; bark of larger branches yellow-green. 7. Narrow-leaf Cottonwood.
        Leaves ovate, bark of larger branches white.
                8. Pointed-leaf Cottonwood.

2. MacDougal Poplar (*P. MacDougalii* Rose). A tree 30-50 feet high, occasionally 100 feet; branchlets finely hairy; leaves broadly ovate, 1½-3 inches long and broad, thin, blue-green, finely hairy on veins on under surface

early in season. Found in California, Nevada and Oregon. Used in these states for street plantings.

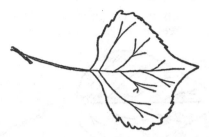

3. FREMONT COTTONWOOD (*P. Fremontii* Wats.). A tree sometimes 100 feet high and 5 feet in diameter; the slender hairless branchlets, light green the current season; older branchlets yellow, leaf scars small, three-lobed, not raised above level of the stem. Winter buds light green and shiny. Leaves ovate, 2-2½ inches long and slightly broader, thickish, shiny above, paler beneath, teeth tipped with glands, veins slender. Stalks of fruit shorter than the pods.

FREMONT HAIRY COTTONWOOD, var. *pubescens* Sarg., has hairy branchlets. Found in California, Nevada, Utah and Arizona. Planted as a shade tree in southern California.

4. WISLIZEN COTTONWOOD (*P. Wislizenii* Sarg.). Tree with hairless branchlets, orange in color; leaves ovate, 2-2½ inches long and about 3 inches wide, thickish, shiny above; veinlets conspicuous. Winter buds shiny, somewhat hairy. Stalks of fruits 2-3 times as long as the pods. Western Texas, New Mexico and Colorado. Shade tree in New Mexico.

5. SARGENT POPLAR (*P. Sargentii* Dode.). A tree often 100 feet high with a trunk diameter of 6 feet; branchlets yellow, angular, conspicuously roughened by leaf scars; leaves ovate, 3-3½ inches long, somewhat wider; at least some of the leaves with one or two small glands at the junction of the petiole and blade. Found in the eastern

foothills of the Rocky Mountains from Saskatchewan to Texas. It is often used as a street tree in this region.

6. BLACK COTTONWOOD (*P. trichocarpa* Hook.). A tree growing to 100 feet in height with a trunk diameter of

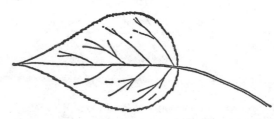

about 3 feet; the branchlets of current year are reddish brown dotted with orange-colored lenticels. The winter buds are fragrant and resinous. The leaves are ovate, 3-4 inches long, finely saw-toothed, dark green and shiny above, rusty or white below. The wood is used in the manufacture of sugar barrels. Found in the Pacific Coast States and British Columbia.

7. NARROW-LEAF COTTONWOOD (*P. angustifolia* James). A tree attaining a height of 50 feet with trunk 1½ feet in diameter; branchlets of the current season at first yel-

low-green, soon orange; bark of large branches yellow-green. The leaves are lanceolate, 2-3 inches long, ½-1 inch wide, yellow-green above, paler below, margins curled back. Widely distributed in the western region.

8. POINTED-LEAF COTTONWOOD (*P. acuminata* Rydb.). A tree about 40 feet high with trunk diameter of 1½ feet; branchlets yellowish brown; bark of large branches white; leaves ovate, 2-4 inches long, dark green and shiny above, pale green below. Found in eastern foothills of the Rocky Mountains.

Willow (*Salix* L.)

(See p. 64.)

Key to the Western Willows.

Margin of leaf entire.
  Leaf thin; shiny, yellow-green above.
                             1. Scouler Willow.
  Leaf thick; dull green above. 2. Beak Willow.
Margin saw-toothed only above middle. 2. Beak Willow.
Margin saw-toothed to base of leaf.
  Leaves linear-lanceolate. 3. Longleaf Willow.
  Leaves lanceolate or lance-ovate.
    Petiole grooved. 4. Red Willow.
    Petiole not grooved.
      Petiole with warty outgrowths near blade.
                           5. Yellow Willow.
      Petiole without warty outgrowths.
                        6. Peachleaf Willow.

1. SCOULER WILLOW (*S. Scouleriana* Barr.). A shrub or occasionally a tree of 30 feet; branchlets yellowish in their first year, dark red the second. The leaves are 1-4 inches long, narrowly obovate or elliptical, tapering to base, margin entire and curved back, dark yellow-green above, paler beneath. Found from Alaska to California eastward to Idaho and Montana. It is the most abundant willow in the Pacific States.

2. BEAK WILLOW (*S. Bebbiana* Sarg.). See p. 70. It is mostly northern in distribution. In the western region it extends from Alaska through Canada to Idaho and Montana along the Rockies to Colorado.

3. LONGLEAF or SANDBAR WILLOW (*S. interior* Rowl.). See p. 67. It reaches into the western region in Wyoming and Colorado.

4. RED WILLOW (*S. laevigata* Bebb.). A tree attaining a height of 20-30 feet, sometimes 50 feet; branchlets orange or dark red in color. The leaves are 3-7 inches long, lanceolate, bluish green and shiny above, whitish

beneath, margin finely saw-toothed. Petiole grooved. Found along streams in southern Oregon, California, Arizona, Utah and Nevada.

5. YELLOW WILLOW (*S. lasiandra* Benth.). A tree reaching 60 feet in height with a trunk diameter of 3 feet, or a shrub; branchlets at first yellow, later purplish. The leaves are 1½-3 inches long (much longer on vigorous shoots), lanceolate, dark green above, whitish beneath, margin finely saw-toothed. Petiole thin, with warty outgrowths near blade. Distributed from the Yukon River, Alaska, to southern California; also found in New Mexico and Colorado.

A variety *caudata* with leaves green on both surfaces and long-pointed at the tip may be found in Oregon, Washington, Idaho, Wyoming, Colorado, Utah, and Nevada.

6. PEACHLEAF WILLOW (*S. amygdaloides* Anders.). See p. 72. This species is found in the West in Colorado, Utah, Nevada, Oregon and Washington.

California Wax-Myrtle (*Myrica californica* Cham.)

A small tree or shrub, growing along the Pacific Coast, 10-35 feet high; leaves oblanceolate, 2-4 inches

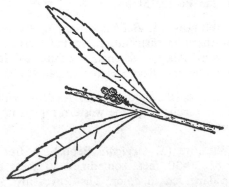

long, dark green and shiny above, paler beneath, evergreen, margin with remote teeth. See also p. 75.

Walnut (*Juglans* L.)

(See p. 77.)

Key to the Western Walnuts.

Leaflets 9-13; nuts longitudinally grooved.   1. Nogal.
Leaflets 15-19; nuts not grooved.
                                2. California Black Walnut.

1. NOGAL (*J. major* Hell.). Occasionally 50 feet high;
leaves 8-12 inches long, with 9-13 leaflets, oblong or

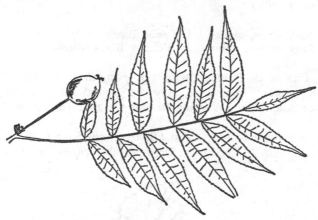

ovate, 3-4 inches long (the lowermost pair about half as
long), thin, yellow-green with conspicuous yellow veins,
coarsely saw-toothed; petiole and rachis hairy. The fruit
is spheroidal in shape, 1-1½ inches in diameter, having
a thin husk covered with short brownish hairs; the nut
has deep longitudinal grooves and is sweet to the taste.
New Mexico and Arizona.

2. CALIFORNIA BLACK WALNUT (*J. Hindsii* Rehd.).
Usually about 30-40 feet high, sometimes 75 feet; the
leaves 9-12 inches long with 15-19 lanceolate to lance-
ovate leaflets, 2½-4 inches long, thin, bright green and
shiny above, paler below, the lower surface furnished
with tufts of hairs and long hairs on veins and midrib; the

petiole and rachis are hairy. The fruit is spheroidal, 1-2 inches in diameter, with a thin, hairy husk. The nut is not grooved, or only slightly so, and is sweet to the taste. California, often cultivated.

Birch (*Betula* L.)

(See p. 88.)

There are two Birches in the western region, one of which, the Canoe Birch, also occurs in the north region. (See p. 90.)

Bark white, chalky. 1. Canoe Birch.
Bark brown, shiny. 2. Western Black Birch.

1. CANOE or PAPER BIRCH (*B. papyrifera* Marsh.). In the western region it may be found in Wyoming, Montana, Idaho, Washington and Oregon. (See p. 90.)

2. WESTERN BLACK BIRCH (*B. fontinalis* Sarg.). A small tree about 25 feet high, or a shrub; leaves ovate, 1-2

inches long, pointed at the tip, doubly saw-toothed, thin, dull green above, paler and dotted with small glands below. Widely distributed in the western region.

Alder (*Alnus* L.)

(See p. 91.)

Key to the Western Alders.

Leaves somewhat lobed and doubly saw-toothed.
  Rusty hairs on lower surface. 1. Red Alder.
  Hairless or slightly hairy on lower surface.

2. Thin-leaf Alder.

Leaves not lobed; singly or doubly saw-toothed.
  Tufts of hairs in the angles of the veins.

3. Mountain Alder.

  Without tufts of hairs. 4. White Alder.

1. RED ALDER (*A. rubra* Boug.). A tree attaining a height of 40 feet or so; branchlets of the current season light green covered with a white woolly mat; leaves 3-5 inches long, ovate, slightly lobed, margin curled back, serrate with glandular-tipped teeth, thickish, dark green above, rusty hairs below; veins are green on upper surface, orange below; petioles are orange. The wood is used for smoking salmon. Found from Alaska to California near the coast.

2. THIN-LEAF ALDER (*A. tenuifolia* Nutt.). A small tree occasionally 25 feet high; the branchlets of the current

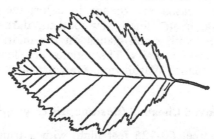

season are hairy and marked with orange-colored lenticels; leaves 2-4 inches long, ovate or oblong, slightly lobed, the margin doubly saw-toothed, thin, dark green above, paler beneath and smooth or slightly hairy; the midrib is orange-colored on upper surface; the petiole is also orange. Widely distributed in the western region, it attains its greatest height in Colorado and New Mexico.

3. Mountain Alder (*A. oblongifolia* Torr.). A small tree 20-30 feet high, branches of the current season slightly hairy, leaves 2-3 inches long, oblong in shape,

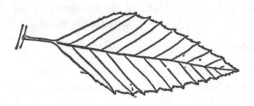

saw-toothed, covered with black glands, especially early in the season; yellow-green above, paler below, with tufts of reddish hairs in the angles of the veins. The petiole is slender and hairy. New Mexico and Arizona.

4. White Alder (*A. rhombifolia* Nutt.). A tree to 70 feet with trunk diameter of 2-3 feet; the branchlets of the current season are orange in color; the leaves 2-3 inches long, ovate, finely saw-toothed, dark green and shiny above, with small glands on the midrib, pale below and somewhat hairy. The petioles are slender, yellow and hairy. Idaho, Washington, Oregon and California.

Golden-Leaved Chestnut (*Castanopsis chrysophylla* DC.)

A large tree, 50-125 feet high, with a trunk diameter up to 6 feet; branchlets of the current season covered with small bright golden scales; leaves are 2-6 inches long, lanceolate, or oblong, the margin entire and curled back; thickish, dark green and shiny above, yellow or golden on the lower surface; fruit, 1-1½ inches in diameter, composed of a spiny outer covering and one, or sometimes two, nuts which are edible. Washington, Oregon and California.

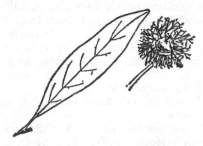

Tanbark Oak (*Lithocarpus densiflora* Rehd.)

A large tree 80 feet high; branchlets of the current season covered with dense woolly coating of yellowish tufted hairs; the leaves are 3-5 inches long, oblong in shape,

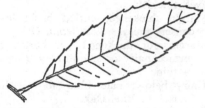

margin toothed (occasionally entire), pale green and shiny above, rusty-woolly or with age bluish-white below; petioles woolly; the fruits are acorn-like borne on a woolly stalk 1 inch long; nut ¾-1 inch long, ovoid; the cup is shallow, clothed on the outside by rigid, linear, brown hairy scales, and on the inside by shiny reddish hairs. The bark is a valuable source of tannin and is used for converting hides into leather. Found in Oregon and California.

Oak (*Quercus* L.)

(See p. 95.)

Key to the Western Oaks.

Leaves deeply pinnately lobed.
Leaves bristle tipped. 1. California Black Oak.

Leaves without bristles.
  Margin of leaf curled back.
    Leaf thickish; petiole with coarse, stiff hairs; buds woolly; acorn ovoid, 1 inch long.
      2. Garry White Oak.
    Leaf thin; petiole with soft, short hairs; buds hairy; acorns conical, 1¼-2¼ inches long.
      3. Valley White Oak.
  Margin not curled back.
    Leaf thickish, soft hairy below. 4. Utah Oak.
    Leaf thin.
      Petiole slender, hairy. 5. Colorado Oak.
      Petiole stout, woolly. 6. Blue Oak.
Leaves not pinnately lobed; entire or toothed.
  Leaves blue-green in color; shell of nut smooth on inner surface.
    Leaves less than 1 inch long. 7. Toumey Oak.
    Leaves 1 inch long or longer.
      Leaves thickish.
        Margin thickened, curled back; lower surface densely hairy. 8. Arizona Oak.
        Margin not thickened nor curled back; lower surface hairy or smooth. 9. Engelmann Oak.
      Leaves thin.
        Hairy below; pale blue above with scattered hairs. 6. Blue Oak.
        Smooth; blue-green and shiny above, paler below. 10. New Mexico Oak.
  Leaves dark green or yellow-green in color; shell of nut silky-woolly on inner surface.
    Leaves whitish and woolly on lower surface.
      Leaves fall* in spring soon after the appearance of new leaves; shape lanceolate. 11. Silver Oak.
      Leaves fall* in their third or fourth year; shape oblong-ovate. 12. Maul Oak.
    Leaves greenish; not woolly on lower surface.
      Smooth; tufts of hairs absent.
        13. Western Live Oak.
      Smooth or hairy.
        Tufts of rusty hairs in angles of veins.
        14. Coast Live Oak.

* Age of the leaf may be determined by the bud-scale scars encircling the twig.

Two large tufts of hairs at base of midrib.

15. Emory Oak.

1. CALIFORNIA BLACK OAK (*Q. Kelloggii* Newb.). A tree at times 100 feet high with a trunk diameter of 4 feet; leaves 3-6 inches long, oblong or obovate, seven-lobed, sometimes nine, the lobes having several sharp teeth toward the apices, dark green and shiny above, light green below, smooth, hairy, or sometimes woolly; petioles yellow, slender; acorn, 1-1½ inches long, ellip-

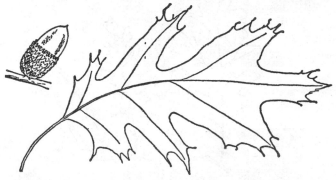

soidal, enclosed one-fourth of its length in the cup. Southwest Oregon and California.

2. GARRY WHITE OAK (*Q. Garryana* Hook.). A tree growing to a height of 60 feet; leaves 4-6 inches long, ob-

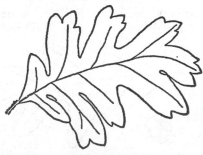

long or obovate in shape, 7-9 lobed, dark green and shiny above, light green or brownish below, hairy or smooth;

midrib stout and yellow; margin of the leaf slightly thickened and curled back. Acorn 1 inch long, ovoid, enclosed about one-fourth of its length by the cup. The wood is used for tight cooperage and cabinet work. Washington, Oregon and California.

3. VALLEY WHITE OAK (*Q. lobata* Née). A tree often reaching a height of 100 feet with a trunk diameter of 4 feet; the branchlets of current season covered with short,

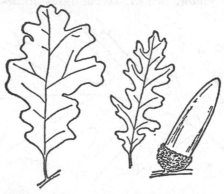

silky white hairs; leaves 2½-3 inches long, oblong or obovate, 7-11 lobed, dark green and hairy above, pale and hairy below, margin slightly thickened and curled back; acorn conical 1¼-2¼ inches long, enclosed about one-fourth or less of its length in the cup. California.

4. UTAH OAK (*Q. utahensis* Rydb.). A small tree, occasionally 30 feet in height; leaves 2½-7 inches long, ob-

long or obovate, 7-9 lobed, thickish, dark green above, pale and hairy beneath; acorn ovoid, ½-¾ inch long, enclosed about one-half of its length in the hemispherical cup. Found from southwestern Wyoming to Colorado, Utah, Arizona and New Mexico.

5. COLORADO OAK (*Q. leptophylla* Rydb.). A small tree sometimes attaining a height of 45 feet; leaves about 4 inches long, oblong or obovate, seven-lobed, thin, dark green and shiny above, yellow-green below with short hairs, especially on the midrib and veins; acorn ovoid, ½ inch long, enclosed about one-half its length in the thin cup. Colorado and New Mexico.

6. BLUE OAK (*Q. Douglasii* Hook. and Arn.). A tree often reaching 60 feet in height, with a trunk diameter

of 4 feet; branchlets brittle at the joints, white-woolly during the current season; leaves variable: 2-5 inches long, oblong, 7-lobed; or 1-2 inches long, oval, entire or with shallow-wavy or toothed margin; thin, pale blue above with scattered hairs, pale and hairy below. Acorn ellipsoidal, ¾-1 inch long, enclosed at the base by the shallow cup. California.

7. TOUMEY OAK (*Q. Toumeyi* Sarg.). A small tree, to 30 feet in height, divided near the ground into several large branches; leaves ½-¾ inch long, oblong or ovate, entire or with remote spiny teeth, thin, light blue-green and shiny above, pale and hairy below. The acorn is ovoid, ½ inch long, enclosed about one-third of its length in the cup. Found in southeastern Arizona. See illustration of leaf on following page.

8. ARIZONA OAK (*Q. arizonica* Sarg.). A tree usually about 30 feet high; branchlets covered with a woolly yel-

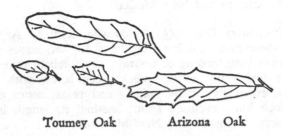

Toumey Oak   **Arizona Oak**

low coating during the first season; leaves 1-4 inches long, lanceolate or oblong, margins revolute, entire, wavy or spiny-toothed, dull blue-green above, densely hairy below. Acorn oblong, ¾-1 inch long, enclosed for one-half of its length in the cup. Arizona and New Mexico.

9. ENGELMANN OAK (*Q. Engelmannii* Greene). A tree to 50 feet; branchlets woolly during the current season; leaves 1-3 inches long, oblong, entire or with wavy or spiny-toothed margin, thickish, blue-green above, yellow-green below, hairy or smooth. Acorn oblong, ¾-1 inch long, brown marked with darker longitudinal stripes, enclosed about one-half its length in the cup. Southwestern California.

Engelmann Oak   **Maul Oak**

Silver Oak

10. NEW MEXICO OAK (*Q. oblongifolia* Torr.). A small tree sometimes 30 feet high; branchlets woolly the current season; leaves 1-2 inches long, oblong, thin, blue-green and shiny above, paler below, entire or wavy re-

curved margins. Acorn ovoid, $\frac{1}{2}$-$\frac{3}{4}$ inch long, enclosed in the cup for about one-third its length. New Mexico, Arizona and western Texas.

11. SILVER OAK (*Q. hypoleuca* Engelm.). A small tree usually 25 feet high; branchlets with a dense white, woolly coating during the current season; leaves 2-4 inches long, usually lanceolate, margins curled back, entire or at times with small, spiny teeth, thickish, yellow-green and shiny above, the lower surface silvery and woolly. Acorn conical, enclosed about one-third of its length in the cup. Western Texas, New Mexico and Arizona.

12. MAUL OAK (*Q. chrysolepis* Liebm.). A tree 20-40 feet high; branchlets densely woolly the current season; leaves 1-4 inches long, ovate or elliptical, margins entire, somewhat thickened on old trees, spiny-toothed on young trees; thickish, yellow-green above, woolly below the first year, becoming smooth and whitish. Acorn ovoid or conical, enclosed about one-third or less of its length in the cup. The wood is used for wagons and farm tools. Southern Oregon, California, Arizona and New Mexico.

13. WESTERN LIVE OAK (*Q. Wislizeni* DC.). A tree to 70 feet; leaves 1-1$\frac{1}{2}$ inches long, oblong-lanceolate, entire, saw-toothed or spiny-toothed; thickish, dark green and shiny above, yellow-green below. Acorn conical, $\frac{3}{4}$-1$\frac{1}{2}$ inches long, enclosed for more than one-half its length in the cup. California.

14. ENCINA, COAST LIVE OAK (*Q. agrifolia* Née). A tree to 80 feet, usually much less; leaves $\frac{3}{4}$-4 inches long, oval or oblong, margin curled back, entire or spiny-toothed; thickish, dull green above, paler and shiny below, smooth or hairy with tufts of rusty hairs in the angles of the veins. Acorn conical, $\frac{3}{4}$-1$\frac{1}{2}$ inches long, enclosed for one-third of its length in the cup. The wood is largely used for fuel. California.

15. EMORY OAK (*Q. Emoryi* Torr.). A tree usually 30 feet in height; branchlets of the current season woolly; leaves 1-2½ inches long, oblong-lanceolate, margin en-

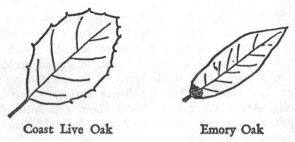

Coast Live Oak   **Emory Oak**

tire or with widely separated teeth; thickish, dark green and shiny above, pale below, smooth or short-hairy, with two tufts of white hairs at the base of the midrib. Acorn oblong, blackish, ½-¾ inch long, enclosed for about one-third of its length in the cup. The acorns are collected and sold as an article of food. Western Texas, New Mexico, and Arizona.

Western Hackberry (*Celtis Douglasii* Plan.)

A small tree of about 20 feet, or a shrub; with ovate leaves unequal at the heart-shaped base, saw-toothed on

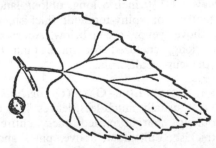

the margin, rough to the touch on the upper surface, pale with prominent veins below; the fruit is ⅓ inch in diameter, "cherry-like," orange-brown and shiny. Idaho, Washington, Oregon, California, Arizona and Colorado.

Oregon Myrtle. California Laurel
(*Umbellularia california* Nutt.)

A medium-sized tree, 20-75 feet, of which the branchlets of the current season are green; leaves are 3-5 inches

long, lanceolate, pointed at both apex and base, thick and shiny, the margin entire, aromatic; fruit ovoid, 1 inch long, green, tinged with purple, the six-parted enlarged calyx lobes covering the stem-end. The fruit is borne in bunches of two or three. The wood is very valuable for the making of fine furniture. Oregon and California.

Sycamore (*Platanus* L.)

WESTERN SYCAMORE (*Platanus racemosa* Nutt.). A large tree with alternate "maple-like" leaves 6-10 inches

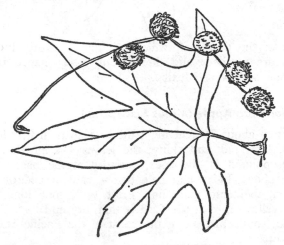

long, thickish, deeply five-lobed, the lobes themselves may or may not be toothed, light green above, paler beneath and densely woolly; bark of young trees and branches is whitish; buds are enclosed within the swollen base of the petiole. California.

ARIZONA SYCAMORE (*P. Wrightii* Wats.). This differs from the Western Sycamore in the usually more elongate

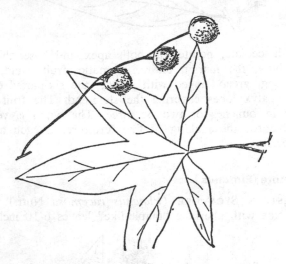

lobes of the thin leaf, which are mostly entire, but at times are toothed, and their deeply heart-shaped base. Arizona and New Mexico.

Oregon Crab Apple (*Malus fusca* Schn.)

A tree about 30 feet high; the branchlets at first long-hairy, later red and shiny; the leaves 1-4 inches long, ovate, pointed at the apex, rounded at the base, dark green above, hairy and pale below, saw-toothed on the margin, the teeth glandular. Fruit ½-¾ inch long, oblong, yellow or red; the flesh is thin, dry and tart. From Alaska southward along the coast of the Pacific States.

Saskatoon. Western Serviceberry (*Amelanchier florida* Lindl.)

A shrub or small tree to 40 feet with dark red, shiny branchlets; leaves 1½-2½ inches long, oval or ovate,

margin sharply toothed, dark green above, paler beneath. From the Yukon River southward, Washington, Oregon and Idaho.

Mountain Mahogany (*Cercocarpus* HBK.)

Small trees or shrubs with short spur-branches marked by crowded leaf scars of previous seasons. The leaves are small and thickish, alternately arranged; the fruits narrowly cylindrical, the calyx remaining on the blossom-end, and at the apex the much elongated feathery style covered with long white hairs.

Key to the Species of Mountain Mahogany.

Leaves obovate.
    Toothed above the middle, margin not curled back.
                            1. Hard Tack.
    Entire or finely saw-toothed above the middle, margin curled back. 2. Mountain Mahogany.
Leaves lanceolate. 3. Mountain Mohogany.

1. HARD TACK (*C. betuloides* Nutt.). Leaves 1-1¼ inches long, obovate, rounded at the apex and tapering at the base, toothed above the middle, dark green above,

pale below, hairy or woolly or becoming smooth; the straight veins sunken on the upper surface of the leaf. Styles of the fruit 2-3 inches long. California.

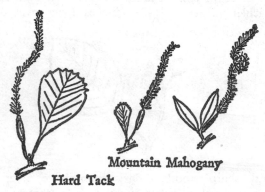

Mountain Mahogany

Hard Tack

2. MOUNTAIN MAHOGANY (*C. paucidentatis* Britt.). Leaves ½-1 inch long, oblong-obovate, rounded at the apex, tapering at the base, margin revolute and entire, or serrate above the middle, gray-green above, paler and woolly below; styles of fruit 1-1½ inches long. In dry situations: western Texas, New Mexico and Arizona.

3. MOUNTAIN MAHOGANY (*C. ledifolius* Nutt.). Leaves ½-1 inch long, lanceolate, tapering at both ends, dark green and shiny above, pale and hairy below, margins curled back, entire, midrib sunken on the upper surface; fruit woolly; styles 2-3 inches long. Dry elevations in the western region.

Plum. Cherry (*Prunus* L.)

(See p. 134.)

Key to the Plums and Cherries of the West.

Margin of leaf toothed and spiny.   1. Holly-leaf Cherry.
Margin saw-toothed, not spiny.
  Leaf broadly ovate (almost circular); fruits ½-1¼ inches long, in groups of 2 or several, stalks arising from a common point.   2. Western Wild Plum.

Leaf ovate, long-pointed at apex; fruit about 1 inch long, 2 or several arising from a common point.

> 3. Wild Plum.

Leaf ovate or oblong, short-pointed at apex; fruit about ¼ inch in diameter, many arranged along an elongate peduncle.   4. Choke Cherry.

Leaf oblong-lanceolate.

> Long-pointed at apex.   5. Pin Cherry.
> Rounded or short-pointed apex.   6. Bitter Cherry.

1. ISLAY. HOLLY-LEAF CHERRY (*P. ilicifolia* Walp.). Leaves ovate with thickened margins, spiny-toothed, 1-2½ inches long, thick, dark green and shiny above, paler beneath; fruit spherical, ½ inch in diameter, purple or blackish, flesh tart and astringent. A small tree or shrub native to California and also widely cultivated there.

2. WESTERN WILD PLUM (*P. subcordata* Benth.). A tree to 25 feet or a shrub, with spiny branches; leaves broadly ovate, almost circular, saw-toothed, 1-3 inches long, dark green above, paler beneath; fruits ½-1¼ inches long, short oblong, bluish; the stone flattened. Oregon and California.

Holly-leaf Cherry

Bitter Cherry   Western Wild Plum

3. WILD PLUM (*P. americana* Marsh.). See p. 134. Extending in its distribution into the Rocky Mountain region, where it is mostly shrubby.

4. CHOKE CHERRY (*P. virginiana* L.). See p. 139. Existing in several varieties in the western region.

5. PIN, RED, or BIRD CHERRY (*P. pennsylvanica* L.). See p. 138. Appears as a variety in the Rocky Mountain region.

6. BITTER CHERRY (*P. emarginata* Walp.). A small tree, to 30 feet, or a shrub; leaves oblong-lanceolate, 1-2½ inches long, saw-toothed, dark green above, paler beneath, with 1-4 glands at the base near the petiole; fruits ¼-½ inch in diameter, spherical, dark red or black, bitter and astingent, 4-5 in a bunch, the stalks attached near one another, but not at the same place on the stem. British Columbia, Montana, Idaho, Washington, Oregon, California, Nevada and Arizona.

Cat's Claw (*Acacia Greggii* Gray)

A small tree sometimes 25 feet high; branchlets with hooked and flat spines ¼ inch long; small bipinnately compound leaves 1-3 inches long, having 2-3 pairs of pinnae each bearing 4-6 pairs of leaflets, the terminal leaflets absent. Leaflets up to ¼ inch long, obovate, unequal, rounded at apex, white-hairy, with a short stalk. The petiole of the leaf has a small brown gland. The fruit is a twisted pod 2-4 inches long, the thin walls thickened at the margins. Western Texas, New Mexico, Arizona, Nevada, and southern California. Four other species of Acacia may be found in southwestern Texas.

Mimosa (*Leucaena Greggii* Wats.)

A small tree, the zigzag branchlets without spines, but the stipules at the base of the petiole become spiny; leaves bipinnately compound, 6 inches long, with 5-7 pairs of pinnae, each bearing 15-30 pairs of leaflets; leaflets ¼ inch long, lanceolate, gray or blue-green, oblique. There is a bottle-shaped gland between each of the pairs of pinnae. The pods are 6-8 inches long, straight, thickened on the margins. Western Texas. Two additional species may also be located in Texas.

Mesquite (*Prosopis*)

MESQUITE (*Prosopis juliflora* DC.). A small tree or shrub, with bipinnately compound leaves 5-10 inches long, composed of a single pair of pinnae (occasionally 2 pairs), the stalk projecting as a short spine from between them. Each pinna bears 6-11 pairs of leaflets. A small gland is present on the petiole near the attachment of the pair of pinnae. Spines occur on the branchlets above the attachment of the leaf. The pods are straight, linear, 4-9 inches long. The wood is very resistant to decay and is used for fence posts, ties, etc. Western Texas, New Mexico and Arizona. See illustrations of *Prosopis juliflora* var. *glandulosa*, p. 224.

SCREW-POD MESQUITE (*P. pubescens* Benth.). A small tree similar in general characteristics to the Mes-

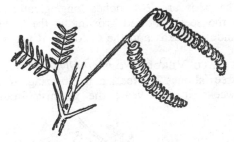

quite. Leaves 2-3 inches long; the stipules become spiny; leaflets white, hairy. The pods are twisted into a close spiral. They are sought as fodder by animals. Western Texas, New Mexico, Arizona, Utah, Nevada and southern California.

Retama. Male Palo Verde (*Parkinsonia* L.)

RETAMA. HORSE BEAN (*Parkinsonia aculeata* L.). A small tree about 15 feet high with spiny branches; bipinnate leaves, the 2-4 secondary branches (pinnae) of which arise near the point of attachment to the stem, giving the appearance of 2-4 pinnate leaves arising from a short stem. The petiole projects between the pinnae as a spine. This spine remains after the fall of the leaflet-bearing stalks and usually attains a length of about 1 inch, bearing the scars of the 2 or 4 fallen pinnae at its

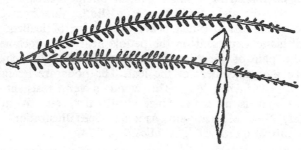

base. Each pinna has 25-30 pairs of remotely placed, small leaflets, diminishing perceptibly in size toward the apex. The pods are 2-4 inches long, greatly constricted between the seeds. Found growing in the valleys of the Rio Grande in Texas and the Colorado River in Arizona.

MALE PALO VERDE (*P. microphylla* Torr.). A small desert tree about 20 feet high, bearing foliage only a few weeks in the year; the greenish branches and

branchlets end in a spine. The leaves are small, 1 inch long, with 2 pinnae originating near the point of attachment of the leaf. Each pinna bears 4-6 pairs of leaflets. The pod is about 2 inches long, bearing two seeds usually and with a deep constriction between them. Found in the deserts of southern Arizona and California.

Palo Verde (*Cercidium Torreyanum* Sarg.)

A much branched small tree about 25 feet high, with yellowish-green, spiny branches bearing leaves only several weeks in the year. The leaves are bipinnate, about 1 inch long, with a pair of pinnae on a short petiole. Each pinna has 4-6 small leaflets. The pod is 3-4 inches long, only slightly constricted, if at all, between the seeds. Arizona and southern California.

Smoketree (*Dalea spinosa* Gray)

A small tree about 15 feet high, or a shrub; the branchlets end in sharp spines and bear only a few small, simple, white, hairy leaves about 1 inch long, obovate, falling within a few weeks of their appearance. The small pod is ovoid, about ⅛ inch long, the lower half enclosed in the persistent calyx. Arizona and California.

Western Locust (*Robinia neo-mexicana* var. *luxurians* Dieck.)

A small tree about 20 feet high with spiny branches; branchlets of the current year covered with brown glandular hairs. The leaves are pinnately compound, 6-12 inches long, with 7-10 pairs of lateral leaflets and a terminal leaflet; the leaflets are oblong, 1½ inches long, blue-green, the apex tipped with a short bristle, smooth except for the slight hairiness of the midrib on the lower surface. The pod is about 3 inches long, covered with glandular hairs. Growing near mountain streams in Colorado, New Mexico, Arizona and Utah.

Desert Ironwood (*Olneya tesota* Gray)

A small tree of the desert regions of Arizona and California, occasionally 30 feet high; the spiny branchlets of the current season are covered with white hairs;

leaves pinnately compound, white and hairy, 1-2½ inches long, with 10-15 leaflets.

Maple (*Acer* L.)

(See p. 153.)

Key to the Western Maples.

Leaves simple.
    7-9 lobed.　1. Vine Maple.
    5-lobed, very large (8-12 inches broad).
                              2. Broad-leaved Maple.
    3-lobed, smaller (2-5 inches broad).
        Lobes doubly saw-toothed.　3. Dwarf Maple.
        Lobes entire or with small secondary lobes.
                            4. Western Sugar Maple.
Leaves compound.
    3 leaflets, terminal one not stalked; serrate usually to base.　3. Dwarf Maple.
    3-7 leaflets (usually 3), terminal one stalked; coarsely serrate or toothed above middle.　5. Box Elder.

1. VINE MAPLE (*A. circinatum* Pursh.). A tree occa-

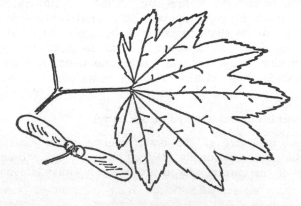

sionally 30 feet high, often a woody vine or shrub. The leaves are as broad as long, 2-7 inches, with 7-9 palmate lobes, pointed at the tip and with saw-toothed margin. Wings of the fruit 1½ inches long, widely spreading. Found along streams from British Columbia to California.

2. BROAD-LEAVED MAPLE (*A. macrophyllum* Pursh.). A large tree reaching a height of 100 feet, with very large leaves, 8-12 inches broad, deeply 5-lobed, the

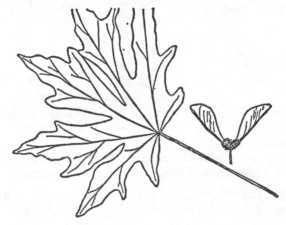

lowermost two much smaller. The lobes have a wavy or lobed margin and the uppermost lobe is often shallowly 3-lobed; thick, dark green and shiny above, pale below. The petioles are 10-12 inches long, the bases of each pair encircling the twig. Wings of the fruits are 1½ inches long, almost parallel. The wood is greatly valued for furniture manufacture. Mostly coastal from Alaska to California, especially abundant in Oregon, and frequently cultivated.

3. DWARF MAPLE (*A. glabrum* Torr.). A shrub or small tree, attaining a height of 25 feet. The leaves are quite variable, shallowly or deeply 3-lobed, or sometimes with three leaflets; thin, 3-5 inches broad, dark green and shiny above, paler below. Wings of fruit ¾-1 inch

long, parallel or somewhat spreading. Widely distributed in the Rocky Mountain region from Montana to New

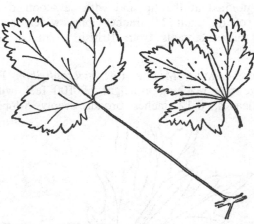

Mexico, westward through northern Arizona, Utah and Nevada to California; and in western South Dakota and Nebraska.

A var. *Douglasii* Dippel, with broad-winged fruits, occurs in Washington, Oregon, Idaho and Montana.

4. WESTERN SUGAR MAPLE (*A. grandidentatum* Nutt.). A small tree, sometimes 40 feet high; branches red with

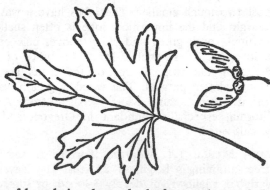

bands of long hairs above the leaf scars; leaves 2-5 inches broad, 3-lobed, margins of lobes are entire, wavy or cut into small lobes; thick, dark green and shiny above, pale beneath, with fine hairs, especially on the veins. Wings of fruit ½-1 inch long, spreading. Idaho, Montana, Wyoming, Utah, Arizona, New Mexico and western Texas. It is sometimes cultivated.

5. Box ELDER (*A. negundo* L.). See p. 154. It occurs in the western region in several recognized varieties. Found in the Rocky Mountain region, Montana to New Mexico, Arizona and Utah; also in California.

California Buckeye (*Aesculus californica* Nutt.)

(See also p. 159.)

A tree 15-40 feet high, trunk enlarged at base, sometimes 5 feet in diameter; winter buds resinous; leaves

usually with five stalked leaflets 4-6 inches long, with finely toothed margins; fruits spherical or obovoid, 2-3 inches long, shell thin, brown, and without prickles. California. Sometimes cultivated in the Pacific States.

Wild China Tree (*Sapindus Drummondii* Hook and Arn.)
(See p. 231.)

Cascara Buckthorn *(Rhamnus Purshiana* DC.)

A shrub or small tree, occasionally 40 feet high; winter buds white, woolly; leaves oblong or elliptical, 2-6 inches

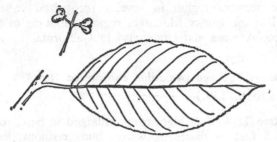

long, margins very finely toothed or entire, thin, brown-woolly on veins below. An extract of the bark is used as a cathartic. Montana, Idaho, Washington, Oregon, California and Arizona.

Blue Myrtle. California Lilac (*Ceanothus.*)

BLUE MYRTLE (*Ceanothus thyrsiflorus* Eschs.). A shrub or tree, occasionally 35 feet high; leaves with three

veins meeting at the base, 1-1½ inches long, oblong, smooth and shiny on upper surface, paler and slightly hairy below, margin with very fine teeth. Fruit a small, black, dry capsule, separating into three parts. California.

CALIFORNIA LILAC (*Ceanothus spinosus* Nutt.). A shrub or small tree 20 feet high, with spiny branchlets;

leaves 1 inch long, elliptical or oblong, leathery, usually with but a single main vein; red on upper surface, greenish below. Capsule black, 3-lobed. Southern California.

Flannel Bush (*Fremontia californica* Torr.)

A shrub or tree 20-30 feet tall; leaves 1½ inches long, ovate, 3-lobed, dark green above, red hairy or roughened on the lower surface; petiole brown-woolly. Fruit an ovoid capsule covered with long brown hairs, opening into five segments. California.

Koeberlinia (*Koeberlinia spinosa* Zucc.)

A much branched shrub or small tree, occasionally 20 feet high, with spiny, pale green branchlets; mostly leafless, the very small leaves (⅛ inch long) falling early.

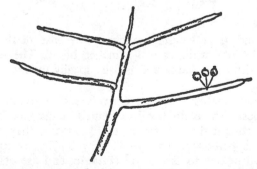

The fruits are black berries containing one or two seeds. Forming thickets in dry situations in western Texas, New Mexico, and Arizona.

Cacti

There are several *Cacti* in the United States which are tree-like. They are most abundant in Arizona, less frequent in southern California and New Mexico.

SUWARRO (*Carnegeia gigantea* Britt. & Rose). A tree sometimes 60 feet high, with a straight, fluted, columnar

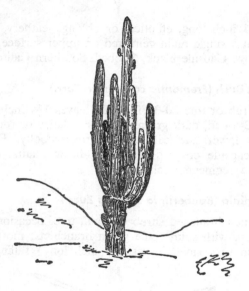

trunk and several erect branches. The base of the trunk has 8-12 ribs which are 4-5 inches broad. The wood is very resistant to decay and is used locally for fencing and building.

Several smaller tree-like *Cacti* are also found in the Southwest. These do not have fluted stems, but because of the constrictions between the branches, they have a jointed appearance. The joints may be flat or rounded. They all belong to the genus *Opuntia,* and are called locally by such names as Prickly Pear, Cholla, Tasajo, and others. The *Opuntias* are used for hedges and also for cattle feed, after the spines are burned off.

Western Dogwood (*Cornus Nuttallii* Aud.)

A tree 40-60 feet tall; branchlets of the current season green, somewhat hairy; the opposite leaves are ovate, short-pointed at the tip, 3-5 inches long, thin, bright

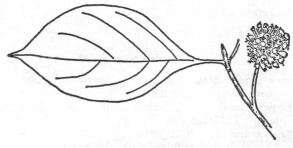

green above with some appressed hairs, white and woolly below; petioles grooved, short-hairy. The minute flowers are grouped in showy clusters surrounded at the base by large white or pinkish, oblong leaves, 1½-3 inches long; fruits are bright red or orange, ½ inch long, in crowded clusters of 30-40. Found growing in the shade of coniferous forests in the Pacific States.

Madroña (*Arbutus Menziesii* Pursh.)

A tree sometimes attaining a height of 125 feet, common in the redwood forests. Leaves oblong, 3-5 inches

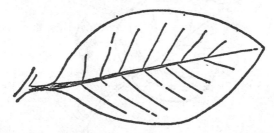

long, leathery, dark green and shiny above, whitish below, margin usually entire and curled back, sometimes finely toothed. The urn-shaped flowers appear in clusters

6 inches long; the fruit is spheroidal, ½ inch in diameter, and a reddish-orange color. The wood is sometimes used for furniture. Found in British Columbia and the Pacific States.

Ash (*Fraxinus* L.)

(See p. 174.)

Key to the Western Ashes.

Leaves simple, broadly ovate. 1. Single-leaf Ash.
Leaves pinnately compound.
    Leaves small, 1½-3 inches long, leaflets ½-¾ inch long. 2. Gregg Ash.
    Leaves and leaflets larger.
        Lateral leaflets without stalks, or nearly so.
            Leaflets 3-7 inches long. 3. Oregon Ash.
            Leaflets smaller, 1-2½ inches long.
                3-5 leaflets. 4. Arizona Ash.
                7-9 leaflets. 6. Standley Ash.
        Lateral leaflets on distinct stalks, ⅛-1¼ inches long.
            Leaves 3½-6 inches long, stalks of leaflets slender, not grooved. 5. Toumey Ash.
            Leaves 10-12 inches long, stalk of leaflet stout, grooved. 7. Green Ash.

1. SINGLE-LEAF ASH (*F. anomala* Wats.). A shrub or small tree, to 20 feet; leaves simple, broadly ovate, 1¼-

2 inches long, dark green above, paler beneath (sometimes with two or three leaflets), margin entire or very

slightly scalloped. Fruits are obovate, ½ inch long, the wing round and surrounding the flat body. Found near streams, Colorado, New Mexico, Arizona, southwestern Nevada and adjacent California.

2. GREGG ASH (*F. Greggii* Gray). A shrub or small tree to 25 feet; leaves 1½-3 inches long, with 5-7, or occa-

sionally 3 leaflets, each ½-¾ inch long; leaflets oblong-obovate, entire or scalloped above the middle, leathery, dark green above, pale with black dots below. Fruit with obovate wing, ½-⅔ inch long. Western Texas.

3. OREGON ASH (*F. oregoniana* Nutt.). A valuable tree, often 80 feet high, with a trunk diameter of 4 feet;

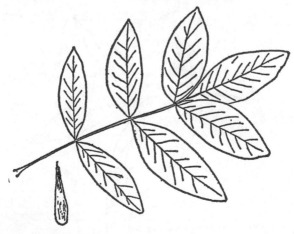

the leaves are 5-14 inches long; petioles grooved; leaflets usually 7 or 5, rarely 3 or 9, ovate, 3-7 inches long, the lateral ones usually without stalks, margins entire or obscurely fine-toothed, light green above, paler below, usually woolly-hairy, but this characteristic is variable. A var. *glabra* Rehd. is smooth below. Fruits 1-2 inches long, the wing oblanceloate, oblong, or elliptical, extending to the middle, or occasionally to the base of the body. Near streams, British Columbia, Washington, Oregon and California.

4. ARIZONA ASH (*F. velutina* Torr.). A tree about 30 feet high; branchlets of the current season white, woolly; leaves 4-5 inches long, petiole hairy and grooved; leaflets 3-5, 1-1½ inches long, elliptical to ovate, finely scalloped above the middle, pale green above, woolly below. Fruit ¾ inch long, wing linear and terminal, shorter than the body. Arizona and New Mexico.

A var. *coriacea* Rehd., with leathery leaves, is distributed from Utah to southern California.

5. TOUMEY ASH (*F. velutina* var. *Toumeyi* Rehd.). A tree about 30 feet high; branchlets gray and slightly hairy becoming smooth during the current season; leaves 3½-6 inches long, petiole hairy, leaflets 5-7, 1½-3 inches

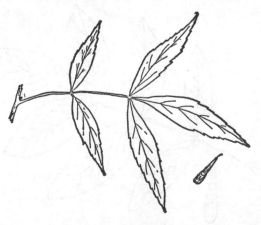

long, elliptical, finely toothed above the middle, the lower surface covered with fine, very short, appressed hairs. Found with the species, but more abundant in Arizona than in New Mexico; used as a shade tree in southern Arizona.

6. STANDLEY ASH (*F. Standleyi* Rehd.). A small tree, occasionally 30 feet high, leaves 5-7 inches long, petiole slender, smooth, leaflets 7-9, 1½-2½ inches long, ovate, yellow-green above, somewhat whitish below. Fruit ¾-1½ inches long, wing oblong-obovate, extending halfway down the body. New Mexico and Arizona.

7. GREEN ASH (*F. pennsylvanica* var. *lanceolata* Sarg.). See p. 178.

Desert Willow (*Chilopsis linearis* DC.)

A shrub or small tree to 30 feet; leaves 2-5 inches long, linear (⅛-¼ inch wide), opposite, or some alternate,

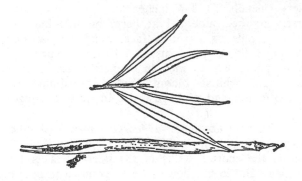

gray-green or yellow-green, margin entire. Flowers ¾-1½ inches long and broad, similar to the Catalpas. The fruit is a narrow pod 7-12 inches long. In dry, well-drained soils and stream beds in the deserts: Texas, New Mexico, Arizona, Utah, Nevada and southern California.

Blue and Red Berry Elder (*Sambucus*)

BLUE BERRY ELDER (*Sambucus cœrulea* Raf.). Shrub or tree occasionally 30 feet high with opposite, pinnately

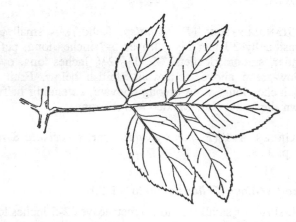

compound leaves, 5-7 inches long, petiole grooved, 5-9 leaflets (usually 5) 1-4 inches long, ovate or oblong, coarsely toothed, unequal at base, on petiolules ¼-½ inch long, pale on lower surface. Small whitish flowers in a large, flat-topped cluster 4-10 inches broad. The fruit is spheroidal, ⅓ inch in diameter, dark blue, covered with a whitish bloom. Widely distributed in the West; common and of largest size in western Oregon.

RED BERRY ELDER (*S. callicarpa* Greene). A tree occasionally 30 feet high. It differs from the Blue Berry Elder in the shorter stalks of the lateral leaflets (⅛-¼ inch long) and in the flowers being grouped in pyramidal clusters about 3 inches high and broad. The fruits are spheroidal, ½ inch in diameter, red. Found along river banks from Alaska to California.

DEFINITIONS

FORMS OF LEAVES

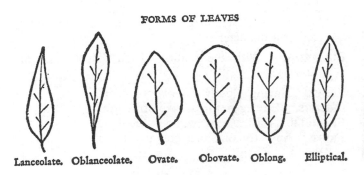

Lanceolate. Oblanceolate. Ovate. Obovate. Oblong. Elliptical.

LEAF MARGINS

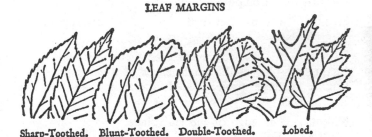

Sharp-Toothed. Blunt-Toothed. Double-Toothed. Lobed.

ALTERNATE. A term applied to the arrangement of leaves, twigs, etc., that are scattered singly along a stem but never opposite each other.

AROMATIC. Having a sweetish pleasant odor.

BARK. The outer covering of a stem or branch.

BLADE. The flat part of a leaf.

BLOTCHED. Having irregular spots.

BRANCH. One of the large divisions formed by the forking of the stem of a tree.

BRANCHLET. A small branch.

315

COMPOUND. A term applied to a leaf that is made up of several leaflets.

CONE. A dry fruit with overlapping scales covering the seed.

CYLINDRICAL. Resembling a cylinder, having nearly uniform diameter.

ELLIPTICAL. With the outline of an ellipse (see fig. above).

FELTY. Having closely interwoven hairs.

FIBROUS. Having a thread-like structure.

FLEXIBLE. Easily bent without breaking.

FRUIT. Any structure that contains the seed.

GLAND. A cell or group of cells producing various substances, as resin, gum, water, etc.

GLANDULAR. Having glands.

GRANULAR. Composed of grains or particles.

HYBRID. A cross between two species or varieties of plants.

LANCEOLATE. Lance-shaped (see fig. above).

LEAFLET. One of the small leaves of a compound leaf.

LOBE. A large projection of a leaf margin (see fig. above).

MARGIN. The edge of the leaf blade.

MATURE. Full-grown.

MOTTLED. Marked with spots of different colors.

MUCILAGINOUS. Resembling mucilage, slimy or gummy.

OBLANCEOLATE. Inverted lance-shaped (see fig. above).

OBLONG. Longer than broad, with rounded ends and nearly parallel sides (see fig. above).

OBOVATE. Egg-shaped in outline, broadest toward the tip (see fig. above).

OPPOSITE. A term applied to a pair of leaves placed opposite each other on the twig.

OVATE. Egg-shaped in outline, broadest toward the base (see fig. above).

Ovoid. Applied to a body that is egg-shaped.

Pendulous. More or less hanging or drooping.

Petiole. The stem of a leaf.

Pith. The small, central, soft part of a branch or twig.

Pod. In this book, a term applied to any thin or dry structure holding the seed.

Pollen. The dust-like particles (cells) produced in certain parts of the flower.

Prickle. A small spine-like outgrowth.

Pyramidal. Tapering to a point, pyramid-like.

Ravine. A deep narrow gorge, usually formed by a stream.

Resin. The thick, sticky (usually aromatic) juice of certain trees.

Resinous. Containing resin.

Scale. One of the small, thin, leaf-like coverings of a bud, usually brownish; also applied to thicker flat structures of a cone, and to the flakes of bark.

Scurfy. Having very small, thin, bran-like scales.

Shrub. A small woody plant with several stems branching from the same root.

Sinus. The space between two lobes.

Species. A term applied to a group of plants that are essentially alike.

Spine. A sharp-pointed, woody outgrowth.

Stipule. A small leaflet or scale at base of petiole.

Teeth. The small projections on the margin of the leaf.

Thorn. A stiff, sharp-pointed, woody projection.

Tree. A woody plant with one large stem.

Trunk. The main stem of the tree.

Twig. A small branchlet.

Veins. The fine lines (usually branching) seen in a leaf.

Wand-like. Resembling a long, slender rod.

Whorl. The arrangement of three or more leaves or twigs in a circle around a stem or branch.

Woolly. Covered with long, tangled hairs.

BIBLIOGRAPHY

The following list of books may be referred to for more intensive study:

Barret, M. F. A LEAF KEY TO FLORIDA BROAD-LEAVED TREES. Montclair, N. J.

Britton. NORTH AMERICAN TREES. Henry Holt & Co., N. Y.

Britton & Brown. FLORA OF NORTHEASTERN AMERICA. Scribner's, N. Y.

Coker, W. C. TREES OF THE SOUTHEASTERN STATES. University Press, N. C.

FOREST TREES OF OKLAHOMA, Ed. 5. Division of Forestry, Oklahoma City, Okla.

FOREST TREES OF TEXAS—HOW TO KNOW THEM. *Bulletin 20* Texas Forest Service.

GRAY'S MANUAL OF BOTANY. American Book Co., N. Y.

Green, R. TREES OF NORTH AMERICA. Edward Bros., Ann Arbor, Mich.

Hough, R. B. TREES OF NORTHERN STATES AND CANADA. Lowville, N. Y.

Mathews. FIELD BOOK OF AMERICAN TREES AND SHRUBS. Putnam, N. Y.

McMinn, H. E. and E. Mains. ILLUSTRATED MANUAL OF PACIFIC COAST TREES.

Sargent. MANUAL OF NORTH AMERICAN TREES. Houghton, Mifflin & Co., N. Y.

Shirley, J. C. THE REDWOODS OF COAST AND SIERRA. University of California Press.

Index

Note—Northeastern, Southern, and Western trees are each listed under their separate headings so that specific information concerning any tree indigenous to the region in which the reader is interested may be easily located.

Both common and botanical names are listed separately throughout and appear in their proper alphabetical order.

Index to Northeastern Trees

Index to Southern Trees

Index to Western Trees